Authentically Emergent

Authentically Emergent

In Search of a Truly Progressive Christianity

by

R. SCOTT SMITH

CASCADE *Books* · Eugene, Oregon

AUTHENTICALLY EMERGENT
In Search of a Truly Progressive Christianity

Cascade Books
An Imprint of Wipf and Stock Publishers
199 W. 8th Ave., Suite 3
Eugene, OR 97401

www.wipfandstock.com

PAPERBACK ISBN: 978-1-5326-4039-1
HARDCOVER ISBN: 978-1-5326-4040-7
EBOOK ISBN: 978-1-5326-4041-4

Cataloguing-in-Publication data:

Names: Smith, R. Scott, 1957–, author.

Title: Authentically emergent : in search of a truly progressive Christianity / R. Scott Smith.

Description: Eugene, OR: Cascade Books, 2018 | Includes bibliographical references and index.

Identifiers: ISBN 978-1-5326-4039-1 (paperback) | ISBN 978-1-5326-4040-7 (hardcover) | ISBN 978-1-5326-4041-4 (ebook)

Subjects: LCSH: Postmodernism—Religious aspects—Christianity. | Evangelicalism. | Church and the world.

Classification: BR115.P74 S68 2018 (paperback) | BR115.P74 (ebook)

Manufactured in the U.S.A.   08/03/18

Unless noted otherwise, all of my Scripture references are to the *New American Standard Bible*, Anaheim: Foundation Press Publications, for the Lockman Foundation, 1977.

Material taken from *Truth and the New Kind of Christian* by Ronald Scott Smith, © 2005, pp. 67–69. Used by permission of Crossway, a publishing ministry of Good News Publishers, Wheaton, IL 60187, www.crossway.org.

For my evangelical brothers and sisters,
my "emergent" friends, and others shaped by their views

Contents

Illustrations and Tables

Preface

In September 2006, about ten months after my book *Truth and the New Kind of Christian: The Emerging Effects of Postmodernism in the Church* (Crossway) was released, I taught a weekend seminar at Biola for our Christian Apologetics program. I was learning more, and Tony Jones had graciously offered to let me interview him by phone for the class. So, I felt the class was shaping up to be a very good learning opportunity. Little did I know, I was the one who would learn the most!

I had asked the Lord if there was something specific he wanted me to ask Tony, and I believe he answered me through a "word" given to me through a person I believe hears from God. But the question I was given to ask seemed unusual to me; it wasn't about anything that at that time I had written or studied in relation to Tony's or Brian McLaren's views. I am glad I asked. The discussions in the class made me realize that there was much more I needed to research and study than I had perceived to that point . . . and I thought I was the teacher of the class!

The insights I gained from that weekend class propelled me to start reading much more of these authors' views, along with those of Doug Pagitt, Rob Bell, Stan Grenz, and many more. Along the way, I started to see more connections, far beyond their epistemological concerns, which was my focus in *Truth*.

Interestingly, I also began to see a growing sense that the "emergents" were seen as "yesterday's news," at least among evangelical academics and publishers at places like the Evangelical Theological Society national meetings. To my concern, I also noticed a marked decrease in willingness to really try to understand and carefully assess their views. An attendee at one of my presentations summed up the attitude I was detecting when he blurted out something like, "Can't we just call them heretics and move on?!"

Though not as much on evangelicals' radar screens, I noticed instead that the emergents' influence actually had morphed and increased.

Moreover, I started to see that they were raising not just philosophical concerns, but also ethical ones, ones about patterns they noticed amongst evangelicals. At the same time, I too started to become aware of some patterns amongst evangelicals, ones that seemed to explain why I think, all too often, we are not seeing the biblically promised power and presence of the Lord. As I investigated this, I came to realize that McLaren, Jones, Pagitt, and Bell actually were much more on target about what has gone wrong with the church than I understood when I wrote *Truth*.

So, this book gives me an opportunity to reconsider my earlier work in *Truth*, as well as carefully consider the emergents' updated thoughts. Yet, I think there is a much deeper set of factors at work in *both* these emergents' more recent views, and amongst evangelicals. I hope to offer not just a different, compelling analysis, but also a fruitful way forward for both groups. I believe that then, and only then, will we find a truly progressive Christianity, one that leaves behind the stale kind of Christianity that all too often we have been taught, and enters into the fullness of Christ. That kind of Christianity will be authentically emergent from what we experience all too often these days.

Along the way, several people have encouraged and helped me, such as Michael Wittmer, Craig Hazen (my director at Biola's Christian Apologetics program), Joe Gorra, John Franke, Steve Sherman, Todd Mangum, and others. My sister, Lynne Young, has been very helpful, too. And, Grace Hansen helped greatly with references. Most of all, I would not have many of the ideas herein without Jesus' involvement in my scholarship. However, if I have made mistakes in this text, they are due to my faults, of course.

And, I wish to express my deep, abiding love and appreciation for my wife, Debbie, and our daughter, Anna, who is quite a good student of postmodernism, even at her young age.

Introduction

WHATEVER HAPPENED TO THE emerging church movement? And, whatever happened to the leaders associated with it and Emergent Village, such as Brian McLaren, Tony Jones, Doug Pagitt, and others? Not that long ago, it seems, these emergents and the phenomenon they were helping to giving voice and leadership to was the talk of many, many Christians. It became the subject of conferences, and it gave rise to numerous popular articles, blogs, radio talk shows, books, and more. These ranged from being enthusiastically supportive to extremely critical, even labeling some of their ideas as heretical.

I wrote one of these books, *Truth and the New Kind of Christian: The Emerging Effects of Postmodernism in the Church* (Crossway, 2005), in which I tried first to describe the movement carefully and accurately, and then assess their views, both in terms of strengths and weaknesses. That book's publication gave me many opportunities to teach and speak at evangelical churches and conferences. It also helped me to have opportunities to meet, listen to, and talk with people such as Jones, Pagitt, and McLaren; academics like John Franke, Todd Mangum, and Myron Penner; and many others who were supportive of, and attracted to, the overall phenomenon. Those opportunities have resulted in some good relationships, fruitful dialogue, mutually improved understanding and appreciation, much challenge and research, and more.

I have written various essays on the views of emergents since that book's publication, but only one more recently.[1] Yet, the heyday of the emerging church now can seem to be a thing of the past. Indeed, it doesn't seem like evangelical Christian publishers put out many books on it nowadays.

---

1. For example, see my "Reflections on McLaren and the Emerging Church"; "'Emergents,' Evangelicals, and the Importance of Truth"; "Emerging Church"; "Emergents and the Rejection of Body-Soul Dualism"; and "Are Emergents Rejecting the Soul's Existence?" Seven years later, this one was published: "God and Relationships on the 'New Kind' of Christianity."

There are reasons for this, which Scott Burson identifies in his very thorough book, *Brian McLaren in Focus*.[2] Several Calvinist evangelicals already had concerns from McLaren's *A Generous Orthodoxy* (2004) and even earlier works.[3] But, when his *A New Kind of Christianity* (2010) came out, a much stronger, more "strident biblicist critique" became evident.[4] Indeed, Burson suggests that many Calvinists today just consider McLaren to be a liberal, and thus he is reviled or written off.

In addition to this, *World Magazine* published an article in 2010 that basically announced the demise of the emerging church.[5] John Piper declared that the leadership of the emerging church was in shambles in 2010.[6] While emerging church blogger Andrew Jones did not announce the death of the emerging church, he did write on his blog that in his opinion, "2009 marks the year when the emerging church suddenly and decisively ceased to be a radical and controversial movement in global Christianity. In many places around the world, the movement has already been either adopted, adapted, or made redundant through the traditional church catching up or duplicating EC efforts."[7]

Yet, this dismissal might be shortsighted. In just 2005, *Time* identified McLaren as one of the most influential evangelicals in the US.[8] Moreover, as Burson observes, in 2011 Jonathan Brink posted on the Emergent Village website that while the stereotype—that the emerging church was a "slick marketing model aimed at middle class, white hipsters saddled in the corner of Starbucks with their Macs"—had died, nonetheless the "underlying questions that had fueled the movement in the first place" had not.[9]

Since then, their influence has broadened and deepened. They (and other authors, speakers, and activists) have morphed their forms of influence into longer-term platforms. For instance, Jones and Pagitt have their own websites and ministries, which include blogs, speaking, and book publishing. Holding a PhD in Practical Theology, Jones teaches in seminaries

---

2. Burson, *Brian McLaren in Focus*. One of the great strengths of his book is that McLaren himself wrote the introduction after having read the manuscript. Plus, Burson draws upon several e-mail conversations and interviews with McLaren, many of which are printed in an appendix. Thus, his book gives McLaren's own words in response to many questions, issues, and arguments.

3. For example, see Carson, *Becoming Conversant*.

4. Burson, *Brian McLaren in Focus*, 164.

5. Bradley, "Farewell Emerging Church."

6. Piper, "John Piper—The Emergent Church."

7. Jones, "Emerging Church Movement (1989–2009)?"

8. "Influential Evangelicals: Brian McLaren."

9. Brink, "A State of Emergence 2010."

and now is the senior acquisitions editor for the "theology for the people" books with Fortress Press. Pagitt leads Solomon's Porch in Minnesota and hosts his own radio talk show. They also have teamed up and head the JoPa Group (http://thejopagroup.com/), which sponsors very innovative events on local, regional, or national levels, such as Church Planters Academy and Christianity 21, "inventive, relational gatherings such as Big Tent Christianity, the Great Emergence," Funding the Missional Church, and Progressive Youth Ministry.[10] They publish their own books through JoPa, yet they also have published through major houses (e.g., Jones with HarperOne, and Pagitt with a division of Random House), thereby reaching much broader audiences. And, they now seem to write within the broad stream of "progressive" Christianity.

McLaren probably still is the author who is selling the most books of anyone writing within this overall position, and his emphasis is upon Christians' praxis today. While he used to publish, for example, with Zondervan, thereby targeting an evangelical audience, more recently he too has published with these large houses. His assessments and recommendations are widely influential and not just in more popular circles. McLaren has been invited to help teach seminary classes, and academics are engaging with his thought, with even dissertation(s) being written about it.[11] Moreover, I think that by examining his views, we will have the opportunity to see clearly some very important issues for Christians in the West today.

There is another highly visible, influential author, speaker, and former pastor who has been part of the larger emerging church conversation, who I think should be considered here, too. Rob Bell has published bestselling books, such as *Love Wins*. Already known as the founding pastor of Mars Hill Bible Church located in Grandville, Michigan, Bell also developed the highly influential "Nooma" video series. Not only through many books, he and his views have become widely publicized, now extended through his podcast, an e-course available through Oprah.com, and a television show on her network.[12] Like the others, he too has published with a large house, HarperOne. While I have not seen Bell identified with emergent (or its earlier forms), I will include use of the term *emergents*, for lack of a better umbrella term, to refer to him, McLaren, Pagitt, and Jones.

10. See http://thejopagroup.com/about/.

11. For example, Burson's book, *Brian McLaren in Focus,* is based upon his dissertation, "Apologetics and the New Kind of Christian."

12. For the e-course, see http://www.oprah.com/app/rob-bell-joy-meaning.html. For the show, see http://www.oprah.com/own/The-Rob-Bell-Show-Premieres-on-OWN-Video.

So, while technically "emergent" (i.e., the loosely defined "organiza-tion") may be passé, the views and influences of these men are anything but that. Instead, their means of influence have morphed. Further, their scope of influence seems to have grown significantly.

In *Truth*, I gave attention to earlier works of McLaren and Jones. For Jones, I focused on his 2001 book *Postmodern Youth Ministry*. I looked at three works from McLaren, all dated in 2003 or before.[13] One of my em-phases was on their descriptions of modernity's shaping influences upon culture and the church, and how things are changing in postmodernity.[14] Here are two tables I used there to summarize their descriptions of moder-nity, and how these traits have impacted the church and broader culture:[15]

Traits of modernity (and issues these concern)	Broad, cultural effect	Impact on the church
Desire to control and conquer *(issues of power)*	Evidenced scien-tifically, politically, technologically, and philosophically	By adopting coercive methods, and even terms, in (e.g.) evangelism, such as "winning" people, or having an evangelistic "crusade"; by treating apologetics as a defense; by attempt-ing to impose our values politically
Age of the machine *(issues of being, truth and knowledge, and power)*	People treated as (re-duced to) mechanisms	By treating the Christian life, and our relationship with God, as simple steps to perform; Christian life as a system to be believed (without any doubts); by reducing the gospel to simple, absolute truths
Age of analysis *(issues of truth and knowl-edge, and power)*	The most highly valued form of thought; science as the discipline to master all of reality	By trying to systematize for all time theological truths in elaborate systems (system-atic theologies)

13. McLaren, *A New Kind of Christian*; *More Ready*; and *Story*.

14. I still think McLaren's focus on practical shaping factors (rather than philosoph-ical ones) gives insights that we cannot gain just from reading philosophical discussions of postmodernism. The influences of modernity and postmodernity are much more than just a matter of philosophical considerations.

15. Adapted from my *Truth*, 52–53.

Quest for certainty and absolute, totalizing knowledge *(issues of being, in terms of shriveled souls; truth and knowledge; and power)*	Foundationalism in epistemology	By not being able to have doubts, or question God; by becoming rigid and legalistic
Critical age *(issues of truth and knowledge, and power)*	Must debunk any who disagree with you	By having to prove anyone wrong who disagrees with us; by becoming defensive against such comments or criticisms
Modern nation-states *(issue of power)*	Also, the rise of global corporations	
Emphasis upon the individual *(issue of being)*	In particular, the autonomous individual	By an inordinate focus on the individual and his or her relationship with God, apart from the body of Christ
Protestantism *(issue of being — i.e., the focus on the individual; also issues of truth and knowledge, and power)*	The rise of Protestantism through the Reformation, against the Roman Catholic Church	
Consumerism *(issue of being)*	Widespread emphasis upon acquiring more and more to fulfill ourselves	By the church being a purveyor of religious goods and services

Here is a table of Jones's observations of contrasting values:[16]

Modern Values	Postmodern Values
Rational: A key Enlightenment emphasis was upon the adequacy of human reason to comprehend universal truths, and this primarily is achieved through science and the scientific method.	*Experiential*: Postmoderns want to experience things rather than just read or hear about them. For example, they want to experience interactive video games, or high-adventure vacations.

16. Adapted from my *Truth*, 67–69.

Scientific: So strong has been the belief in the superiority of science to any other discipline that scientism (the belief that only what science tells us is true and reasonable, is in fact true and reasonable) has become deeply embedded in our cultural mind-set. Scientists have been the high priests of this worldview. Even God can and should be studied scientifically.	*Spiritual*: While popular interest in spiritual things waned under the influence of modern science, today spirituality is in! And, people are willing to take innovative means to try to be spiritual.
Unanimity: Communities tended to be homogeneous, not multicultural. Religious options were few, even for dating (certainly not Catholics with Protestants).	*Pluralistic*: Spirituality takes on many forms, some of which have nothing to do with believing in God. Others will want to know who or what you mean by "God." As Jones wisely observes, technology has made "everything available to everyone," and religiously the "choices are overwhelming."[A]
Exclusive: Most Americans agreed with the Judeo-Christian worldview, at least morally speaking.	*Relative*: The emphasis on pluralism leads people to think that "all faiths contain elements of truth and any religion is a perfectly good way to express your spirituality."[B]
Egocentric: Modern philosophers stressed the importance of the self. In ethics, that stress focused on the autonomy of the self. Culturally, this view gave birth to the name the "Me" generation for the Boomers, with an emphasis upon self-fulfillment.	*Altruistic*: Here, Jones notes an important paradox—Millennials seem to be even more "consumeristic" than their parents, yet they also highly value giving away their time and resources.
Individualistic: With the heavy emphasis upon self-fulfillment, modern marketing efforts targeted the individual consumer.	*Communal*: In response to the emphasis upon the self, postmoderns are returning to the family and community, but in "untraditional ways such as cohousing."[C] TV shows such as *Survivor*, *Big Brother*, *Friends*, and others capitalize on this interest.
Functional: The stress in modern architecture and technology has been on usefulness to serve a purpose. For instance, the "worship center" replaced the "sanctuary."	*Creative*: Here Jones observes that "Gen-Xers and Yers are known for their aesthetic sensibilities."[D] Beauty for its own sake is highly valued.

Industrial: The goals of the industrial age were "efficiency and material bounty,"[E] and machines were highly valued for their ability to contribute to these goals.	*Environmental*: In response to exploitation of the Earth's resources, students are concerned about the environment and its longer-term viability.
Local: Peoples' interests were largely local, despite transportation improvements. Youth group overseas missionary trips were "virtually unheard of,"[F] and communication with missionaries took place via snail mail.	*Global*: Jones puts it best when he writes: "With no major wars or economic depressions to unite us, students believe they're citizens of the world, and their loyalties may be stronger to the entire human race than they are to nations. CNN and the Internet only strengthen this conviction."[G]
Compartmentalized: One's life and character at work could be separated from life on Sundays at church. We could live segmented lives. People did not practice what they preached in all areas of life.	*Holistic*: Integrity in *all* aspects of life is very important. Postmoderns are *rightly* suspicious of those who live segmented, compartmentalized lives.
Relevant: Make the gospel relevant to peoples' daily lives. Be seeker-sensitive.	*Authentic*: Be real. Be full of integrity in all areas of life. Jones puts it well: "Today, the younger generations respond [to appeals to relevance of the Bible to our daily lives], "Don't tell me how to apply this Bible passage to my life. You don't know anything about my life. Just tell me what it really means. I'll decide how to apply it."[H]

A. Jones, *Postmodern Youth Ministry*, 31.
B. Jones, *Postmodern Youth Ministry*, 33.
C. Jones, *Postmodern Youth Ministry*, 35.
D. Jones, *Postmodern Youth Ministry*, 35.
E. Jones, *Postmodern Youth Ministry*, 34.
F. Jones, *Postmodern Youth Ministry*, 36.
G. Jones, *Postmodern Youth Ministry*, 37.
H. Jones, *Postmodern Youth Ministry*, 37.

Besides their descriptions of modernity's influences, I also addressed a philosophical shift emergents endorse in the theory of how we have knowledge, namely, away from "foundationalism" to a kind of "holism." Foundationalism is a view that our beliefs can be structured in such a way that the justification of some beliefs can be used to support other beliefs. Some of those former kinds of beliefs are "foundational," much like a building's foundation. They are anchored, or grounded, in reality, and even knowably so—these are called *basic* beliefs. And, I examined various changes emergents recommend for the practice of the Christian faith, in order to be faithful to the gospel story in postmodern times.

In my assessment, I tried to highlight several good, practical concerns and suggestions emergents raise, such as about the church's need to be authentic. As for criticisms, I first suggested that they had not described accurately the options within philosophy about foundationalism. I argued mainly that they misconstrue foundationalism as requiring that we have "bomb-proof" *certainty* in our beliefs. Instead, I pointed out that, among philosophers, there is a widely recognized version called "modest foundationalism," which does not require invincible certainty in our beliefs. Yet, in that more "modest" view, we still can know directly, immediately, that some of our beliefs are justified by reality.

Yet, interestingly, Jones replied to me that *in practice* many pastors and Christian leaders act and preach as though they have "bomb-proof" certainty. This claim is not about the philosophical status of foundationalism; rather, he was observing how attitudes that were shaped by modernity have affected Christians practically. This claim is much more significant than I realized at the time, and I will return to it later in some detail.

Relatedly, I observed in *Truth* that emergents deny that we could ever have *direct* access to know reality. Instead, I suggested that for their views, each community has its own language, and that language "stands between" us and reality itself. Moreover, the real world in itself is indeterminate. So, we end up "constructing" our own worlds by how we talk about them, according to the grammar (story) of our community. This in turn has major implications for Christian doctrines, as I then argued.

However, through dialogues with James K. A. Smith and Alasdair MacIntyre, I learned since the publication of *Truth* that this interpretation of their claim was mistaken. Smith and I both contributed to *Christianity and the Postmodern Turn*, which appeared in 2005. There, I reiterated the same interpretation I gave in *Truth*. But Smith countered that I was claiming that "we are imprisoned in language—that there is a world 'out there,' but it is a kind of noumenal realm that we can never reach, because we are confined by the strictures of language that come 'between' us and the world."[17] To him, my criticisms are off base because I have a "restrictive understanding of language."[18] Instead, as he suggested, language is *part* of the world, and so are we. Further, he claimed that the world we inhabit is "always already *interpreted* within a framework of signs or a semiotic system."[19] Nevertheless,

17. Smith, "Who's Afraid of Postmodernism?," 221.
18. Smith, "Who's Afraid of Postmodernism?," 222.
19. Smith, "Who's Afraid of Postmodernism?," 222 (emphasis in original).

this view does not entail the "kind of stilted Kantianism that Scott paints."[20] Instead, for him, "the very experience of the things themselves is a matter of interpretation."[21] Or, put a bit differently, *everything is interpretation*.

The more I have considered his (and others) comments, I think Smith is right that this is a better understanding of what people like McLaren and others are trying to say. However, this means that I need to return and reconsider my earlier assessments of such views. This book gives me an occasion to do that in regards to these emergents.

Additionally, McLaren, Jones, Pagitt, and Bell have developed their views significantly over the years. I believe we now can see that there are many shaping influences on their ideas and suggestions, including but not limited to those specifically from postmodernity. Indeed, they are addressing questions and topics of concern to the broader public. For instance, they have developed their thought ethically, such as about colonialism and its influences, even upon the church, and how we should live in postcolonial times.[22] They also have raised questions and advanced several provocative claims that relate to the nature of the gospel itself and traditional doctrines of the faith, such as about heaven, hell, and the status of followers of other religions; the nature of sin and why Jesus died on the cross; what kind of thing humans are (e.g., are we really a unity of body and soul?); the nature of God's relationship to creation; and even more. I did not really address these topics in *Truth*, yet the emergents' stances are vitally important for Christians to consider. To what extent should we embrace their thoughts?

So, in chapter 1, I will try to explain the development of their thought in at least these aspects. I will consider McLaren and Pagitt's appeal to an older story line than that of modernity, namely a Greco-Roman version of the gospel story. In chapter 2, I will provide my own sketch of the major shaping influences of the predominantly Western and, in particular, Americanized version of Christianity, the one with which people like McLaren find such fault in terms of the practice of Christianity. Doing this will help in part to assess the accuracy of their concerns with evangelicalism and conservative Christian churches and organizations. Yet, I also will suggest that the root problem is not so much the shaping influences of modernity as it is something more specific, something which I think we will see later that these emergents *also* embrace. If so, that may have important implications

20. Smith, "Who's Afraid of Postmodernism?," 222.

21. Smith, "Who's Afraid of Postmodernism?," 218.

22. Burson *(Brian McLaren in Focus)* shows how for McLaren, this shift is tied to a shift in emphasis from postmodernism to postcolonialism (e.g., 51), the latter of which I will develop more in chapter 1.

for their proposed correctives for how to be faithful as Christians in our time.

In chapter 3, I will turn to surface some contributions these men have made. While I attempted to surface helpful observations of their contributions in *Truth, I did not realize then just how accurate they were (and still are) in many of their observations and criticisms of all too many of today's evangelicals and their churches.* It is important then for me to try to do justice to their important points.

Then, in chapters 4 and 5, I will assess their more recent views, including the trajectories of their thought. I will divide my attention between considering philosophical issues (including, but not limited to, the claim that everything is interpretation) and biblical, theological ones. Finally, in chapter 6, I will offer a suggestion for a more faithful way forward for both evangelicals and these emergents, and those influenced by their thought. Here I will propose what I think is the overarching story line of the entire Bible, and how this actually fits with the findings for which I will have argued. It also fits my own story, of which I will sketch some key parts in hopes of my readers having a better understanding not only of what shapes and influences me (factors in my "situatedness"), but also as an example of how my suggested story line of the Bible has explanatory power in real life.

All in all, what I hope to accomplish is to point to, and illustrate, *the utter importance for both evangelicals and emergents of living in the fullness of life that God has for us in Christ.* That is the key to a great, new, and *authentic emergence* of the church from its present captivity, which I will argue is due to subtle, yet deeply naturalistic influences. In all too many ways, the church today in the west, and particularly North America, has been *naturalized.* This clearly is not in the sense that Christians no longer believe God exists; rather, it is the more subtle sense that God has become, to various extents, irrelevant for how we live our lives. My proposed solution will be an authentic kind of Christianity that emerges from being deeply united with the Lord, and it is truly progressive—fresh, full of life, and full of God's power and presence. This more authentic kind of Christianity comes from recapturing and embracing the fullness of life God promises in Scripture.

1

The Development
of Emergents' Thought

Introduction

Brian McLaren writes as a concerned Christian thinker, former pastor, and speaker/activist who is deeply concerned that Western Christians have been so co-opted by the influences and values of modernity that they do not even realize how the way they live out the faith has become "modernized."[1] He also has pointed out to me that he is more concerned with ethics (orthopraxis) than right doctrine (orthodoxy) or philosophy. For example, why have particular views helped foster and sanction the use of violence in association with the gospel?

> I am less concerned to argue for or against foundationalism [a view in epistemology] than I am to ask questions like these: why did so many Christians of the modern era—whom [sic] I assume were as sincere, intelligent, pious, and honest as any of us, likely more so—find it so easy to participate in colonialism, racism, slavery, environmental irresponsibility, mistreatment of women, militarism, and a careless attitude toward the poor? Why did their theologies make them concerned about scores of rather petty issues while ignoring these larger issues, or even worse, while defending the wrong side of these larger issues?[2]

1. See the charts in the introduction. See also McLaren's *A New Kind of Christian*.
2. McLaren in the second part of his "Cordial Response to R. Scott Smith" (bracketed

He has emphasized the importance of orthopraxis as *the point* of orthodoxy, and so he is not as concerned with generating a "right" system of beliefs (which would seem to him to be a modern project) as much as he is with helping us to live faithfully as Christians in our contexts.[3] Indeed, in *A New Kind of Christianity*, McLaren expands these to a more holistic set of emphases of orthodoxy, orthopathy, ortho-affinity, and orthopraxy.[4] Of course, that does not mean he does not have theological views that shape and inform his ethics. Indeed, in *A New Kind of Christianity*, he reaches even further back in history than the modern era, to trace the roots of those issues.

One of the main emphases that surfaces in McLaren, Jones, Pagitt, and Bell is the importance of relationships, something that McLaren sees as being undermined by the modern emphasis on the autonomous individual. This ethical emphasis ends up influencing many aspects of his thought; for instance, the importance placed upon *living in* community and *living out* the "one anothers" of Scripture. Another facet is the emphasis placed upon embodiment, which is crucial for our living out these relationships. Yet another influence is the "turn to relationality," which has implications for what kind of things we are. For instance, should we understand ourselves in the more "conventional" way, as being both body and soul, or in a way that is more holistic in terms of our relationships? Of course, this will have implications for what God is like, so that we can be in relationship with God.

My focus here will not be on McLaren's, Bell's, Pagitt's, or Jones's specific, applied ethical exhortations as much as their shaping influences, to help us understand the *whys* behind their thought, and then to assess them constructively later. To do that, I will try to summarize McLaren's understanding of the story of Jesus when it has been stripped of its distorting influences, to get to his radical, "secret" message, one that is set in its Jewish narrative context. In that process, I will explain his view that Jesus' kingdom comes in nonviolent, non-coercive, and non-controlling ways, which will have implications for his views of Christ's work on the cross, hell, and more. I will look at his notion of "purposeful inclusion" and just what enables one to be a member of his kingdom. Along the way, I also will bring in Pagitt's, Bell's, and Jones's respective views to help flesh out their understanding of these kinds of topics. I will take these steps to show why they come to their particular ethical emphases.

inserts mine).

3. McLaren, *Generous Orthodoxy*, 31.

4. McLaren, *A New Kind of Christianity*, 29.

But, I should note that I am not trying to force their views to fit into McLaren's framing story. For some time now, McLaren has been developing an extended explanation of how Christianity in the West has gotten into a mess, as well as a recommended set of solutions for how to go forward now as Christians. He thus provides a way to examine in some specifics, but also in broad terms, why many think we now need to embrace a new kind of Christianity, beyond the traditional evangelicalism that these men have left. So, his views provide a way to see touch points with what Bell, Pagitt, and Jones also are saying, yet with their own distinctives.

Deconstructing the Story:
Finding the "Secret Message" of Jesus

McLaren wisely wants to consider carefully the contexts in which Jesus lived and taught, and this leads him to an exploration of the political, religious, and social dynamics and dreams of Jesus' day. A key concern for McLaren is that by focusing today extensively on a framing story of Jesus that emphasizes his dying for our sins so that we can go to heaven when we die, we not only bring certain aspects of his story to light, but we also might miss or even suppress other dimensions, ones that might prove to be even more important.[5] Part of McLaren's motivation is a concern that we have domesticated Jesus, whether by materialistic science or conventional religion, and so his stated objective is to find a more radical vision of him, one that is more faithful to the Gospels.[6] He will try to peel "back the layers of theology and history," to find the core of Jesus' message.[7]

But, why is this even needed? To McLaren, today we have inherited a version of the gospel story that has been filtered through the lens of a different framing story, one that even predates and helped give shape to modernity's own overarching story and subplots.

The Greco-Roman Narrative

McLaren thinks that today we have been reading Jesus' story through the received lens of the Greco-Roman story, and not the Jewish story that developed through the Jewish patriarchs, Moses, and the prophets. Put differently, we have been reading Jesus' story (and even that of the whole Bible)

5. McLaren, *Secret Message*, 3.

6. McLaren, *Secret Message*, x.

7. McLaren, *Secret Message*, 26.

backwards rather than *forwards*. Under this influence, McLaren claims that since about the fifth of sixth century in the West, being a Christian "has required one to believe that the Bible presents one . . . storyline by which we assess" all history and experience.[8]

According to him, there are six main steps in this story. First, the garden of Eden was an absolutely perfect creation. Second came the fall into original sin, which, third, led to a "state" of condemnation, i.e., the fallen world. Fourth, there is salvation, justification, and atonement. Then, there are two options: fifth is the state of heaven, or eternity, whereas the other, sixth option is the state of hell with eternal conscious torment. McLaren depicts these as follows:

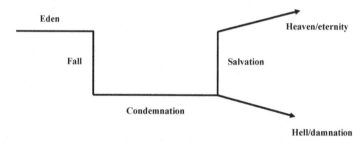

But McLaren questions this received narrative. He notices that it begins with one classification of things, all being good, yet ends with two very different ones (good versus evil), as though this story can be reduced to a "manufacturing process" that sorts its products into their appropriate bins. It's as though their eternal destinies are predetermined, so that those who are deemed evil (or good for that matter) are selected due to nothing they deserve.[9]

Now we should observe the kinds of questions McLaren raises to get us to enter into his thinking, such as rhetorical ones to get us to question our own preconceived notions. For instance, "can we dare to wonder" if it would have been better if this story never arose, since there is more suffering at its end than its start? He also asks us questions such as these: Did biblical characters, such as Abraham, Moses, Jesus or Paul, hold the Greco-Roman story? Does Scripture teach it directly? Did the church in its first three centuries accept it? Does it help us love God, our neighbors, enemies, and strangers more?[10]

8. McLaren, *A New Kind of Christianity*, 34.

9. McLaren, *A New Kind of Christianity*, 35.

10. McLaren, *A New Kind of Christianity*, 37 (bracketed insert mine).

To him, the answers are clearly "no." Instead, the Greco-Roman narrative is a marriage of Greek philosophy (that of Plato, seen through Plotinus, and Aristotle) with the Roman political, economic, and military empire. McLaren portrays Plato as maintaining that ultimate reality is immaterial, eternal, and unchanging (the realm of the "forms," or essences). Material reality, which is temporal and changing, is like shadows of the "forms" on the dark wall of a cave. In contrast, according to McLaren, Aristotle taught that the changing, material world (for example, chairs, people, etc.) is real. "Chair" and "people" are just unchanging words or names we impose on those things.[11]

For McLaren, at least three results stemmed from this treatment. First, the Greco-Roman mind was dualistic. On the one hand, the profane, physical world of matter is always changing, but the metaphysical world of ideals and spirit is sacred and changeless. Second, the Greco-Roman mind developed a sense of superiority and supremacy. Using Aristotelian resources, the Greeks and Romans developed amazing engineering feats, whereas using Platonic ones, they developed the life of the mind, thinking they could grasp absolute, transcendent, universal truths. Third, a social dualism and sense of superiority developed: "we" the civilized are superior, whereas "others" are barbarians and inferior. The social order was characterized by order and stasis, and it was imperial in outlook.[12]

Now we can transpose this narrative on the six-step received version of the Bible's story line, to see how McLaren understands its impact on our inherited version of the Bible's story:

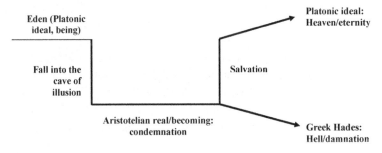

For him, there are several key shifts resulting from the Greco-Roman framework's influence. First, there is a shift from the biblical view of a good garden of Eden to one that is a perfect and unchanging Platonic ideal, or state. Second, the fall is not simply a move from obedience to disobedience.

11. McLaren, *A New Kind of Christianity*, 38.
12. McLaren, *A New Kind of Christianity*, 38–39.

Rather, it becomes a fall from Platonic perfection to Aristotelian change and becoming, which involves a shift from *state* to *story*.

God's character becomes skewed, too, according to McLaren, so that God (whom McLaren dubs "Theos") is like Zeus. Theos is a perfect Platonic god who loves spirit, state, and being, but hates matter, story, and becoming, since there's only one way to go from perfection. What is becoming is pathetic, detestable, and imperfect, so Theos wants to destroy it. The doctrine of original sin suggests God is hostile toward humans and his perfection "requires God to punish all imperfect beings with eternal conscious torment in hell. So in this popular view of original sin, God's response to anything that is less than absolutely perfect must be absolute and infinite hostility."[13] Salvation means being forgiven, that is, souls are restored to a plane of perfection, so Theos can love them again.

What about hell? In a world that has been purged of becoming, it too must be a state, a permanent condition that is unchanging. Taken together with these other aspects, McLaren sarcastically claims this story is the "good news" taught by much of Western Christianity.[14]

Pagitt embraces a similar understanding of how the Jewish story of the good news was translated into Greek thought and thereby changed in the process. As he explains, under Constantine, "Christianity started moving from a faith committed to multicultural unity to one requiring monocultural uniformity," and this took place during the embrace of the Greek worldview.[15] Even before that, during the first century and the spread of the gospel by Jesus' followers farther and farther away from Jerusalem and into the rest of the Mediterranean area, they "used Greek understandings . . . to tell the story of the Hebrew faith."[16] By the time of Constantine, Christianity became the official religion of the Empire. This is highly significant for Pagitt, for he reasons that in so doing, Christianity became a Greek expression. But, "when the telling of the gospel changes, the meaning of the gospel changes with it"; thus, "we have ended up with a changed faith."[17] The result of this assimilation meant that in terms of understanding the gospel, there was less Hebrew influence and more Greek dominance, so much so that Pagitt claims our theology today has been shaped profoundly by first-century Greco-Roman influences.[18]

13. McLaren, *Why Did Jesus,* 106.

14. McLaren, *A New Kind of Christianity,* 41–44.

15. Pagitt, *Christianity Worth Believing,* 41.

16. Pagitt, *Christianity Worth Believing,* 44.

17. Pagitt, *Christianity Worth Believing,* 45.

18. Pagitt, *Christianity Worth Believing,* 45.

Reinterpreting Jesus' Context

In contrast to the Greco-Roman story, McLaren thinks that if we understand Jesus' story as situated in *his* context, then we can see that politically, Jesus announced that the kingdom of God is here and now, that we are to believe this and follow him. This is a new political, social, and spiritual reality, one that is radically unlike the Roman Empire or modern, imperialistic nation-states, for in his kingdom, there are no violent responses, even to evil, for violence is defeated with forgiveness.[19]

For Jews, this "good news" comes with an announcement of judgment on injustice and hypocrisy, but this too does not mean that sinners will be sent to hell. On the contrary, McLaren observes that the ancient prophets did not mean by "judgment" that people would be sent to hell.[20] Instead, judgment is about the exposing of, naming of, and dealing with evil.

In *The Secret Message of Jesus*, McLaren begins to develop his version of the story in which we find ourselves, which includes three episodes.[21] The first episode he calls *creation*, in which God is not a removed, deistic creator, but rather a relational participant in creation's story. In McLaren's earlier trilogy, his character Neo explains that for the Jews, this episode does *not* mean that there were two worlds, a morally superior "ideal" world before the fall, and a morally evil, material world after the fall. That, he explains, is a Greek notion that was imported into our thinking, which, as we have seen, fits with McLaren's understanding of Plato and Aristotle's influence upon Greek thought as passed down through Plotinus.[22] Instead, the universe is not to be seen as dichotomies between the natural and supernatural, or physical and spiritual; rather, the world is deeply integrated "with matter and life and God."[23]

The second episode, *crisis*, is marked by disconnection from God. There is a series of crises, as Neo explains, "a disintegration of the primal harmony and innocence of creation. In a sense, they all involve human beings gaining levels of intellectual and technological development that surpass their moral development."[24] Adam and Eve's decision to be like gods themselves resulted in their going "beyond the limits that they know they should keep" and thereby "*disrupting the balance, going beyond their proper*

---

19. McLaren, *Secret Message*, 18. Nor, as we shall see, are sinners damned to hell, for in Jesus' kingdom we refuse to judge (17).

20. McLaren, *Secret Message*, 23.

21. See also a discussion in McLaren, *Story*, 71–75.

22. McLaren, *A New Kind of Christianity*, 37.

23. McLaren, *Story*, 51.

24. McLaren, *Story*, 53–54.

limits as . . . part of creation."[25] Disobedience has resulted in shame, alienation, disharmony, and more.

In the third episode, *calling*, God calls Abraham, Sarah, and others to know him and make him known, to "be part of this movement of people who want to bring God's blessing back to the world,"[26] to rescue God's creation from *human* evil.[27] Fourth, the *conversation* between God's people with and about God and their special, covenant relationship carries on across generations. There also is conflict in this episode of the story, for "remaining faithful to God and God's calling involves great struggle with both internal and external antagonists."[28]

The Jewish Story, and What God is Like

Now, in *A New Kind of Christianity*, McLaren has extended and modified these themes somewhat. Instead of focusing upon these four episodes of the Bible's story line, he now tries to develop a more particular statement of the overall "Jewish" story line in the Bible, which sets the context within which Jesus' story needs to be seen.[29] In this way of framing the Bible's story, McLaren draws upon three motifs: Genesis, Exodus, and Isaiah.

In Genesis, McLaren sees a story of God's good, evolving, *sacred creation*, yet one that has been marred by human evil, and then *reconciliation*. It would include the episode he entitled "calling" before, such as God's calling of Abraham and the patriarchs. The book of Genesis gives us a sacred vision of the past, but that does not mean it (at least in its entirety) should be read as literal history. For instance, he does not interpret Eden's story literally.

McLaren interprets Exodus to be a story of *sacred liberation* and *formation*. Interestingly, he gives some space to understanding the story of Israel's bondage, suffering, and then deliverance from Egypt. In his account, it is a story of injustice and oppression, but, importantly, it is *not* a story of God acting violently toward the Egyptians, despite his acknowledgment that there are at times "troubling" details in Exodus. For instance, he explains

25. McLaren, *Story*, 54 (emphasis mine).

26. McLaren, *Story*, 73.

27. McLaren, *Secret Message*, 28.

28. McLaren, *Secret Message*, 28.

29. It is interesting that McLaren writes as though there is a *single* Jewish story— "the" one he tells (privileges?)—when in his view it seems everything is interpretation, thereby rendering *many* versions of "the" Jewish story, and as many as there are those doing the telling.

the Nile's turning "red like blood" as due perhaps to "a red tide."[30] It is not God who uses a plague to strike dead the firstborn in Egypt, but instead it is just "a plague."

Indeed, "God never works directly, only indirectly," working through people like Moses, or natural phenomena like frogs, diseases, and weather.[31] Instead, "God sides with the oppressed, and God confronts oppressors with intensifying negative consequences" until the victims are freed, and the victimizers are humbled.[32] God is not passive about injustice, but he also does not "force compliance."[33] In all this, God works as liberator from external and internal oppression.

Similarly, for Bell, God does judge people, but it is *not* forever; that is not even a biblical category, he claims.[34] In an example from the Old Testament, yet as used by Jesus, Bell discusses references to Sodom and Gomorrah *after* their destruction in Genesis 19. For instance, he notices that Ezekiel records God's promise that he will "restore their captivity, the captivity of Sodom and her daughters" (Ezek 16:53), and they "will return to their former state" (v. 55). So Bell reasons that according to Ezekiel, after destruction there will be restoration. Similarly, as Jesus warns the people in Capernaum that it will be more tolerable for Sodom and Gomorrah than for them in the day of judgment (Matt 10:15; cf. 11:23–24), so Bell understands this to mean that there *still* is hope for Sodom.

So, God judges, but always with restoration in view. Bell observes that the prophets teach that "God crushes, refines, tests . . . but always with a purpose."[35] This is the case even with delivering someone over to "Satan," for even in such cases, God's purpose is to teach people not to blaspheme (as in 1 Tim 1:20).[36] Bell concludes that "no matter how far people find themselves from home because of their sin, indifference, and rejection," we can be assured that this will not be their condition for all time.[37] So, the purpose of God's judgment seems to be to rehabilitate us, so we can learn from the consequences of our bad choices.[38]

---

30. McLaren, *A New Kind of Christianity*, 57.

31. McLaren, *A New Kind of Christianity*, 58.

32. McLaren, *A New Kind of Christianity*, 57–58.

33. McLaren, *A New Kind of Christianity*, 58.

34. Bell, *Love Wins*, 88.

35. Bell, *Love Wins*, 85–86.

36. I put "Satan" in quotes, as Bell does (*Love Wins*, 89).

37. Bell, *Love Wins*, 86 (emphasis in original).

38. Thanks to Michael Wittmer for this suggestion.

What else is this Jewish God like? McLaren says God is compassionate, not violent; gentle, not cruel; good, not evil; forgiving, not retaliatory toward some; and just and fair to all, not biased toward some. Indeed, according to Burson, McLaren's "bedrock belief" is that God is good.[39] Unlike Theos, God is not capricious, bloodthirsty, hateful, or prone to fits of vengeful rage. Nor is God tribal, imperial, or a violent god of profit. Nor is God a dictator, as would be the case, he thinks, if God exhaustively determines the future, for history is unscripted. Instead, God loves justice, kindness, reconciliation, and peace. In the end, his "grace gets the final word."[40]

To help dislodge the notion that God's justice requires wrath to be poured out on sinners, Tony Jones goes to great lengths in *A Better Atonement* to stress the idea that God, as to his *essence*, and not a mere attribute, is love. Jones draws upon Orthodox Christianity to try to show that the Western Church's idea that justice and love are *attributes* of God is not necessarily the only, or best, understanding of the atonement. Rather, for Orthodox Christians, "their starting and ending point is 1 John 4:8—'God is love.'"[41] Citing the Antiochian Orthodox priest, Father James Bernstein, this means that "His love is not just an expression of His will towards creation, or simply an attribute, but rather God loves by nature—because of who He is."[42]

Later, Jones suggests this kind of mind-set fits better with our own experience of God. A stress upon God's wrath "contradicts the experience that most of us have with God, and that a lot of us have with the Bible. Our experience of God is not of wrath, but of love. Indeed, that's how most people experience God even before they accept the idea that Christ stands between us and God. So it seems odd to first have to convince people that God's wrath burns against them, then to convince them that Jesus lovingly took on that wrath."[43]

Bell suggests in *Love Wins* a similar view of God's very essence as love.[44] He complains that in the received view of (evangelical) Christianity, if people don't believe the right things in the right ways (i.e., how the person doing the telling believes), they'll go to hell.[45] This strikes him as untenable; this God is fundamentally different from the One whose essence is love.

---

39. Burson, *Brian McLaren in Focus*, 155, 206–7.

40. McLaren, *A New Kind of Christianity*, 102.

41. Jones, *A Better Atonement*, locations 414–15.

42. Bernstein, https://preachersinstitute.com/2014/09/22/the-original-christian-gospel/, cited in Jones, *A Better Atonement*, locations 419–20.

43. Jones, *A Better Atonement*, locations 584–87.

44. Bell, *Love Wins*, 177, where he explicitly says this twice.

45. Bell, *Love Wins*, 173.

Here is his depiction, with vivid imagery: "A loving father who will go to extraordinary lengths to have a relationship with them would, in the blink of an eye, become a cruel, mean, vicious tormenter."[46] Such a God seems utterly unlike how we know our earthly fathers should behave. If there was one who behaved like that, we would call the police!

For McLaren, it is the God of fundamentalists, whether Christian, Jew, or Muslim, who is most like Theos. This God is a competitive warrior, jealous of rivals, and determined to defeat them in disgrace. The God of the fundamentalists is superficially exacting, exclusive, loving one "in group" but rejecting (and maybe even hating) others.[47] It is this God that is deterministic and never moved by events; not interacting, but controlling.

Ultimately, this God is violent and will explode with unquenchable rage if pushed too far.[48] Indeed, a God who intentionally would commit genocide through a flood is unacceptable to McLaren, hardly being "worthy of belief, much less worship. How can you ask your children—or nonchurch colleagues and neighbors—to honor a deity so uncreative, overreactive, and utterly capricious regarding life?"[49]

Now, Burson makes it clear that McLaren had been taught and embraced five-point Calvinism as a teenager.[50] Yet, over time, he came to see it as the "chief propagator of this kind of distorted Christian narrative."[51] As recounted in *A Generous Orthodoxy*, he came to see the God of Calvinism as the "chief engineer, [who was] controlling the whole machine" of creation.[52] Moreover, to him, the determinism in Calvinism leads to an illusion of freedom, leaving us as just puppets.[53] If that is the case, then creation (and humans in particular) does not really have dignity and authenticity.[54] However, McLaren now makes clear that he is not trying to single out five-point Calvinism, but rather "fundamentalism and the broader inflexible, self-protective, and (sadly) racist Christian identity that so often takes refuge in fundamentalism."[55]

---

46. Bell, *Love Wins*, 173–74 (bracketed insert mine).

47. For McLaren, under the Greco-Roman view, homosexuals have been rejected simply due to how they were born. See *A New Kind of Christianity*, 178.

48. McLaren, *A New Kind of Christianity*, 102.

49. McLaren, *A New Kind of Christianity*, 109.

50. Burson, *Brian McLaren in Focus*, 13, 96.

51. Burson, *Brian McLaren in Focus*, 24.

52. McLaren, *Generous Orthodoxy*, 187.

53. McLaren, *Generous Orthodoxy*, 186.

54. Burson, *Brian McLaren in Focus*, 112.

55. McLaren, "Five Questions You Might be Asking," 14.

Bell's view of God is very similar to McLaren's. The God who has been taught to many Christians is unlovable.[56] A God who can be loving one moment, but cruel and terrifying the next, is not only schizophrenic, but also unacceptable. Moreover, a God who would punish people forever for their sins which they committed in only a short time seems repugnant. Again, Bell expresses himself very powerfully: "no amount of clever marketing or compelling language or good music or great coffee will be able to disguise that one, true, *glaring, untenable, unacceptable, awful reality*."[57]

In his more recent book, *What We Talk About When We Talk About God*, Bell wants to address misconceptions that many people have about God today. The God that Christians talk about often can seem to cause harm and fail many people, whether through allowing suffering or even commanding wars and genocides.[58] To trust in that God can seem like "a step *backward*, to an earlier, less informed and enlightened time."[59] This God can seem tribal (e.g., by being *for* the elect), irrelevant, narrow (requiring only one way to God), mean (due to the problem of evil), and perhaps not very smart (in light of science).[60]

For Pagitt, the received version of Christianity portrays a God who is "up and out," who utterly determines all events, so that "all that happens, good or bad," is God's doing.[61] And, we cannot please this God. Pagitt, like Bell and McLaren, draws upon many pastoral (and personal) examples that show how people need (and many want) a God who is "down and in," who is intimate and will identify with us, and who will comfort us. I think a strength of his book *A Christianity Worth Believing* is the deep pathos with which he writes, whether expressing his own pain and brokenness (e.g., "I knew pain. I had been both the violated, lonely victim, and the oppressing, bullying offender") or that of others, such as victims of sexual abuse.[62] In these stories, Pagitt powerfully expresses his heart's cry (and that of many others) for a God who will be intimate with us, comfort us, and dwell with us.[63]

---

56. Bell, *Love Wins*, 175.

57. Bell, *Love Wins*, 175 (emphasis mine).

58. Bell, *What We Talk About*, 3.

59. Bell, *What We Talk About*, 7 (emphasis in original).

60. Note: the parenthetical explanations are my suggestions. Bell simply lists the adjectives in this perception of God.

61. Pagitt, *A Christianity Worth Believing*, 102.

62. Pagitt, *A Christianity Worth Believing*, 95.

63. I deeply resonate with this heart cry. I will try to explain this aspect of my story later.

Yet, to him, in the received view, which he chalks up to the Greco-
Roman "hybrid God," God is perfect and removed, yet loves us, but only
conditionally (for the right kind of follower). This God is opposed to most
people, and he mostly wants obedience.[64] He is unmovable, "wholly other
and nothing like" us, and not really immanent in the world.

We have been taught, according to Pagitt, that the biblical language
that seems to portray God as being close, intimate, and involved with our
suffering and daily lives really is just poetic and has "nothing to do with the
reality of God's nature. . . . [which is] summed up in the prescribed list of
qualities of God—the omnis."[65] Indeed, these poetic uses of language are to
be treated as culturally bound, but not the understanding of God as immovable, distant, and removed.[66]

Like Bell, Pagitt is highly engaging and at his best, I think, when he
describes the hearts of people he has known and counseled who have tried
to live with this "up and out" view of God. He describes the impact of this
view upon Amy, who describes her mind-set and feelings as never being
able to please God, that she "could never be repentant enough," for God
could never forget her sins.[67] Could such a God love her completely? No; if
honest with herself, she felt that "that powerful, vengeful God" could "barely
stand to look at me."[68]

Pagitt describes how the view that sin separates us from God implies
also that it separates God from us. Yet, from what he has experienced, he
still knew that "God was with me even when I was an 'unrepentant sinner.'"[69]
But, as he suggests, if sin causes distance between us, that implies sin is more
powerful than God (which is not true) and that God is not active in the lives
of both saints and sinners. Yet surely God does seek out the sinner; after all,
Jesus came to seek and save the lost.

These considerations move Pagitt to reconceive of sin not as distance,
but in terms of *disintegration*. Instead of being separated from God, Pagitt
describes his own conversion as a "new connection with God": "God hadn't
been waiting for me to do something before God was willing to get involved
in my life. God had been involved all along. The disconnection ended not
when God decided I was righteous enough or clean enough or enough of

64. Pagitt, *A Christianity Worth Believing*, 99.

65. Pagitt, *A Christianity Worth Believing*, 108–9.

66. Pagitt, *A Christianity Worth Believing*, 109.

67. Pagitt, *A Christianity Worth Believing*, 111, where he quotes her own comments
about her story.

68. Pagitt, *A Christianity Worth Believing*, 111.

69. Pagitt, *A Christianity Worth Believing*, 112.

a believer to cross the bridge but when I saw what it looked like to live life with God and understood the invitation to join in."[70]

In Pagitt's mind, the received "Greek" view we have inherited about God and our separation from him leaves us with devastating effects. To him, this theology might help bridge the gap by the cross, but it never really closes that gap because we have to be perfect for this God, which will never happen until after we die. Our sins won't count against us, but until then we will be imperfect and flawed.[71] These positions leave us with an "afterlife-focused faith," with little motivation for living now for God. Instead, we are left to "bide our time in this miserable life until God decides it's time for us to escape to heaven."[72]

In the third part of "the" Jewish story, McLaren uses Isaiah to show that, having been liberated and on a journey, Israel's narrative culminates in the "sacred dream of the peaceable kingdom," first in which Israel will enjoy the blessings of the promised land.[73] But then Israel lives under many failed, corrupt regimes, is plagued by enemies, and finally is exiled. But then this dream of a peaceable kingdom expands to a promised time, with "a sacred vision of the future," one of love and hope.[74]

But McLaren's understanding of this eschatological hope is not the same as the one many evangelicals tend to find in eternity, in heaven with the Lord, or in a millennial reign of Christ on earth, views that McLaren finds to be children of the Greco-Roman narrative.[75] Instead, he asks us to imagine a different understanding: "What if we were to receive these images [i.e., of God's peaceable kingdom, as in Isa 2:4, 11:6–9, or 65:17–25] as a vision of the kind of future toward which God is inviting us in history . . . [and] not a perfect state beyond time?"[76] For McLaren, this way of rein-terpreting these prophetic visions (i.e., more as poetry within his overall "Jewish" story) liberates us from seeing the future as utterly determined, for the future is unfolding along with us and our actions now.

---

70. Pagitt, *A Christianity Worth Believing*, 113. The "bridge" is a reference to dia-grams, such as used by Campus Crusade, now Cru, that the cross of Christ provides, to bridge the gulf between us and God that is caused by our sins. For example, see http://www.crustore.org/fourlawseng.htm.

71. Pagitt, *A Christianity Worth Believing*, 113.

72. Pagitt, *A Christianity Worth Believing*, 114.

73. McLaren, *A New Kind of Christianity*, 59.

74. McLaren, *A New Kind of Christianity*, 65.

75. McLaren, *A New Kind of Christianity*, 62.

76. McLaren, *A New Kind of Christianity*, 62 (inserted brackets mine).

For McLaren, God doesn't determine all events; instead, the future is genuinely open to God. McLaren is a kind of open theist.[77] For him, the "future . . . is waiting to be created."[78] Moreover, God's peaceable kingdom is "a potentiality to which God from the future is inviting humanity as 'junior partners' to help establish in this space-time matrix."[79] The story we find ourselves in is an evolving one.

For McLaren, this openness requires that humans have free will, in a libertarian sense; i.e., according to Burson, people have "the ability to choose between two or more live options . . . without any predetermining cause."[80] Another key reason for such freedom is that it seems necessary for an authentic faith. Connecting this to Jesus' use of parables, McLaren observes that "if it's the heart that counts, then hearts can't be coerced; nobody can be forced. They can be invited, attracted, intrigued, enticed, and challenged—but not forced."[81] Still, while human freedom is an important position for McLaren, he also has said it is not the *most* important, which is that God is good.

Moreover, this interpretive shift affects our understanding of prophetic visions as literal truths, instead allowing, for instance, to understand Isaiah's reference to beating swords into plowshares more in contemporary terms, such as "Christians and Jews and Muslims throwing a picnic together."[82] Or, having the knowledge of the Lord covering the earth "would mean a deep kind of universal and egalitarian spirituality."[83]

This kind of vision that McLaren casts for the various religions (and their adherents) has further development in his book, *Why Did Jesus, Moses, the Buddha, and Mohammed Cross the Road? Christian Identity in a Multi-Faith World.* There, he explores in detail his religious pluralism, which is quite reminiscent of John Hick's views in at least two ways.[84] First, for McLaren, it seems the goal of all religions is a moral makeover, or transformation. Consider, for instance, his comments about the way of Jesus as one of liberation. He then explains that in terms of addressing injustices; of be-

---

77. See McLaren's reply to e-mail correspondence in Burson, *Brian McLaren in Focus,* 291. See also 75–77 and 96–102. Pagitt agrees that God does not determine all events; see his *Flipped,* 136.

78. McLaren, *A New Kind of Christianity,* 62.

79. Burson, *Brian McLaren in Focus,* 77.

80. Burson, *Brian McLaren in Focus,* 128. See Moreland and Craig, *Philosophical Foundations,* 267–84.

81. McLaren, *Secret Message,* 48.

82. McLaren, *A New Kind of Christianity,* 63.

83. McLaren, *A New Kind of Christianity,* 63

84. Hick, "A Pluralist's View."

ing in solidarity with the poorest and the marginalized; meeting the needs of the homeless, thirsty, and hungry; developing opportunities for work and education; and more.[85]

Additionally, he is quite explicit that he is not saying that all religions teach the same things, nor is he denying the presence of "unique divine revelation in any one religion."[86] But, there is a second point of commonality with Hick. By appealing to the Spirit's omnipresence, and that "all people are encountering the Holy Spirit simply because we live, move, and have our being in the Spirit's domain, we can understand human religions—all human religions, including our own—as imperfect human responses to our encounters with the Spirit who is present in all creation."[87]

As I have argued elsewhere, McLaren affirms the epistemological view that we do not have direct access to reality as it truly is, in itself, apart from how we interpret it.[88] To even have an experience, whether of God, anyone, or anything else, requires interpretation. This is quite similar to the view of Hick and his religious pluralism, who, by applying Kant's epistemology, has contended that no one religion has direct access to ultimate religious reality (the "Real"); instead, our various experiences of the Real inevitably are shaped by our conceptual grid.[89] So, McLaren seems to follow that kind of path when he proposes that "each religion, based on its unique location and history, would have a unique, particular, and evolving perspective from which to encounter the Spirit in a unique way. That would mean that differences between religions would not necessarily mean contradictions. They could simply mean additional data, expressed in different systems of local imagery and language, based on differing encounters with the same Spirit of God, present in all creation across all time."[90]

On the Bible and Its Interpretations

These three books, or perhaps "motifs," of the Jewish framing story shed considerable light for us on how McLaren sees the Bible and its authority. Clearly, he does not see it as a legal kind of code to be followed. By approaching it as if it were, he claims we have developed deep problems in relation to

85. For example, see McLaren, *Why Did Jesus*, 236–37.

86. McLaren, *Why Did Jesus*, 152.

87. McLaren, *Why Did Jesus*, 151–52.

88. For example, see my "Reflections on McLaren and the Emerging Church," 237–41.

89. See, e.g., Hick, "A Pluralist's View."

90. McLaren, *Why Did Jesus*, 152.

science, ethics, and peace. With science, fundamentalism has painted "itself into a corner by requiring that the Bible be treated as a divinely dictated science textbook providing us true information in all areas of life," but that approach has placed Christians on the wrong side of truth over and over again, whether that was with Galileo, Darwin, or even with some present-day attitudes such as toward psychological and psychiatric help.[91]

By this way of understanding the Bible, McLaren thinks that ethically we do not have any "clear categories" for many deeply significant social and ethical issues, such as abortion, capitalism, and more, which he says are not directly discussed therein.[92] In terms of peace, he is deeply concerned that due to this same framing story, too many Christians end up using the Bible as "a box cutter or suitcase bomb," to deeply wound and harm others.[93] Finally, he thinks that it has been all too easy to rationalize our stands for immoral positions, like slavery in the United States, due to this way of seeing the Bible.

McLaren posits that this way of reading the Bible is due to seeing it as a "legal constitution," an approach with which we are familiar since we have been raised in such an era. As such, the Bible would be an encyclopedia of facts. So, like lawyers quote specific sections of the constitution to win their case, so we too do that with Bible. We look for precedents in past cases of interpretations. We also look for the "spirit" versus "letter" of the law, and we are concerned with authorial intent. In short, we treat it like an annotated code that resolves all questions and thus should be read literally. Pagitt amplifies this image, noting that in encyclopedias we don't need to read the surrounding entries to get a sense of context for the entry (or facts) we want to find.

Instead, McLaren thinks we need to see the Bible as a community "library" which contains poems, prophecies, histories, fables, parables, letters, sage sayings, quarrels, etc. It is a library of the culture and community that traces back to Abraham, Isaac, and Jacob. The Bible is a carefully selected

91. I think McLaren shines when he puts his finger on a very dangerous attitude that some well-meaning Christians have held. He tells the sad story of a sister of a seminary president who took her life because she was counseled that the only biblical way to deal with her depression was to fast and pray (see *A New Kind of Christianity*, 68). At one point such attitudes led my wife and me to move to a different church, since we were dealing with anxiety and depression while in a church where many also held these kinds of attitudes.

92. McLaren, *A New Kind of Christianity*, 68.

93. McLaren, *A New Kind of Christianity*, 69. Pagitt echoes this same, painful observation, that too often people have used the Bible to "beat others into ideological submission," making it more of a "sword of spite" than the sword of the Spirit (*A Christianity Worth Believing*, 56–57).

group of ancient documents of paramount importance for a people who want to belong to the community of people who seek the God of Abraham, Isaac, Jacob, and Jesus. Similarly, Bell writes that the Bible is "a library of radically progressive books . . . that tells stories about human interactions with the divine being who never, ever gives up on us . . . never stops calling . . . and inviting us into new and better futures."[94]

Indeed, the Bible's inspiration preserves, presents, and inspires an ongoing, vigorous conversation with and about God. Moreover, Bell thinks "God breathes life into the Bible, and through it into the community of faith and its members, and into my soul."[95] So, for McLaren, the Bible is the word of God in the sense that "if we enter the text together and feel the flow of its arguments, get stuck in its points of tension, and struggle with its unfolding plot in all its twists and turns, God's revelation can happen to us."[96]

So McLaren's goal is not to have us learn supposedly "timeless truths," extract them from the Bible, and then call them God's words. Instead, he wants to put *us* in the text and the conversation, so we are immersed in the story and the Spirit.[97]

But, how do we make sense of the seemingly different various portraits of God in the Bible, especially passages in the Old Testament that speak of God as being violent? His answer is that we tend to see God through the lens of our experience. So, if a group was violent or tribal, they'd probably tend to see God that way. The Bible, then, seems to be a collection down through time of the community of faith's members' interpretations of God: "I *am* saying that human beings can't do better than their very best at any given moment to communicate about God as they understand God, and that Scripture faithfully reveals the evolution of our ancestors' best attempts to communicate their successive best understandings of God."[98] As an implication, it is clear from statements like this that McLaren does not endorse biblical inerrancy; indeed, it would seem to be a modern notion to him.

Here, we can make connections between Calvinism and McLaren's ethical emphases. For instance, consider Burson's summary of McLaren's view about five-point Calvinism, which is *"a tightly formulated, highly rationalistic systematic theology that provides a universalized explanation of how the divine judge and king unconditionally determines all individuals to either eternal salvation or eternal damnation. This ideology has infused excessive*

---

94. Bell, *What We Talk About*, 165–66.
95. Bell, *What We Talk About*, 83.
96. McLaren, *A New Kind of Christianity*, 91.
97. McLaren, *A New Kind of Christianity*, 96.
98. McLaren, *A New Kind of Christianity*, 103.

confidence into the hearts and minds of many who have viewed themselves as a member of the chosen elect, which, in turn, has often fueled colonizing superiority and oppression."[99]

McLaren sees Calvinism's doctrine of unconditional election as affecting "the us-them and in-grouping and out-grouping that lead to prejudice, exclusion, and ultimately to religious wars."[100] Why? In part, Burson explains that McLaren sees it as a question of God's being able to play favorites: "If God can choose some people for privilege and others for fodder, then as humans who is to say we do not also have a divine precedent and edict to do the same?"[101]

For another kind of connection, McLaren exhibits great "postcolonial sensitivity to contemporary marginalized voices due to oppressive Western colonization and imperialism."[102] In *A Generous Orthodoxy*, he links this mind-set to Calvinism, which he argues has been shaped by colonialism and modernity.[103] McLaren explains that he began to lose confidence in Calvinism when he witnessed it "allying itself with Theonomy and the hard-core Religious Right."[104] In e-mail discussion with Burson, McLaren explains more about this connection and his concerns thereof: "I started to see that the slaughter/land theft/apartheid of the Native Americans, the enslavement of Africans, segregation in the Deep South, Apartheid in South Africa, and now the anti-gay, anti-Muslim, we're gunning-for-world-war-three, culture-war mentality of American Evangelicals all had something in common . . . and it was the hyper-confidence of Calvinism (or Greco-Romanism, or Imperial thinking)."[105]

So, ethics has become a greater concern than epistemology for McLaren. Yet, there still are important epistemic ideas at work that we should surface. McLaren denies that anyone has direct access to reality, whether that is religiously speaking or otherwise. To do so would require that we can set aside our "situatedness," that is, our *particularity*. But, as Merold Westphal explains, due to our finitude, we have epistemic limitations and

99. Burson, *Brian McLaren in Focus,* 111 (emphasis in original).

100. McLaren, *Generous Orthodoxy,* 109. See also Burson's discussion, *Brian McLaren in Focus,* 141–45.

101. Burson, *Brian McLaren in Focus,* 207–8. For McLaren's own words on this, see *A New Kind of Christianity,* 193.

102. Burson, *Brian McLaren in Focus,* 240.

103. McLaren, *Generous Orthodoxy,* 188.

104. McLaren, in reply to Burson's e-mail, July 20, 2009, in Burson, *Brian McLaren in Focus,* 293. See also 25, note 26, for other references that discuss this association.

105. McLaren, in reply to Burson's e-mail, July 20, 2009, in Burson, *Brian McLaren in Focus,* 295.

thus "blindness" due to our limited perspective. And due to our fallenness, we have blindness due to our sin and perversity.[106] This means that no human being can ever hope to achieve an unbiased "God's eye" standpoint, be blind to nothing, and have exhaustive, pristine knowledge. To even think we could know reality directly suggests a willfulness to play God.

Now, these views have implications for revelation, including Scripture. While evangelicals claim that the Bible is God's inscripturated revelation to us, nonetheless for McLaren, that is *their* interpretation, and not a good one, based on the various kinds of practical effects we have seen in and through evangelicals' lives. Moreover, while God could speak to us, nonetheless we will not be able to receive his intended meanings as such, but only as we interpret them.

Jones has echoed such thought in the past. In *A Better Atonement*, he more forcefully states this position: "I do not think it possible to 'begin with the Bible.' We always begin with our own hermeneutical assumptions." Indeed, we cannot "escape" our own hermeneutical horizons.[107]

Pagitt too seems very inclined in similar directions epistemologically. In *A Christianity Worth Believing*, he too is concerned with treating the Bible like an encyclopedia, with timeless, universal truths than can be extracted from their contexts without doing violence to them.[108] Moreover, the Bible's authority comes from both God *and* the communities who grant that to it.[109] The story we have today is not the pure, unadulterated gospel story.[110] And, "every theology is grounded in a . . . set of culturally based assumptions and concerns."[111]

Moreover, in his chapter in *Listening to the Beliefs of Emerging Churches*, Pagitt is more explicit. A particular theology cannot be separated from a particular culture, and it cannot give us universal truths that are divorced from that context. It is as though we cannot have direct access to God in his view.[112] Our understandings are "useful but temporary," and "complex understandings meant for all people, in all places, for all times, simply are not possible."[113] Indeed, it seems we cannot be objective; as he explains, "at the atomic level, the observation of something affects the specimen. In this

---

106. See Westphal, "Phenomenologies and Religious Truth," 121.

107. Jones, *A Better Atonement*, locations 78–81.

108. Pagitt, *A Christianity Worth Believing*, 58.

109. Pagitt, *A Christianity Worth Believing*, 64.

110. Pagitt, *A Christianity Worth Believing*, 35.

111. Pagitt, *A Christianity Worth Believing*, 48.

112. Pagitt, "The Emerging Church and Embodied Theology," 125.

113. Pagitt, "The Emerging Church and Embodied Theology," 137.

sense, there is no way to be an 'objective observer.' So if we connect truth to objectivity, we are in a bad place in light of our understanding of the world."[114]

What then is the view of God in the Bible that we should adopt? McLaren contends that the "mature" view of God's character is what we see in Jesus. According to McLaren, we see a God who is not violent or tribal, doesn't decree ethnic cleansing or genocide, isn't sexist, homophobic, or a warmonger, or one who decrees eternal conscious torment.[115]

There are more interpretive considerations to note here. As we have noticed already, McLaren considers the Bible to be presenting in narrative form peoples' evolving interpretations of God, which he uses to explain why we see God use violent means in earlier stories, such as the flood, in which he acts "in his insecurity" and "drowns helpless children."[116] This implies an important consideration, that we can understand God's character in a mature way only in light of the story's end, in light of Jesus' story.[117] It is *not* the case for McLaren that God's character itself changes; indeed, as Burson notes explicitly, God's ontological being is not evolving.[118] Rather, *how we perceive his character* does evolve.

The Emphasis upon Relationality and Relationships

Before continuing McLaren's understanding of Jesus' story, we should pause and reflect upon the emphasis McLaren has made upon the importance of relationships between humans and God, other humans, and the rest of creation. As we will see shortly, McLaren sees the "conventional," "received" view of the gospel as advocating that the soul is what is saved and goes to heaven when we die, but the body is bad. In this view, our need is to develop our souls and look forward to our escape from the body. But this leads to little concern for developing a social or environmental ethic and related actions.

---

114. Pagitt, "The Emerging Church and Embodied Theology," 142. As a brief aside, it is interesting that Pagitt makes at least one bold assertion as "fact" that is not without significant controversy, to say the least: "What do we do with the *fact* that there is not a single 'verse,' a 'universe,' but rather many 'universes,' a 'multiverse'?" (emphasis mine). Compare this with William Lane Craig's arguments against many worlds hypotheses in Moreland and Craig, *Philosophical Foundations*, 487–89.

115. McLaren, *A New Kind of Christianity*, 118.

116. McLaren, *A New Kind of Christianity*, 110.

117. McLaren, *A New Kind of Christianity*, 114.

118. Burson, *Brian McLaren in Focus*, 86.

In contrast to the modern emphasis upon individual autonomy and the good being found in a society that is simply an aggregate of individuals, McLaren and others have stressed the importance of embodiment as key to relationships. For him, the good is found in relationships in community, particularly the body of Christ. There we are to live out the "one anothers" of Scripture and love our neighbors as ourselves, thereby witnessing to the truth of the story of Jesus.

His emphasis upon our need for relationships reflects what some have called the *turn to relationality* in terms of how we view the nature of what is real, especially of human persons. For the (former) postfoundationalist philosopher-theologian LeRon Shults, who also has influenced Pagitt, this is a turn away from substance metaphysics (in which we are understood as a unity of two kinds of things, body and soul) to a form of monism, in which our human *essence* is understood in terms of our relationships with ourselves, the world, and others, including God.[119] *To be real, one must stand in actual, existing relations. Essentially, we are beings-in-relation.* In that model, "human knowing is no longer understood as wholly self-determined nor as undetermined, but rather as conditioned and mediated by the embodied communal relations of the knower."[120] Put differently, we are completely embedded in creation; not even our minds escape this continuity, and we are beings-in-relation, even with God.[121] For Shults, this leads to a nuanced form of *panentheism*. As he contends, our relationality in God entails that "we cannot step back from our relation to the *infinite* trinitarian God and compare this divine object to other objects."[122]

A key reason why Shults rejects body-soul dualism is that he views essences as being static: "human being is not a static substance but a becoming—a dynamic, historically configured movement in search of a secure reality."[123] McLaren echoes this kind of view in *A New Kind of Christianity*, in which he portrays and then criticizes a Platonic view, inherited from the Greco-Roman narrative, as affirming that essences (and souls would be one example) as being perfect, fixed, and immutable, yet thereby being

---

119. See Pagitt, *Flipped*, 9, 11, and 17, for information on Shults's influence on Pagitt. I say "former" about Shults in that more recently Shults has become an atheist.

120. Shults, *Reforming Theological Anthropology*, 183–84.

121. Shults, *Reforming Theological Anthropology*, 164.

122. Shults, *Reforming the Doctrine of God*, 164. Notice that I do not think he is focusing on God's being incomparable. Rather, I think he is focusing on how we are embedded in creation in and relationship with God, such that we cannot abstract ourselves from our situatedness and *know* God as he truly is, apart from our being in relation with him and creation.

123. Shults, *Reforming Theological Anthropology*, 217, note 1.

incapable of being subjects of stories.[124] But if so, they are unable to enter into relationships, for relationships unfold, become, and develop over time, and they require stories to be told about them. But, how can a story be told about a static essence? For this kind of reason, Shults and the late Stanley Grenz have thought that we should shift in our view of God from an essence/substance kind of view to a more relational one.[125]

Even with this move away from an essentialist view of God, we have seen that McLaren does not want to say that God's character, or being, is evolving. However, he seems to think he needs to "think of God outside of neo-Platonic categories."[126] Along those lines, McLaren believes the Greco-Roman narrative assumes "a bipolar world of matter/spirit, physics/metaphysics, natural/supernatural, and male/female."[127] But, to have a creation that truly is free and open, without essences which (supposedly) prohibit change, development, and relationships, McLaren seems to think we need an *organic* vision of the universe (including ourselves) in terms of its relationship with God. We are important "elements" in a whole. This vision fits well with McLaren's theistic evolution, too, for in such a view, creation is not fully determined and populated with essences that make it static.

So, McLaren's vision fits well with panentheism. He clearly wants to avoid a "transcendent Platonism," but also an "immanent pantheism." For him, it is important to distinguish God and the universe.[128] Moreover, when we consider many of the influences upon McLaren that he and Burson acknowledge, there is a long list of panentheists. For example, there are Hans Küng, John Haught, Jürgen Moltmann, Wolfhart Pannenberg, Karl Rahner, and Thomas Jay Oord.[129]

Now, for McLaren, his emphasis upon relationality does not entail that we do not have souls. Indeed, as we will see, he has a place for the soul, but not as one's essence. As for Pagitt, in 2007 to 2008, he seemed to be heading more clearly toward panentheism, like Shults. Then, Pagitt tended to see modern thought often as dichotomous, or dualistic, stressing two polarities

124. McLaren, *A New Kind of Christianity*, 43.

125. For example, see Shults, *Reforming the Doctrine of God*, 1–12. For Grenz, see "The Relational God," especially 88–89.

126. McLaren, in reply to Burson's e-mail, July 20, 2009, in Burson, *Brian McLaren in Focus*, 296.

127. McLaren, *A New Kind of Christianity*, 175.

128. McLaren, in reply to Burson's e-mail, July 20, 2009, in Burson, *Brian McLaren in Focus*, 296.

129. See Burson, *Brian McLaren in Focus*, 100, 153. See also McLaren, in reply to Burson's e-mail, July 20, 2009, 295–96.

that imply distinction.[130] He observed a wide range of dualistic categories, such as religious or secular; earthly or spiritual; orthodox or heretical; those who have the Spirit, and those who don't; and "in" the world, but not "of" it. Other dualisms imply conflict, such as flesh versus spirit; God on one side, with humans on another; "God separate from creation"; etc.[131] As he remarked, under this framing story, he assumed his body was one thing and his spirit another, that he himself is "a collection of distinct parts."[132]

Many have made these kinds of observations, but Pagitt tied this mind-set to a Greek way of thinking that separated flesh (which was seen as bad) from spirit or soul (which was seen as good). He claimed this kind of Gnosticism had been adopted by Christians, and its influence continues to this day.[133] Under this Greek influence, Pagitt argued that we have inherited many concepts that promote a mind-set of "disconnection" and "separation" in our theology and praxis.

In *Listening to the Beliefs of Emerging Churches*, Pagitt pursued a theology of "integrated holism," and one aspect he considered was the "nature" of creation at the smallest level. What is matter? Pagitt introduced the idea that matter is "made of energy packets and not 'little hard balls of matter,'" and this idea required "not only different theological conclusions but different presuppositions."[134] Apparently, one such presupposition that he was reconsidering was "the idea that there is a necessary distinction of matter from spirit, or creation from creator."[135]

Pagitt also described that he had been released from thinking of the spiritual and material worlds as two different things. Instead, in *A Christianity Worth Believing*, it seemed that "everything is made of the same . . . energy, interaction, and movement."[136] So, this idea naturally extended to how he saw humans as interconnected wholes, and not as body being one thing, while spirit is another. In contrast, he thought dualism fosters a deep, multifaceted separation, which he saw as contrary to God's purposes.

Pagitt's stress on "holistic connection," integration, interconnection, and so forth seemed to press him further. If creation is like this, what is God's relationship to the creation? He realized the implication, claiming that

---

130. For example, see Pagitt, *A Christianity Worth Believing*, 78–79.

131. Pagitt, *A Christianity Worth Believing*, 81.

132. Pagitt, *A Christianity Worth Believing*, 78.

133. Pagitt, *A Christianity Worth Believing*, ch. 8.

134. Pagitt, "The Emerging Church and Embodied Theology," 142.

135. Pagitt, "The Emerging Church and Embodied Theology," 142.

136. Pagitt, *A Christianity Worth Believing*, 76–77.

"holism is the goal of God for the world."[137] Sin is disintegration, whereas God's design is for integration.[138] Pagitt posited that God is connected to his creation, including mountains, oceans, embryos, etc. As Pagitt stated explicitly, he is not endorsing pantheism, but instead is highlighting the congruency and symmetry between Creator and creation.[139] In his theology of holism, "the good news of Christianity is that we are integrated with God, not separated from God."[140] Indeed, his "assumption is that God is present in all things."[141] So, while Pagitt was not endorsing *pantheism*, in which everything is God, in these works he did seem to be moving away from a more traditional monotheistic conception to a more *panentheistic* one, in which the creation (which is one kind of stuff) is *in* God, which he saw as fitting well with his overall emphasis upon relationality.

In his more recent *Flipped*, he develops even more explicitly his turn to panentheism. Pagitt describes the received view of Christianity as a "religious transactional system," in which we are separated from God.[142] As he understands this view, humanity is "completely other" than God, with different essences.[143] To bridge that gap, we need an "adapter" to connect us, which is Jesus in such views.[144] To him, though, in this approach, "the spiritual search is reduced to working out the right technical specifications," much like an input-output system.[145] But, the good news to Pagitt is that we are "In God"; this fits with his understanding of Paul's expression in Acts 17:28: "in Him we live and move and exist."[146]

So, what are God and creation like in Pagitt's view? Pagitt claims that "all things are held together In God. And all of creation is being reconciled or seeking to live harmoniously with God."[147] Indeed, "God is the very existence of all things."[148] In terms of Pagitt's ontological views, he makes some sweeping claims. For example, "*everything* that exists is made of only one

---

137. Pagitt, "The Emerging Church and Embodied Theology," 135.

138. Pagitt, "The Emerging Church and Embodied Theology," 132.

139. Pagitt, *A Christianity Worth Believing*, 88.

140. Pagitt, *A Christianity Worth Believing*, 90.

141. Pagitt, *A Christianity Worth Believing*, 91.

142. Pagitt, *Flipped*, 54.

143. Pagitt, *Flipped*, 155.

144. Pagitt, *Flipped*, 54.

145. Pagitt, *Flipped*, 54.

146. Note: Pagitt capitalizes "In" for "In God," apparently to stress this holistic connection. For his appeal to this verse, see *Flipped*, 36.

147. Pagitt, *Flipped*, 13.

148. Pagitt, *Flipped*, 14.

hundred types of atoms," yet also is energy.[149] Now, he might be overgeneralizing, for by "everything," he has included God as also made of atoms, and yet also is energy. Yet, he repeats this generalization, where he asserts that "all of existence is energy."[150]

Though we are In God, we still are "unique parts of the whole."[151] Unlike pantheism's view, we retain our individuality, as does God, who "*wants people to live free from sin*."[152] We are In God and yet also particular beings, which is made possible because "energy moves as particles and waves."[153] Pagitt draws upon Einstein's work to explain: "As captured in the equation $E=mc^2$, energy is the same thing as matter and the other way around. In science parlance this is called wave-particle duality (wave and particle at the same time)."[154] Pagitt draws the connection; for him, "We are In God, but we do not lose our individuality. We live as wave and particle."[155] Yet, Pagitt also claims that "God is not a separate subject that we talk about or relate to through belief, behavior, faith, or practice."[156]

Like Pagitt, in *Love Wins*, Bell also seemed to be inclining toward panentheism. Themes of integration and connection abound. Early, he mentions occasionally our being connected with God. For instance, he describes eternal life as being "a quality and vitality of life lived now in connection with God," as opposed to a kind of life that is becoming more and more disconnected from God and has increasing degrees of "despair and destruction."[157] Yet, *both* kinds still have some degree of connection with God.

But as he progresses with the book's argument, Bell delves more and more into our relationship and connection with God. For instance, he claims that the Bible teaches that "people . . . are inextricably intertwined with God."[158] To support this, he refers to Psalm 24:1, that the earth is the Lord's, and everything (and everyone) in it. Moreover, in Acts 17:28, Paul says that in God we live and move and have our being.

---

149. Pagitt, *Flipped*, 151 (emphasis added).
150. Pagitt, *Flipped*, 159.
151. Pagitt, *Flipped*, 189. See also 149.
152. Pagitt, *Flipped*, 170 (emphasis added, to stress God's own desires).
153. Pagitt, *Flipped*, 151.
154. Pagitt, *Flipped*, 151.
155. Pagitt, *Flipped*, 152.
156. Pagitt, *Flipped*, 14.
157. Bell, *Love Wins*, 59, 66.
158. Bell, *Love Wins*, 98.

To Bell, the scriptural authors teach that "we're all part of the same family."[159] Since God wants all to be saved, his love is what "a parent has for a child [which pursues and bonds] . . . and always works to be reconciled with, regardless of the cost."[160] So Bell proceeds to give a list of verses that he says show that God will be "reconciled" with everyone, without fail.[161]

Here are some examples: (1) Psalm 65:2: "To Thee all men come."[162] (2) Isaiah 52:10b (lit.): "And all the ends of the earth will see the salvation of our God."[163] (3) Philippians 2:10–11 "Every knee should bow . . . and every tongue should confess that Jesus Christ is LORD, to the glory of God the Father."[164] (4) Psalm 22:27–29: "All the ends of the earth will remember and turn to the LORD, and all the families of the nations will bow down before Thee . . . . All the prosperous of the earth will eat and worship, all those who go down to the dust will bow before Him."[165] (5) Psalm 30:5a: God's "anger is but for a moment, His favor is for a lifetime."[166] And, in all these purposes, God will not fail; for example, Jer 32:27b: "Is anything too difficult for Me?"[167]

But Bell has in mind a much broader connection with God than just for humanity. He appeals, for instance, to Colossians 1 to support the idea that in Jesus' resurrection God will "renew, restore, and reconcile 'everything on earth or in heaven.'"[168] Jesus is "everywhere," Bell asserts, and he is the "*divine* life-giving energy that brought the universe into existence."[169] In this connection with creation and all humanity, Jesus is "saving and rescuing and redeeming not just everything, but everybody."[170] Jesus even contains "every single particle of creation,"[171] and he is present in all of it.[172]

So, in *Love Wins*, it seems he was (at the least) gravitating in the direction of panentheism. But, in *What We Talk About When We Talk About God*,

---

159. Bell, *Love Wins*, 99.

160. Bell, *Love Wins*, 99.

161. Bell, *Love Wins*, 100.

162. Bell, *Love Wins*, 99.

163. Bell, *Love Wins*, 99.

164. Bell, *Love Wins*, 99.

165. Bell, *Love Wins*, 100.

166. Bell, *Love Wins*, 101.

167. Bell, *Love Wins*, 101.

168. Bell, *Love Wins*, 134.

169. Bell, *Love Wins*, 146.

170. Bell, *Love Wins*, 151.

171. Bell, *Love Wins*, 155.

172. Bell, *Love Wins*, 159. See also 60–61.

he seems to embrace it more clearly. He echoes Paul Tillich, a panentheist, when he claims God is the "ground of our being."[173] The *ruach* (divine breath, spirit) of God is the "life force that brings everything into existence," and God's *ruach* is present always in all created beings.[174] So, God is present in our experiences, yet transcends them too: God is the "transcendent presence in our . . . sensations of the depth and dimension and fullness of life."[175]

In terms of God's transcendence, then, Bell describes this as "something very real and yet beyond our conventional means of analysis and description" (which I take, e.g., to be modern, scientific conceptions).[176] God is "a reality that is . . . *beyond* words."[177] Though God transcends us and our experiences, God is "not distant or detached or indifferent" to us and our condition; rather, "God is present among us in Jesus."[178] This is the significance, Bell explains, of the meaning of Immanuel, which is a radical claim about reality: God is with us and is *for* us.[179] And, God is "moving everything forward so that God will be *over all and through all and in all*," a reference to Ephesians 4:6.[180]

What then is creation like? Bell describes fundamental reality as particles in motion, such that the universe is unpredictable on a small scale.[181] This means miracles cannot be dismissed out of hand due to the behavior of subatomic particles.[182] Moreover, "the primary essence of reality is energy flow. Things . . . are ultimately relationships of living energy."[183] These points lead Bell to suggest that while we have been taught that there are clear distinctions between what is material versus immaterial, and physical versus spiritual, "what we're learning from science, however, is that that distinction isn't so clear after all."[184] Perhaps there is not a distinction between them

173. Bell, *What We Talk About*, 15.

174. Bell, *What We Talk About*, 108.

175. Bell, *What We Talk About*, 15.

176. Bell, *What We Talk About*, 63.

177. Bell, *What We Talk About*, 87.

178. Bell, *What We Talk About*, 131.

179. Bell, *What We Talk About*, 131.

180. Bell, *What We Talk About*, 187 (emphasis in original). Interestingly, the context for the verse is about God's relationship with the body of Christ.

181. Bell, *What We Talk About*, 36–38.

182. Bell, *What We Talk About*, 70.

183. Bell, *What We Talk About*, 45.

184. Bell, *What We Talk About*, 45.

at all.[185] This would seem to fit his depiction of cells as both matter and memory.[186]

So, if we are ultimately living energy, then, since matter is ultimately energy, it seems we are made of matter, as is the rest of creation. Thus, due to the "interconnected web of relationships" in creation, including our own, "our interactions with energy alter reality because we're involved."[187] This interconnectedness is something that science tells us.[188] Being part of creation (and yet still retaining our individuality), we are embedded in this holistic web of relationships, such that we cannot "step back" from them and achieve a separate, "disconnected" view of reality, as though we can stand apart from it. Furthermore, for him, this "good news" of integration should be expressed in terms of ever-increasing "connectivity" and "levels of hierarchy leading to holism," not only in ourselves, but also beyond us, so that God may be all in all.[189]

Moreover, Bell describes God not only as the life force present in all creation, but also as the "electricity that lights up the whole house."[190] So, in terms of God's relationship to us and the rest of creation, "all matter is permeated by the redeeming energy and power of God."[191] We are interconnected with God, for "everything has a singular, common source and is infinitely, endlessly, deeply connected."[192] Moreover, this means God is present with us at all times and in all places.[193] All of life and creation is sacred because God is immanent, being interconnected with all of creation.[194]

Finally, and more briefly, Jones has been reading and discussing panentheism for some time, as in blogs. But, in his book *The Church is Flat*, he seems to give it his endorsement, at least to Moltmann's form. For instance, Jones introduces the subject in this context:

> In the following sections, I will reference a particular theological doctrine that is central to the theology of Jürgen Moltmann, describe how the emerging church movement has intuitively embraced this theology, and then offer suggestions for the ECM

185. Bell, *What We Talk About*, 45.
186. Bell, *What We Talk About*, 51.
187. Bell, *What We Talk About*, 47.
188. Bell, *What We Talk About*, 202
189. Bell, *What We Talk About*, 186–87.
190. Bell, *What We Talk About*, 15. See also 123.
191. Bell, *What We Talk About*, 187.
192. Bell, *What We Talk About*, 118.
193. Bell, *What We Talk About*, 98.
194. Bell, *What We Talk About*, 181–83.

and the broader Protestant church as to how they can more deliberately embody a relational ecclesiology. It is my contention that Moltmann has not adequately developed actual practices that embody his ecclesiology and the emerging church has not adequately reflected on the practices that have emerged over the past decade. The following will be an attempt [to] ameliorate both of those weaknesses.[195]

Jones then proceeds to explain that "since God inhabits all of creation equally . . . Moltmann's panentheism serves to tear down the sacred-secular divide evident in the ecclesiologies that demarcate the church as unique because it is indwelt by God's Spirit in a special way."[196] For Jones, Moltmann's panentheism "is evident in the practices of the emerging church movement," even though "the emerging church movement has underrealized the extent to which panentheism plays a role in its practices."[197] Moreover, "to embrace panentheism, and to reflect on it in a thoroughgoing manner, will only serve to strengthen the practices that embody panentheism and that will, in turn, strengthen the theological identity of the ECM."[198]

The Jesus Story, Freed from the Greco-Roman Narrative

With the primacy of relationships in mind, let's return now to McLaren's version of Jesus' story, with additional observations from Bell, Pagitt, and Jones.

The Advancement of the Kingdom, and Heaven

Perhaps the most important aspect of this story is how the kingdom advances. If it were just another imperial story, like that of Rome or modernity, then God sovereignly could exercise his will and bring about his kingdom. Or, if God determines the future, as made known through prophecies, then that too would make creation's story "forced" or even coerced, rather than one of its own emergence. But that seems inconceivable to McLaren. If the kingdom were to come by way of power, this would make it just like the earthly, "demonic" powers, which resort to violence and coercion.[199] In

195. Jones, *The Church is Flat,* location 164.
196. Jones, *The Church is Flat,* locations 164–65.
197. Jones, *The Church is Flat,* locations 165 and 166, respectively.
198. Jones, *The Church is Flat,* location 166.
199. For example, see McLaren, *Secret Message,* 69. See also his *Everything Must*

many places, he claims God does not advance his kingdom by violence, bloodshed, revenge, or hatred.[200] Instead, God draws both individual and "corporate or even cosmic evil out from the shadows and into the broad daylight, so that it can be seen and named and rejected and banished."[201] By corporate or cosmic evil, he means a kind of groupthink (e.g., Nazism) that can take over or "possess" a group that never would happen just to individuals alone. So, Jesus' kingdom comes "subtly, gently, and secretly."[202]

Moreover, evil is overcome or transcended by acts of nonviolent resistance and love. For instance, suppose a rich landowner took a poor peasant to court and demands his outer garment (Matt 5:40). According to McLaren, "Jesus says to strip down naked and give them your underwear as well! Your 'generosity' leaves you defenseless and exposed—but in a sense, your exposure exposes the naked greed and cruelty of your oppressors."[203]

God's kingdom will come to earth, McLaren claims, which is contrary to the attitude he finds common amongst evangelicals, of escaping the body and this material world so that the soul goes to heaven.[204] But as disembodied beings, we would "feel free of creaturely restraint, liberated from all duty as embodied, environmented creatures."[205] To McLaren, the kingdom will not come about by the second coming of Jesus, who would enforce his will with power and domination. To him, a popular abuse of this phrase forces us to "see the nonviolence of the Jesus of the Gospels as a kind of strategic fake-out," a trick, "to be replaced by the true jihadist Jesus of a violent second coming."[206] Moreover, McLaren claims that the "kingdom of God never advances *by* or *through* war or violence."[207] Rather, as people trust Jesus, they can begin to live a better way of life now, and "the world will be changed by their growing influence."[208]

Bell echoes very similar thoughts. He criticizes the notion that heaven is some other place *where* we go when we die. To him, the Jewish people of the first century conceived of the world as being restored and renewed, and

---

Change, 144, where he discusses the evangelical view of the "second coming Jesus" as a jihadist, waging holy war (and, thus, by McLaren's lights, unethical).

200. For example, *Secret Message*, 32.

201. McLaren, *Secret Message*, 63.

202. McLaren, *Secret Message*, 66.

203. McLaren, *Secret Message*, 126.

204. McLaren, *Secret Message*, 78.

205. McLaren, *Everything Must Change*, 142.

206. McLaren, *Everything Must Change*, 144.

207. McLaren, *Secret Message*, 158.

208. McLaren, *Secret Message*, 83.

it would be marked by peace.[209] In terms of "when," Bell thinks that having eternal life is not so much what we enter into when we die; rather, it is "more about a quality and vitality of life lived now in connection to God."[210] So, heaven seems to be "both the peace . . . that come[s] from having everything in its right place," with nothing missing, "and the endless joy that comes from participating in the ongoing creation of the world."[211] Heaven is the participation in life in the age to come, which literally is (and will be) heaven on earth.[212] And, that life includes our "growing progressively in generosity, forgiveness, honesty, courage, truth telling, and responsibility."[213] As these happen, we take part in that kind of life, even now.

The Sources of Evil

McLaren acknowledges that individuals act in evil ways, but his focus seems more to be on systemic sources, or the cosmic and corporate types of evil. In *Secret Message*, McLaren does not explicitly rule out the existence of literal demons; however, while "individual evil spirits may be behind the scenes . . .[Jesus'] dominant opposition arises not from dirty personal demons crouching in darkness but rather from dirty systems of power and violence operating in powerful people who function in broad daylight."[214] The kingdom of God will confront not fallen angels as much as "all corrupt human regimes."[215] This is exactly where we see him focus in his attacks on various counterfeit "kingdoms" and "isms" that must be resisted. But in *A New Kind of Christianity*, McLaren seems to have developed a bit further in his thought. Here, it seems "the Satan" was appropriated from the Babylonians as a character in Zoroastrian religion, and then was sustained "in Judaism by . . . the Pharisees."[216]

    Furthermore, from the standpoint of his affinities with panentheism, it makes sense that McLaren would not want to hold that there are such real

---

209. Bell, *Love Wins*, 40 (emphasis in original).

210. Bell, *Love Wins*, 59.

211. Bell, *Love Wins*, 48.

212. Bell, *Love Wins*, 33.

213. Bell, *Love Wins*, 51.

214. McLaren, *Secret Message*, 64. See also *Story*, where Neo suggests that Satan might be a metaphor borrowed from the Zoroastrians, one that is for a "terribly real force in the universe" (103).

215. McLaren, *Secret Message*, 66.

216. McLaren, *A New Kind of Christianity*, 88. In contrast, McLaren claims that the Sadducees were the more conservative Jews, and they never accepted the Satan as legitimate. See also his comments on the Satan in *Why Did Jesus*, 157.

spirit beings who are, as traditionally understood, evil and irredeemably hell-bent on destroying God's works. For if they are real, then that would mean that there is a very significant dualism in reality. Nor would it make sense to say that these beings could somehow be "in" God, for God, who is holy and good, would have irredeemable evil present in his very being.

Bell holds similar views on Satan. There is little mention of Satan in *Love Wins*.[217] In a discussion of Paul's handling Hymenaeus and Alexander over to Satan, Bell observes that, regardless of what (or who) Paul meant, "there is something redemptive and renewing that will occur."[218] It is as though Paul and others have tried everything else to get their attention, so that we would describe their behavior as "hell-bent." But whether there is a literal, angelic person called "Satan" who hates God and is determined to overthrow God's kingdom, Bell does not explicitly tell us in *Love Wins*. Nevertheless, if everything in creation is reconciled to God in Christ, then it is hard to conceive how there (still?) could exist such a being who is evil and "hell-bent" on lying, stealing, killing, and destroying (cf. John 8:44 and 10:10).

For Pagitt as well, at least in *A Christianity Worth Believing*, I don't see him explicitly address whether there is a real fallen angel, Satan, and his followers. But, it seems hard to see how they could fit into his theology of holism, interconnection, and integration. Indeed, in *Flipped*, it seems there is no room ontologically for such literal beings. He even describes sin as a force.[219] And for Jones, he explains that "I don't believe in demons and I don't think I believe in Satan—at least not in the personified form."[220]

What then might we observe about McLaren's views on original sin? McLaren redefines it along the lines of René Girard's mimetic (imitation) theory.[221] As McLaren describes it, this involves a five-step process of imitation, rivalry, anxiety, scapegoating, and then ritualization.[222] The first step is *imitation*, or innocent mimicry, yet when two people compete for a desired object, they become *rivals*. Anxiety is the next step, and violence can result, whether the rivalry is between family, friends, or others. Overall, violence leads to a growing sense of anxiety in a society, which then needs to find an outlet. As McLaren explains, the next step is for the people in a society

217. Bell, *Love Wins*, 70.

218. Bell, *Love Wins*, 89.

219. Pagitt, *Flipped*, 170.

220. Jones, *A Better Atonement*, location 620.

221. Burson, *Brian McLaren in Focus*, 138–39. See also Girard, *Violence and the Sacred*.

222. Burson, *Brian McLaren in Focus*, 139.

to "imitate one another in shared aversion toward and violence against the victim—or scapegoat—and in so doing, all experience a catharsis of anxiety and a euphoria of unity."[223] Since this mechanism was effective, societies "begin to ritualize this maneuver, leading to regularly scheduled rites,"[224] which McLaren suggests now are handled by religious and political systems and sports leagues.[225] So, original sin is not due to a general condition; rather, it is transmitted by the "sociological mechanism of mimesis," and not genetics.[226]

Entering the Kingdom

How then does someone enter this kingdom? What is required for membership? This brings us, of course, to the atonement. In *The Story We Find Ourselves In*, one of McLaren's characters, Kerry, says the penal substitutionary atonement (PSA) theory "sounds like divine child abuse."[227] It would require violence on God's part to inflict suffering on Jesus for our sins by which he would atone for them, and thus such an action would be immoral to McLaren. In contrast, his character Neo suggests a view he calls the "powerful weakness" or "foolish wisdom" theory. In this, "by becoming vulnerable on the cross, by accepting suffering *from* everyone, Jews and Romans alike, rather than visiting suffering *on* everyone, Jesus is showing God's loving heart, which wants forgiveness, not revenge, for everyone. Jesus shows us that the wisdom of God's kingdom is sacrifice, not violence."[228]

Later, Neo explains that God deals with "all our wrongs, all our wickedness and evil, all our sin. . . . They're faced and known by God for all they were. But what if all the guilt and regret and shame of that judgment are absorbed into God's pain, the pain Jesus made visible on the cross, so God forgives us, so none of our wrongs count for anything anymore, and . . .what if God, by judging our wrongs as evil and therefore worthless, actually forgets our wrongs forever because they're worthless now?"[229] So, there does not seem to be a place for God's retributive justice, to be exercised as punishment for sins, in McLaren's view. Though Jesus "absorbed" all of sin's

---

223. McLaren, *Why Did Jesus*, 108.

224. Burson, *Brian McLaren in Focus*, 140.

225. McLaren, *Why Did Jesus*, 109.

226. Burson, *Brian McLaren in Focus*, 141.

227. McLaren, *Story*, 102.

228. McLaren, *Story*, 105.

229. McLaren, *Story*, 153.

guilt and pain, nonetheless his death on the cross was *not* a substitutionary atonement that propitiated the wrath of God against our sins.[230]

How then does someone move from the counterfeit kingdoms of "egotism, racism, consumerism, hedonism,"[231] colonialism, exclusivism, elitism ("and other members of the hostility family") to the kingdom of God?[232] It involves repentance, which McLaren explains has five moves. The first is to "hear from the heart and to think deeply about what you hear."[233] This profound rethinking is what repentance means, he says, for "you begin looking at every facet of your life again in this new light."[234] This seems to be like seeing life under a new aspect (like Wittgenstein) or framing story.

We should explore somewhat further his emphasis upon repenting of hostility. McLaren remarks that many leave the church today due to the inherent hostility in orthodoxy (which I take to mean traditional evangelicalism).[235] The gospel as embraced by evangelicals has distinguished between those who are in Christ, and whose sins have been forgiven, and those who are not in Christ and thus are not forgiven, being destined to eternal punishment. But, to McLaren, evangelicals who share this message are being very imperious, colonizing others and domesticating them, and thus are inherently hostile.[236]

Instead, he advocates that Christians need to abandon this hostile understanding of religious conversion, in which we view our religion as supreme and outsiders are condemned. Furthermore, McLaren understands our hostility not stemming from a fallen, sinful human nature, but something else: "we have learned from our own mistakes that religious people engage in hostility not because they are inherently hostile, but because they perceive things they love are under threat. Their aggression often boils over from a loving defensiveness."[237]

Second is the move of trust: we believe in God, "believing in or having confidence in the good news of the kingdom."[238] Third, we are to stay open to receive forgiveness, acceptance, love, and everything else we need to live

230. Further, it does not seem there is a place for a theory of the atonement in McLaren's three-line narrative (Burson, *Brian McLaren in Focus*, 147).

231. McLaren, *Secret Message*, 105.

232. McLaren, *Why Did Jesus*, 168.

233. McLaren, *Secret Message*, 105.

234. McLaren, *Secret Message*, 105.

235. McLaren, *Why Did Jesus*, 168.

236. For example, see McLaren, *Why Did Jesus*, 180–81, 244, and 255.

237. McLaren, *Why Did Jesus*, 262.

238. McLaren, *Why Did Jesus*, 109.

in God's kingdom. Even more so, we need to receive the Holy Spirit. Fourth, we go public with our repentance, faith, and receptivity, e.g., through baptism. And, fifth, we learn to follow Jesus each and every day of our lives, which will involve development in practices and disciplines.

Nor does it seem that Bell could countenance the PSA view. However, he admits that "when people say that Jesus came to die on the cross so that we can have a relationship with God, yes, that is true."[239] But, he quickly counters that explanation as the "first explanation," for it puts the focus on us, whereas the gospel story is much bigger and grander—it is about God's reconciliation of all creation. Furthermore, the substitutionary atonement view would entail, it seems, that God could be violent, which seems very much like the God who Bell says is untenable. Instead, similar to McLaren, Bell writes that "God is so *for* us that God is willing to take on the worst the world can bring and suffer it, [and] absorb it."[240] He liberates us from our guilt and shame by "announcing who we truly are and then reminding us of this over and over and over again."[241] Our confession then names "the darkness and pain that lies within," which thereby robs "it of its power."[242]

For Pagitt, what Jesus did on the cross was not an appeasement of the wrath of a Greek blood god (who apparently would be much like McLaren's Theos). Instead, "Jesus was sent to fulfill the promise of the Hebrew love God by ending human hostility."[243] That is, Jesus is not a shift from one war motif to another (say, against spiritual forces, or people); instead, he is the ender of war by ending peoples' anger. When he arose, God's love for humanity won out over our capacity for mutual hatred. Indeed, through him, "all humanity is brought into" God's created world, which is marked by "peace and harmony and integration."[244]

For Jones, there are several flaws with the PSA. He claims it hinges on the doctrine of original sin, which, as he puts it, was Augustine's view that "sin is passed biologically."[245] Furthermore, while "most of us easily reject" that view, "we still generally hold to the doctrine. That's because Original Sin is . . . an ontological argument."[246] What does he mean by this latter clause?

---

239. Bell, *Love Wins*, 134.

240. Bell, *What We Talk About*, 144 (bracketed insert mine).

241. Bell, *What We Talk About*, 152.

242. Bell, *What We Talk About*, 191.

243. Pagitt, *A Christianity Worth Believing*, 194.

244. Pagitt, *A Christianity Worth Believing*, 194.

245. Jones, *A Better Atonement*, locations 411–12.

246. Jones, *A Better Atonement*, locations 411–12.

As with above, and elsewhere in *A Better Atonement*, Jones makes references to our physicality, and this relates to how he understands the fall of Adam and Eve in Genesis. According to him, the Bible does not indicate there was a genetic kind of change in Adam and Eve that would be passed on to their posterity.[247] For Jones, hermeneutically, the fall story is not factual, but it is paradigmatic.[248] That is, for him, the fall story is truthful for it is "meant to be paradigmatic of the human condition. . . . The passage seems to teach that each of us would choose the fruit that opens our eyes rather than trusting God who tells us we don't need our eyes opened."[249] It is *truthful* in that it shows us the universal human proclivity to sin, that we are fallible, make mistakes, and die.[250]

But for Jones, it is not *factual* (i.e., historical), for at least a couple reasons. First, the ontology required for inherited depravity seems misguided. Jones rightly sees that the doctrine requires that humans are a unity of both physical and metaphysical properties (i.e., a body and a soul). But Jones seems focused upon a lack of any indication of physical, genetic change in Adam and Eve after their sin, so that he therefore dismisses the doctrine.

Second, he appeals to Abelard to help show that the doctrine of original sin is unjust. According to Jones, Abelard held that though we are sinful and guilty, nevertheless this is not due to an inherited depravity: "Humans cannot be held liable for another person's sin, Abelard argued. That is not justice. We are inclined toward sin because of Adam, but we are not guilty of his sin."[251]

There are at least three more reasons why Jones wants to move beyond the PSA. We already have seen the first, that it seems to require a view of God that cuts against most peoples' experience of him as a God of love, not wrath. Second, Jones suggests that in the PSA, "God might need therapy."[252] God is so angry that he "looks around for someone to punish for that sin."[253] Sending natural disasters and diseases is not enough to satiate his anger. So,

---

247. Jones, *A Better Atonement*, locations 106–7. Additionally, he remarks about our physicality: "We have real DNA, real physical, material properties" (locations 353–54).

248. Jones, *A Better Atonement*, location 106.

249. Jones, *A Better Atonement*, locations 99–101 (bracketed insert mine).

250. Jones, *A Better Atonement*, locations 242–43.

251. Jones, *A Better Atonement*, locations 501–5. Similarly, Jones claims that "just as one person cannot be held liable for another's sin, neither can a person achieve absolution on another's behalf" (locations 504–5).

252. Jones, *A Better Atonement*, location 588.

253. Jones, *A Better Atonement*, location 588.

"finally he finds and [*sic*] innocent victim . . . and only after killing his son does God's anger finally abate."[254]

Third, Jones does not see God as being bound to forgive our sin only through a substitutionary sacrifice, for God's freedom is not bound by anything. Therefore, "God could have forgiven us of our sin however God wanted too [*sic*]—with or without the execution of his son."[255]

These and some other considerations (including that Satan is not a real person) press Jones away from the PSA, or the ransom-to-Satan or Christus Victor theories. Instead, he sees himself inclined toward views that maintain God's freedom, and ones that support God's calling us (because he is love) and setting an example for us: "Ultimately, God invites us into his trinitarian life. That's what the cross is about."[256] So, in his mind, this leads him to Girard's last scapegoat theory, or the solidarity theory of Jürgen Moltmann.

Life After Death (and Hell), and Human Anthropology

Now, as we've seen, McLaren's God cannot act coercively or violently, and, in particular, cruelly, for that would be immoral. To clarify, McLaren has told me that "if God can be cruel, heartless, vicious, careless of human life . . . then for me, the whole thing falls to pieces."[257] I take him to mean that Christianity itself would crash to the ground. Thus, if there is no punishment from God for sin, then it makes sense that there would not be a literal hell either, "where" there would be eternal punishment and torment.

I think there is a second reason for him to reject the idea of eternal punishment in hell. In *A Generous Orthodoxy*, the soul is not the essence of humans:

> From the integration of the faculties of the human body—which includes the brain . . . the mind emerges with its own faculties (will, memory, anticipation, analysis, classification, contrast, cause and effect, imagination, etc.). It can be differentiated from the body (think of someone in a persistent vegetative state), but it is not disassociated from the body (think of mental illness, learning disabilities, the effects of narcotics or alcohol . . .). From the integration of the faculties of the body and mind, the soul emerges with an ethical and aesthetical and relational

254. Jones, *A Better Atonement*, locations 589–90.

255. Jones, *A Better Atonement*, locations 622–624.

256. Jones, *A Better Atonement*, locations 626–27.

257. E-mail correspondence from Brian McLaren, November 10, 2009.

dimension—the person whose story includes a body and mind, but is not limited to a body and mind.[258]

There, McLaren clearly does not see the soul as one's essential nature. It seems to be a higher, emergent reality but never disassociated from the mind-body complex. Accordingly, humans seem to be primarily material bodies with emergent properties that depend upon the body for their existence.

This stance affects the resurrection and life after death, which McLaren clearly affirms.[259] In an earlier work, McLaren's thoughts seem to be expressed through his character, Neo. Speaking of Kerry, who finds her place in God's story but then dies, she does not continue her existence after death as a disembodied soul. Instead, upon death, who she is in that moment will be reconstituted in God with all her past moments. Then, God will identify and judge all her wrongs, forgiving and forgetting all of them, leaving her "full and substantial and free and pure and complete."[260]

So, at death, there is not a strict continuity of the person's identity; rather, we are remembered by God, who then, after judging us, "re-members" us after death. *But* if there was nothing good leftover after that "judgment," then there is nothing to remember. Those people simply would not experience life after death. In that case, since those people had ceased to exist, it seems it would be unnecessary and perhaps even immoral for God to re-member those people, only to cast them into hell for eternal torment.

Later, in *A New Kind of Christianity*, McLaren explains that the Greco-Roman narrative assumes a multiplicity of dualisms, such as between matter and spirit, natural and supernatural, body and soul, etc.[261] But, Burson observes that for McLaren, this bifurcated view is antiquated and "has been discredited by contemporary scholarship and has led modern Christians into scientific, metaphysical, social, and ethical quandaries."[262]

Furthermore, McLaren explicitly rejects the Cartesian kind of body-soul dualism, in which it can be easy to see the soul as the ghost in a machine, which he identifies with the dualism of the Greco-Roman narrative we have inherited. In this view, human beings are ghosts (souls) in machines (bodies), which are so radically different that we cannot really account for how they could interact, much less be integrated, together. McLaren accurately

---

258. McLaren, *Generous Orthodoxy*, 280–81.

259. See Burson, *Brian McLaren in Focus*, 152.

260. McLaren, *Story*, 154. See also 194, for how God saved Kerry.

261. McLaren, *A New Kind of Christianity*, 175.

262. Burson, "Apologetics and the New Kind of Christian," 128. See also McLaren, *A New Kind of Christianity*, 176.

observes that the Cartesian view is widely criticized, for we are not mere souls "riding around as passengers in male or female body-vehicles."[263] He is right; Cartesian body-soul dualism should be rejected.[264]

While embracing a form of monism about creation, McLaren rejects reductive approaches, in which everything can be reduced to its lowest level of parts and properties. To him, that takes away the mystery and beauty of creation. Instead, Burson explains that McLaren has moved much more clearly to a type of nonreductive physicalism, with Nancey Murphy's influences being the most pronounced.[265]

Let me sketch Murphy's nonreductive physicalism. For her, ontologically, creation is physical. That is, she embraces ontological reductionism.[266] However, not all causes can be reduced to the lowest levels of things. There also is top-down, as well as whole-part, causation. Thus, while she adheres to the view that creation is made up of physical stuff, nonetheless she is against reductionism of causes.

Murphy argues that properties or processes emerge that are describable only by concepts available at a higher level of analysis than physics.[267] There are aspects of life that simply cannot be described in the language of physics or other natural sciences. Indeed, there are properties at various levels that can only be described in various languages; e.g., along with the natural sciences, there could be the psychological, sociological, ethical, and even theological levels, all with their specific ways of talking. Put differently,

> The nonreductive physicalist view . . . attributes mental and spiritual properties to the entire person, understood as a complex physical and social organism. Since mental states or attributes are states of the whole person, no special causal problems arise. This view of mental states arising from the functioning of the nervous system is consistent with what we know from science about the interactions between brain states and mental states: measurable effects on the central nervous system have psychological consequences; many psychological or mental states have physiological consequences.[268]

263. McLaren, *A New Kind of Christianity*, 175–76.

264. However, the Cartesian view is not the only way available for defending a dualism of body and soul. There also are the views of Aristotle and Thomas Aquinas.

265. Burson, "Apologetics and the New Kind of Christian," 129.

266. See Murphy, "Human Nature," 18, where she argues against a need for humans to have a soul.

267. Murphy and Brown, *Did My Neurons Make Me Do It?*, 78–84, where she has a section on "emergence."

268. Murphy, *Beyond Liberalism*, 150.

Though new properties emerge, and can be described in various languages, nonetheless ontologically these properties also are physical, due to her ontological reductionism.

Very similarly, from Pagitt's and Bell's views of the nature of creation as matter/energy, there is no ontological room for actual souls (as our immaterial essence) to exist. Bell expands a bit more on his philosophical anthropology. In terms of what is the basis for a person's identity (i.e., what makes someone the same person through time and change), we are a bundle of atoms that changes its membership.[269] But, he appeals to the "pattern" as the enduring reality, not the parts.[270] Like Murphy says, we are a hierarchy of levels of organization, and a whole.[271] The whole emerges from the parts in a proper order.[272]

In regards to hell, in *Love Wins*, Bell criticizes the view that God could at one moment be loving, gracious, going to extremes to seek out people, and yet, immediately after death, be cruel, mean, and a vicious tormenter. Still, Bell affirms a literal hell, but he does not mean eternal separation and conscious torment away from God's presence. Instead, *hell* is a term we use that describes "the very real consequences we experience when we reject the good and true and beautiful life that God has for us."[273] It also is the vast evil that comes from the depths of our hearts, along with the societal "chaos" that comes from our failing to live in the world according to God's ways.[274]

Here I think Bell shines as a writer. His compassionate, pastoral heart extends to many who are suffering from heart-wrenching examples of evil, whether inflicted by individuals, the ravages of war, or other sources. He is quite right: we can choose to inflict all manner of evils upon others and thereby experience a kind of "hell" on earth.

Yet, as we have seen, he thinks there still will remain hope, even for people such as those of Sodom. Bell tries to open up conceptual space for his own view. He explores how there have been different views held by "good" Christians down through the centuries, and that while many today think that there is only this life in which we get to trust in Jesus, others have responded differently. Some, for instance, think that while there are two destinations, still wonder: what happens to those who continue over time to become less humane in their treatment of others? Can we eventually lose

269. Bell, *What We Talk About*, 51.

270. Bell, *What We Talk About*, 52.

271. Bell, *What We Talk About*, 58.

272. Bell, *What We Talk About*, 62.

273. Bell, *What We Talk About*, 93.

274. Bell, *What We Talk About*, 93.

the image of God in us? He also explores a further position, that "there must be some kind of 'second chance' for those who don't believe in Jesus in this lifetime."[275] He claims that even Luther wrote in 1522 that God could restore people through a second chance.[276] He also claims that others suggest that if we can have another chance to repent after death, why could we not have an endless number of opportunities to trust in Christ?[277]

To Bell, these options held by Christians over time help create conceptual space that permits us to be good Christians and yet have freedom to believe that God is able to give many opportunities for all kinds of people, including atheists, followers of other religions, and those who reject Jesus, since the only Jesus they saw was an oppressive person.[278] Moreover, as Bell realizes, there is a key belief at the heart of this view, that given enough time, God's love will melt even the hardest of hearts, so that they will turn to him. *God's love will win.* This stance works together with the belief that all will be reconciled to God through Christ. It also fits with the perspective he suggests, that restoration and reconciliation bring glory to God, whereas eternal torment does not.[279]

So for him, this is a viable stance for Christians; to be a good Christian, one does not have to believe that only a few will go to heaven after death, and the rest will go to hell. Nor do you have to believe it to *be* a Christian, he claims.[280] According to him, this version of the gospel story is not a very good one. This is especially so in contrast to his preferred version, which he says is more loving, expansive, beautiful, and inspiring than any other story about the ultimate course of history.[281]

These views of what humans are also help us understand more about McLaren's concept of our need as sinners. Neo suggests what God might say to someone after this "judgment" (purification?): "Well done! You have lived well! You helped the story advance toward my creative dreams. You fed the hungry, clothed the naked . . . . Wherever you went, you contributed love and peace, generosity and truth, courage and sacrifice, self-control

275. Bell, *Love Wins*, 106.

276. Bell, *Love Wins*, 106.

277. Bell, *Love Wins*, 106–7.

278. Bell, *Love Wins*, 106.

279. Bell, *Love Wins*, 108. His stress on integration and connection with God reminds me of Pagitt's views. There is such a tight connectedness in Pagitt's "holism" that I just don't see how there could be a literal hell with eternal torment.

280. Bell, *Love Wins*, 110.

281. Bell, *Love Wins*, 110–11.

and justice, faithfulness and kindness. You enriched the story, enhanced its beauty."[282]

Who then is "in" the kingdom? And who is "out"? For McLaren, at least in *Secret Message*, though the kingdom is available to all, not everyone will be in it. God does not *force* everyone to be in, so "naïve inclusion" is not an option. Nor is "judgmentalism and exclusion," for that would be coercive and violent. Instead, McLaren opts for "purposeful inclusion," in which all are welcome, but there is a requirement "that those who wish to enter actually have a change of heart—that they don't sneak in to accomplish their own agendas, but rather that they genuinely want to learn a new way of thinking, feeling, living, and being in 'the pastures of God.'"[283] Those who refuse reconciliation, who oppose the kingdom, "who want to ruin it by dividing it against itself" must be excluded, for he recognizes a kingdom divided against itself cannot stand. Still, these people do not face eternal judgment in hell, for evidently they will not be remembered.[284]

The Conventional and Emerging Versions of the Gospel Story

In sum, McLaren contrasts the conventional, or received, version of the gospel story (which seems to be closest to his understanding of the gospel according to evangelicals) with his emerging one in four main ways. First, in terms of the human situation (the framing story we find ourselves in), the conventional view says that because Adam and Eve sinned, God has "irrevocably determined" to destroy the entire universe, and he will send all humans' souls to hell for punishment of their imperfection "except for those

282. McLaren, *Story*, 166–67. In terms of God's "dreams," see *Everything Must Change,* in which the dream of the kingdom of God is tied to God's sacred ecosystem, McLaren's alternative framing story (e.g., 131–32).

283. McLaren, *Secret Message*, 165. Also, it seems that exclusivists (such as traditional evangelicals) could be excluded from McLaren's view of the kingdom, since they might "ruin it by dividing it against itself" (i.e., as McLaren understands it) by trying accomplish their own agenda—of seeing people repent and trust Jesus as the only way to God. Thanks to Michael Wittmer for this suggestion.

284. McLaren, *Secret Message,* 170. His more recent *Why Did Jesus* focuses more on religious pluralism, and it is not clear to me that he has shifted in this basic understanding from what he wrote in *Secret Message*. But in *Why Did Jesus*, McLaren focuses upon the religions as being our imperfect responses to our encounters with the Spirit. Still, the key for him seems to be authentic moral transformation into what *he* calls the way of Jesus. Nevertheless, Burson points out that in terms of the fate of the unevangelized, McLaren thinks such a focus is "idle conjecture and a deterrent to focusing on temporal and social concerns and one's own spirituality" (Burson, *Brian McLaren in Focus,* 158).

specifically exempted."[285] But McLaren's *emerging* view says that humans have "rebelled against God and filled the world with evil and injustice."[286] We are lost, like sheep without a shepherd, and God wants to heal us of our sickness.

In addition to what we have seen from Jones, I might add that in Pagitt's view, we are not inherently depraved, which he understands as the view "that humans start out lacking anything good."[287] Instead, inherent depravity is the product of a culturally based theology, not a timeless, universal truth.[288] It is part of the legal, judicial model, he claims, which was created as a way to help Romans understand Christianity and see a need for God.[289]

On that model, God is the judge, and his commands are the law. Breaking that law brings upon us God's condemnation through death and damnation. Jesus acts as our substitute, to pay the legal debt we cannot pay on our own. But to Pagitt, this model skews our understanding of the gospel in many ways. For one, God is beholden to the law, such that the law is the driving force, not him. Even God, along with his mercy and compassion, seems to be "subject to the law."[290] So, the gospel becomes sin-centered, not Jesus- or God-centered. Second, the law is not the be-all and end-all of faithfulness. Third, God is powerless, despite his own heart's breaking, to do anything other than offer Jesus as a substitute. Fourth, God is an angry judge who is immovable and must assuage his wrath through the death of Jesus.

For Pagitt, then, sin is not an issue of separation from God; that is part of the Greek-influenced version of the gospel. That view is just a culturally bound creation. Instead, sin is more about disintegration and how God has acted to integrate all of us into him.

For McLaren, the second aspect of the gospel involves the questions Jesus came to answer. The *conventional* view claims that since everyone is doomed to hell, Jesus came to answer how individuals can be saved from eternal damnation and go to heaven when they die. But this view also implies a more Gnostic kind of idea, that the soul needs to escape the *flesh*, which is bad. In the meantime, McLaren thinks the conventional view has a very minimal understanding of Christians' role on earth (besides getting

285. McLaren, *Everything Must Change,* 78. Note that by his irrevocable determination, this is a forced story and therefore wrong.

286. McLaren, *Everything Must Change,* 78.

287. Pagitt, *A Christianity Worth Believing,* 124.

288. Pagitt, *A Christianity Worth Believing,* 127.

289. Pagitt, *A Christianity Worth Believing,* 155.

290. Pagitt, *A Christianity Worth Believing,* 155.

as many souls into heaven as possible). To him, its focus is simply how God can help those who are saved to be happy.

If he's right, this kind of understanding would leave Christians with little to no place for a social ethic. Down through history, people writing within the broad Christian tradition have varied in terms of a social ethic, sometimes leaning toward a minimalist view, while at other times embracing a much more confident one. For instance, Augustine saw individuals in society as being in conflict, so his social ethic is not so much about making social progress, but more about maintaining a balance of power and roughly achieving justice. There is *some* room for cooperation and improvement in the city of man, but only in eternity in the city of God will we find perfect justice.[291]

But Aquinas, who was highly influenced by Augustine, came up with a very different social ethic, for he had a more optimistic view of what humans can accomplish. That optimism stemmed in part from his view about the nature and extent of the fall. Society is not just a check against sin; we have abilities here and now to do what is good and improve society.[292]

However, from a very different interpretation of Augustine, Luther had a low expectation of the transformation of people in a society by the love of Christ, even in believers. Thus, in his view, it is impossible to build a Christian society. The goal of God's people is to grow in piety and spread the gospel. In contrast, the goal of civil society is to keep external peace and prevent evil.[293]

Though also a Reformer, Calvin came to a very different conclusion regarding his social ethic. Drawing upon his idea of a "third use" of the law, while Christians do not need to keep the law to be justified before God, they do have the ability to keep the moral law—yet only with the help of the Holy Spirit. Hence, believers can have confidence that they can obey the moral law. The moral law is an invaluable guide to Christians for life, so out of gratitude they keep it. Historically, these reasons for confidence led to much energy to serve God and a belief that the regenerate can discern and do good now. So, believers can make progress in transforming society and in growing into Christlikeness.[294]

In contrast to the conventional view, McLaren's *emerging* view suggests that Jesus focuses on a different question to answer: What must be done about the mess we are in, generally in the human condition, and specifically

---

291. See my *In Search of Moral Knowledge*, 57–58.
292. Smith, *In Search of Moral Knowledge*, 68, 70.
293. Smith, *In Search of Moral Knowledge*, 76.
294. Smith, *In Search of Moral Knowledge*, 79–80.

for those living then under Roman domination? Thus, the very nature of the focus of what is on Jesus' mind leads to a dynamic energy to work to better God's kingdom on earth. McLaren's reasons are not necessarily the same as those of the more optimistic Christians we just surveyed; for instance, he does not draw the same conclusion as Calvin about the nature and extent of the fall, or even our primary need in terms of our relationship with God. But he does land squarely in the conclusions that some other Christians have drawn: that Christians have a moral obligation to better life on earth, and they can do much to help fulfill that duty. On the other hand, McLaren's understanding of the conventional view is also in line with some other historical options suggested by Christians, ones that see little point in trying to redeem society now.

Before leaving this second dimension of the two stories, let me explain a bit more about McLaren's notion of just *what* it is we are trying to redeem here and now. Unlike the more optimistic Aquinas or Calvin, who were interested in redeeming culture or society in order to build God's kingdom here, McLaren sometimes uses the term God's "*sacred ecosystem*" for the kingdom. For Aquinas and Calvin, there was a clear demarcation in a hierarchy of ethical importance between humans and the rest of God's creation, particularly because God created humans in his image, and Jesus has identified permanently with humanity in his incarnation, thus giving humans a unique kind of dignity that no other aspect of creation shares.

But for McLaren, God's kingdom is not only about people; it includes all of creation, which is evolving and unfolding in terms of its own story. Christians need to address systemic issues of our day, including injustice, poverty, the ecological crisis, and more. We are to care for one another and all living creatures, which is a theme that can be traced from his "fiction" trilogy and continues in *Everything Must Change*.

The third question is: how did Jesus respond to the crisis? Under the *conventional* view, his good news is that if you repent of your own individual sins and believe that the Father punished Jesus on the cross as a substitute for your own punishment, you will go to heaven, not hell, when you die, and you will live forever. In the *emerging* view, however, the good news is that God loves humanity and invites all to turn from their respective, current paths and follow his way, which seems primarily to be one of moral transformation. This also seems to include not just individuals, but also cultures and communities, for they have their own societal, group-based sins. If we trust him and become his disciples, we will be transformed, and the world will be transformed, too, which is possible now. In *A New Kind of Christianity*, McLaren explains further that eternal life is not a promise about life after death, or eternal life in heaven, which are linked to the Greco-Roman narrative's influence. Instead, it is "life of the ages" that transcends life in the present age. It's part of God's new Genesis.

Fourth, what was Jesus' purpose? In the *conventional* view, Jesus came to deal with original sin, and he saves people from God's wrath, which they deserve. But in the *emerging* view, Jesus "came to save the earth and all it contains from its ongoing destruction because of human evil."[295] For McLaren, a telling problem with the conventional view is that it does nothing to confront and correct the dysfunction of society's machinery. Instead, it aids and even abets society's "suicidal" tendencies in various ways.[296]

In *A New Kind of Christianity*, McLaren's views have adjusted somewhat. Jesus came to announce a new kingdom, a new way of life, a new way of peace. His is a new kingdom with room for many religious traditions in it. If Christians could set aside the destructive, imperialistic, dualistic, and tribal Greco-Roman narrative, they "could offer Jesus (not Christianity) as a gift to the world," and they would not need to think they had to insult other religions.[297] Moreover, he thinks Christians would be freed from thinking that in the future, all other religions would no longer exist. Christians also wouldn't need to think of who is "inside" versus "outside." Instead, they could look forward to a time "when members of all religions, including our own, learned to be reconciled with God, one another, and all creation."[298]

So this good news is a fulfillment of McLaren's Jewish narrative. For instance, to be born again means to participate in a new Genesis, a new creation that interrupts the death spiral of violence and instead is regenerative. We take part in a new Exodus, a liberation from principalities and powers (but not to be understood as literal demons, i.e., fallen angels) that would oppress us, by entering a new, peaceable kingdom, which is here now.

So, according to McLaren, it seems Jesus' secret message can be summed up as follows: Christ the king is in and among us here and now.[299] The kingdom of God, or heaven, is not something that we go to when we die; instead, the kingdom has come to earth, and we can be members of that kingdom *now* by following the "way of Jesus," thereby being morally transformed, working to transform his kingdom (or sacred ecosystem) *now*. Thus, this is "salvation" in McLaren's view. And, this suggests what Burson

---

295. McLaren, *Everything Must Change*, 79.
296. See McLaren, *Everything Must Change*, 81–82.
297. McLaren, *A New Kind of Christianity*, 215.
298. McLaren, *A New Kind of Christianity*, 215.
299. McLaren, *Secret Message*, 101.

observes, that one can "become a follower of Jesus without converting to the Christian faith or apprenticing oneself to a community of Christ-followers."[300]

For Bell, the good news is better than the typical story we have been told. The gospel is better than we can "go" to heaven when we die if we trust Christ now, in this life. Indeed, it is far deeper. First, will many be cast into eternal conscious torment if they do not trust Christ in this life? No; the good news, according to Bell, is that "Jesus forgives them all. . . . Forgiveness is unilateral."[301] It is something God has done already, since he has reconciled all of us to himself. And, God gets what God wants—he does not want any to perish, and eventually, his love will soften even the hardest hearts.

Second, the eternal life that we are given is not something which starts when we "go" to heaven. So ours is not a gospel of "sin management" now. No, it is a present reality, to be lived and enjoyed now. It is the life of the kingdom of God being realized more and more in our daily lives now.

The Next Step

We now have seen many of the more developed, mature views of McLaren, Jones, Pagitt, and Bell, including their depiction of what has gone so wrong in the church, particularly in the United States, but also throughout the West. Largely, they once portrayed this in terms of the effects of modernity, but now have broadened and deepened that assessment. Now, I want to probe their depiction; to what extent does it accurately account for the problems they have identified in evangelical churches and believers?

To help accomplish this task, I think it will behoove us to revisit the nature of the effects of modernity (and other factors leading up to it) upon evangelicals, to help us evaluate McLaren's and others' stories, analyses, and assessments. So, in the next chapter, I will examine how the church has been shaped by a series of scientific, historical, cultural, and philosophical developments. What we will find, I believe, is that these emergents are quite on target in many of their criticisms of the practice of Western evangelicalism these days, even more so than I realized when I wrote *Truth*. Yet, I think we also will be able to identify another, deeper factor at work, one which they seem to miss.[302]

300. Burson, *Brian McLaren in Focus*, 197.

301. Bell, *Love Wins*, 188–89.

302. Thanks to Michael Wittmer for his valuable feedback on an earlier draft of this chapter.

2

Another Story

The Shaping of Western,
American Evangelical Christianity

Introduction

Scripture is God's special revelation to all people. For evangelicals, it holds core doctrines across cultures, such as God's existence as a Trinity, the deity of Christ, the atoning sacrifice of Christ on the cross for our sins, his resurrection, and more. Still, how evangelicals live that out practically likely will vary somewhat compared to that of other Christians in others times, cultures, and places.

Looking back, it can be fairly easy to notice how Augustine's theology was shaped in part by influences from Aristotle, Plato, and his own experiences with Manichaeism. Aquinas was shaped (again, in part) by being born into a time of the Roman Catholic church's hegemony religiously in Europe, along with reliance on the works of Augustine, Aristotle, and Islamic scholars who had recovered Aristotle's thought. In turn, Luther's theology was influenced not only by the book of Romans, but by also the abuses of the Roman Catholic church and how it had synthesized Aristotle's thought with its theology.

But, at the same time, it can be easy not to realize the extent to which oneself and one's fellow Christians are shaped by cultural, historical, philosophical, and other conditions. These men all lived in and through times that predated ours. Perhaps most importantly, we live on the other side of the Enlightenment and the rise of the modern era, through which our more immediate spiritual predecessors in the faith passed. Western Christianity did pass through that era, with its many kinds of critical cultural, historical, philosophical, religious, and other changes. That overall experience (if it can be labeled in the singular) has had important effects, as we now shall see. Here I will focus mainly on factors in the United States, but several factors have had broader influences too.

A Series of Cultural Influences

By and large, throughout the ancient period and most of the Middle Ages, there was a pretty consistent belief, both philosophically and theologically, in the reality of immaterial entities.[1] Plato believed that there is a sensible realm (the world in which we live, in which we can experience things by our senses) and an intelligible realm (a realm we know by reason). The *forms*, which are archetypes or essences, are "part of" the intelligible realm. The forms are real, but they *themselves* are not located in space or time; thus, they are immaterial.

Some examples may help illustrate what kind of things the forms are. First, consider triangularity, which is the essence of being a triangle. Second, there is humanness, or the essence of being human. There is also justice itself, as well as the true, the good, and the beautiful. Numbers themselves also would be examples. We call these archetypes *universals*, meaning they are *one* kind of thing (triangularity itself, humanness itself, which are immaterial). Yet, they can be present in *many* particular instances (various humans, this triangle $\triangle$, and that triangle $\triangle$), which are located in space and time.[2]

Consider also properties, or qualities, that can be present in different things. For instance, the virtue of justice is a property that humans should have due to the kind of thing they are. In Plato's view, it too is a universal. So also would be things like thoughts or concepts. For instance, though an individual can have a concept of equality in that person's mind, that same concept can be present in many minds.

So, on a Platonic (and Aristotelian) basis, each human being has an essential nature, i.e., a particular, human soul, which is the instance of

1. There were exceptions, however; e.g., from the ancients, there was Democritus, an atomist, and Epicurus, an empiricist.

2. For a discussion of these kinds of issues related to moral forms, see Plato's *The Republic*, book 6, 504d–501b.

the universal, humanness. Thus, all humans literally share that nature in common. While a human's soul is immaterial, it is that universal that has been particularized. Aristotle's biological classification system was based on dividing living things according to their kinds, and their respective natures defined what kind of thing (a dog, a rose, a horse, an oak tree, etc.) something is. His classification system was used until Darwin's theory was embraced.

Augustine (354–430) and Aquinas (1224–1274) followed similarly, in that there are real, immaterial things, such as human souls, and immaterial beings, including God, angels, and demons. Calvin and Luther continued in the same basic direction. In these kinds of views, thoughts, beliefs, experiences, desires, and other "mental states" are real and immaterial, too. Additionally, moral principles and virtues are immaterial, and they are appropriate for us due to our essence as image bearers.

We can call this view a kind of *metaphysical realism*, in that these entities really exist. But these thinkers also believed we could know this to be so—an *epistemological realism*. In general, they all could appeal to reason to know these and other truths. Christians could explain that ability in terms of reason and general revelation (or perhaps natural law). Additionally, Christians had special revelation to which they could appeal. Special revelation would be needed for us to know some of these truths (e.g., specifics about the human soul, such as that it is made in God's image, and that is fallen; that God is triune; that angels exist). On the other hand, some others we could know by reason (e.g., that we do have souls; and that there must be a "prime mover," as Aristotle thought, to be the first cause of the universe).

With the rise to dominance of the Christian worldview in Europe, universities were formed that unified the disciplines across the curriculum. This unity was based in a recognition that all truth is God's truth, and he is Lord of all (Col 2:3). Thus, all the disciplines should be grounded in who God is and what he has revealed both by special and general revelation in his two "books"—Scripture and creation. Therefore, the deliverances of science should fit with what we learn from theology, philosophy, anthropology, and more.

Still, this story was not without some exceptions. For instance, William of Ockham (1280–1349) denied the Platonic view of properties as universals. Instead, he helped champion the view that properties are just particulars, which is a view called *nominalism*.[3] Even so, more or less this broad consensus maintained its vitality through most of the Middle Ages.

---

3. For example, see Brower, "Aquinas on the Problem of Universals." See also William of Ockham, *Quodlibetal Questions*, 5.12–13, 441–48.

But, several additional, crucial changes began to be implemented, and nominalism also came to be much more accepted when Europe transitioned into the modern era.

Modern Science's Prestige

Several important scientists made their contributions, and they were motivated by Christianity. For instance, Nicolaus Copernicus (1473–1543) sought to worship God via astronomy.[4] He developed his revolutionary heliocentric scientific theory, which he saw as compatible with biblical teaching. Galileo Galilei (1564–1642) further developed this theory. He argued that this model is biblically compatible and scientifically superior to the Aristotelian model, which was the accepted model at the time.

According to Aristotle, the earth was the center of the universe. Moreover, the cosmos is eternal, animated by a soul, and has a necessary structure. Aristotle also thought the heavens are perfect and incorruptible. Similar to Copernicus, Galileo was directed by interpreting the cosmos as God's book of creation, which was written in the language of mathematics. Still, reading that book can be challenging and requires techniques, mathematical physics, and experimental equipment. Nevertheless, it is constantly open for investigation. In contrast, he held that Scripture uses observational expressions about heavenly bodies because "the intention of the Holy Ghost is to teach us how one goes to heaven, not [sic] how heaven goes."[5]

Johannes Kepler (1571–1630) also appealed to the influence of Christian teaching in his developments in modern science. In his view, mathematical ideas exist eternally in God's mind. God created the universe according to these ideas, and he manages the universe by them. Contrary to Aristotle, for Kepler the universe does not have a soul. Instead, Kepler understood God's design of the universe to be *like* a clock, or a "celestial machine," but not *merely* a machine.

This new, heliocentric model, coupled with the emphasis upon empirical methods, led to great advances in the prestige of modern science. This prestige seemed to reach its zenith in Isaac Newton (1642–1727) and his work. Though it was debated for much of the eighteenth century, Newton's "theory of gravity had become established among those engaged in research in orbital mechanics and physical geodesy, leading to the *Principia*

---

4. Copernicus, *On the Revolutions of the Heavenly Spheres*, 7.

5. Galilei, "Letter to the Grand Duchess Christian of Tuscany," 119. On the attribution to Cardinal Baronio, see *The Trial of Galileo*, 56.

becoming *the* exemplar of science at its most successful."[6] Moreover, according to philosopher George Smith, the *Principia* was *the* most important factor in the development of astronomy and modern physics.[7]

Meanwhile, these scientific developments fit the pattern of the Enlightenment, or Age of Reason (roughly late seventeenth and eighteenth centuries), in which there was a growing confidence in human reason, even untutored by Scripture or theology. By using reason, and studying the laws of nature, people thought they could learn the fundamental principles thereof. This great confidence of the Enlightenment was expressed succinctly by the German philosopher Immanuel Kant: "'have the courage to use your own intelligence!'—[this] is therefore the motto of the enlightenment."[8] Yet, it seems more accurate to refer to several *Enlightenments*.

The Many Influences of the Enlightenment(s)

The Didactic Enlightenment and "Common Sense"

There were differing impacts of the broad phenomena we call the Enlightenment on Europe and the United States. Thus, following Henry May, George Marsden suggests four European "Enlightenments," or sets of ideas, that influenced the United States.[9] Their influences varied abroad. First, the "early Moderate Enlightenment" emphasized ideals of balance, order, and religious compromise. The thought of people such as John Locke and Isaac Newton seem associated with this first version. In the United States, John Adams and James Madison used these ideals in association with the Revolutionary War. Second, the great skeptic, David Hume, and Voltaire helped shape the "Skeptical Enlightenment," which Thomas Paine indwelt. Third, the radical "Revolutionary Enlightenment" developed the ideas of Jean-Jacques Rousseau. Fourth was the "Didactic Enlightenment," which stemmed from Scottish Common Sense Realism. According to Marsden, only the moderate and didactic Enlightenments had much influence in the States. This is not to say, however, that Hume's philosophy (and that of others) eventually did not have significant influences there, too.

As one of the main expositors of Common Sense (CS), Thomas Reid (1710–1796) developed it as a response against Hume's skepticism.

6. Smith, "Newton's *Philosophiae Naturalis Principia Mathematica.*"

7. Smith, "Newton's *Philosophiae Naturalis Principia Mathematica.*"

8. From Kant, "What is Enlightenment?" 145 (bracketed insert mine).

9. See May, *The Enlightenment in America*, xvi, in Marsden, *Understanding Fundamentalism and Evangelicalism*, 128; hereafter, *UFE*.

Contrary to Hume, Reid argued that our minds can have direct access to reality and know that to be the case.[10] Other contributors to CS included Francis Hutcheson, Adam Smith, and Dugald Stewart.

As the historian Mark Noll explains, according to CS, "all humans possessed, by nature, a common set of capacities—both epistemological and moral—through which they could grasp the basic realities of nature and morality."[11] We can know universal truths as they truly are; we can know (by our own intuition) universal, objective truths *objectively*.[12] In contrast to Hume's skepticism, CS's goal was to establish a solid foundation of truth. Moreover, according to Noll, people believed in CS that these capacities to know objective truths could be studied "as scientifically as Newton studied the physical world," and these studies would yield scientific laws for human behavior and ethics.[13]

Yet, as Noll wisely observes, there is a tension between this confidence in our natural intellectual and moral abilities to recognize and know truths of all kinds and the Reformation's stress upon our fallenness. Jonathan Edwards and all other major evangelical leaders in the mid-1700s in the United States had defended the Reformation view of human nature. It "denied that people had a 'natural' moral sense by which they could understand what was both true and in their best interest," which was the very basis for CS.[14]

Nevertheless, by 1800, US evangelicals came to embrace CS. Noll thinks that the explanations for this lie in how CS philosophy provided "exactly what was needed to master the tumults of the Revolutionary era."[15] CS appealed to intuition, and that provided an "intellectually respectable way to establish public virtue in a society that was busily repudiating the props upon which virtue had traditionally rested—tradition itself, divine revelation, history, social hierarchy, an inherited government, and the authority of religious denominations."[16]

CS helped meet three needs of the Revolutionary generation. First, CS helped justify the rebellion against Britain. Second, CS provided a way to

10. See Marsden, *Fundamentalism and American Culture*, 14, 113; hereafter *FAC*.

11. Noll, *Scandal of the Evangelical Mind*, 85.

12. By an objective truth, I mean one that is what it is whether or not any human believes it. It refers to the way things are in reality (i.e., metaphysically). But *our being objective* is an epistemological notion. It involves our being able to set aside our biases, influences, etc., to consider some claim. (Of course, postmoderns will deny that we can ever be truly unbiased. I will address this in chapter 6.)

13. Noll, *Scandal of the Evangelical Mind*, 85.

14. Noll, *Scandal of the Evangelical Mind*, 86.

15. Noll, *Scandal of the Evangelical Mind*, 87.

16. Noll, *Scandal of the Evangelical Mind*, 87.

found principles of social order without needing to appeal to tradition or autocratic government. And third, CS helped evangelicals preserve Christianity in a time in which those people were rejecting traditional religious structures and any form of absolute sovereignty. Instead of appealing to the authority of a sovereign, or tradition, people could draw upon self-evident truths and unalienable rights. To establish social order, the framers could appeal to "a Constitution infused with the principles of moral philosophy," which are known by the moral sense.[17] Finally, Protestant Christianity could be supported likewise by appealing to common sense, which people believed simply would vindicate the truths of the Bible.

Moreover, CS also held to the Enlightenment "trust in objectivity, its devotion to a principle of privileged scientific inquiry."[18] CS was seen as being scientific, which helped it become deeply accepted by evangelicals and other Americans. John Witherspoon, the president of Princeton, stated that "a time may come when men, treating moral philosophy as Newton and his successors have done natural [philosophy], may arrive at greater precision."[19] If we study moral principles in our own consciousness (evidently without explicitly needing to study Scripture), we can discover *scientifically* the needed principles to be a moral society.[20] Noll summarizes this confidence: "Explicit in the lectures and textbooks of the nation's Protestant leaders was the Enlightenment belief that *Americans could find within themselves resources, compatible with Christianity*, to bring social order out of the rootlessness and confusion of the new nation."[21]

So, CS provided a foundation in America for the continuation of the older synthesis of science and Christianity. Via CS, "modern empirical scientific ideals, the self-evident principles of the American revolution, and evangelical Christianity" could be by reconciled.[22] People wed CS with the thought of Francis Bacon (1561–1626), the seventeenth-century philosopher who had developed an inductive, scientific methodology. That is, people thought that the "careful observation and classification of facts," which they could know by their *objective* common sense, should be applied

---

17. Noll, *Scandal of the Evangelical Mind*, 88.

18. Noll, *Scandal of the Evangelical Mind*, 88.

19. Witherspoon, "Lectures on Moral Philosophy," 3.470, in Noll, *Scandal of the Evangelical Mind*, 89.

20. Noll, *Scandal of the Evangelical Mind*, 89. This appeal to a "scientific" basis for morality might help explain (in part) why theology too was seen as needing to be done as a science, since the Bible has much to say about morality.

21. Noll, *Scandal of the Evangelical Mind*, 90 (emphasis mine).

22. Marsden, *UFE*, 128.

generally to reliably and clearly know facts.[23] To many, then, evangelical Christianity and science were seen as allies, and that alliance was deeply rational. Theologically conservative evangelicals believed this synthesis was so strong that there was a "beatification of Bacon" and deep respect for Newton.[24]

There was such profound respect for Bacon's methodology that its application was not limited to natural sciences. For instance, many thought there are first moral principles that could be a "foundation of certain knowledge" from which, by using Baconian induction, we might arrive at "authoritative conclusions concerning moral, political, and economic laws."[25] Noll sketched this mind-set of nineteenth century evangelicals, for whom "Baconianism" was the "belief that strict induction from verified individual facts to more general laws offered the best way to understand the data on *any* subject," including the facts of Scripture.[26]

Noll observes that the Baconian method gravitated toward a particular hermeneutic. Since, in CS, we are able to discern truths clearly, we should read the Bible in a "simple," "literal," "natural" kind of way.[27] Classical dispensationalist leaders, such as C. I. Scofield and Reuben Torrey, continued this kind of approach to studying Scripture, thereby stressing scientific methods. Torrey himself understood his work as "simply an attempt at a careful unbiased, systematic, thorough-going, *inductive* study and statement of Bible truth. . . . The methods of modern science are applied to Bible study—thorough analysis followed by careful synthesis."[28]

So, people in the States deeply embraced science's great prestige and Bacon's inductive, observational methodology. They saw the "Baconian ideal" as highly desirable, regardless of subject of study—the eternal, fixed truths in nature, or those in the Bible. According to Marsden, the Princetonians in the 1800s "saw themselves as champions of 'impartiality' in the careful examination of the facts, as opposed to 'metaphysical and philosophical speculations'" that the German higher critics used. They were influenced by *philosophical naturalism* and its principles.[29] Largely, evangelicals thought Bacon's methodology should be applied to theology, by arranging truths

23. Marsden, *FAC*, 14.

24. Bozeman, *Protestants in an Age of Science*, 72.

25. Marsden, *FAC*, 16.

26. Noll, *Scandal of the Evangelical Mind*, 178 (emphasis added). On the facts of Scripture, see Marsden, *FAC*, 14.

27. See Noll, *Scandal of the Evangelical Mind*, 197.

28. Torrey, *What the Bible Teaches*, 1 (emphasis in original), in Marsden, *FAC*, 60.

29. It is interesting to wonder if they considered their own philosophical presuppositions.

into a systematic whole, and thereby bestowing the prestige of science upon theology.

Before proceeding, let me define philosophical naturalism. It is a philosophical view about the nature of what is real, and, roughly, it holds that *only the natural* exists. As Carl Sagan, the astronomer, said, "The Cosmos is all that is or was or ever will be."[30] Usually, what is natural can be described as being made up of matter; so, *all that exists is physical stuff,* which sometimes is called *physicalism.*[31] Thus, the "natural" (in this context) is the antithesis of "supernatural." Typically, then, the common understanding of naturalism is there are *no real supernatural (or immaterial) beings or things.* Clearly, this view excludes souls, essential natures, angels, Satan, demons, moral principles and virtues (i.e., as being immaterial), and God.

So, it seems that CS also might fit with the Protestant teaching of the perspicuity of Scripture. Theologically, according to that doctrine, common people could understand the Bible. But, philosophically, CS affirmed the perspicuity of nature.[32] How, though, did CS influence evangelicals' understanding of the doctrine of human depravity, and the extent of its impact upon humans' noetic abilities? Evangelicals still seemed to hold officially to the orthodox doctrine of depravity, but according to Marsden, the influence of CS (that everyone has the ability to know God's truth) was more pronounced.[33] What seemed to emerge was more of a mind-set that humans' intellect suffered only from a "slight astigmatism."[34]

We can see this great confidence from CS for all people to know truth of all kinds, especially from the Bible, in a quote from the great Princeton theologian, B. B. Warfield, in 1903. He claimed that "it is the distinction of Christianity that it has come into the world clothed with the mission to *reason* its way to its dominion. Other religions may appeal to the sword, or seek some other way to propagate themselves. Christianity makes its appeal to right reason, and stands out among all religions, therefore, as distinctively 'the Apologetic religion.' It is solely by reasoning that it has come thus far on its way to its kingship. And it is solely by reasoning that it will put all its enemies under its feet."[35]

---

30. Sagan, *Cosmos,* 1.

31. There also could be a form of naturalism that says some non-physical things (like, minds, thoughts, beliefs, etc.) emerge from the physical, but they depend for their existence completely upon the physical. This might be called a "pluralistic physicalism."

32. Marsden, *FAC,* 16.

33. See Marsden's discussion of this attitude in *FAC,* 111–13.

34. Marsden, *FAC,* 16.

35. Warfield, "Introduction," 26.

Marsden also notices this confidence: "by 1859, evangelicals, both scientists, and theologians, thought they had discovered an impregnable synthesis between faith and reason. Scientific reasoning, the kind they most respected, firmly supported Christian faith."[36] Similarly, Warfield also expressed this high confidence in science, because it "was an objective, unified, and cumulative enterprise" to which all people can contribute.[37] Echoing this same perceived strength of the synthesis between theology and science based on common sense, Warfield thought that theology was the queen of the sciences, and its "truths could be discovered once and for all on the same foundational epistemological principles as the truths of old Newtonian physics had been established."[38]

But, there were other factors at work that soon would broadside evangelicals and this mind-set. In part, the view of the nature of the universe was changing. Naturalism already had been making progress through Darwin's evolutionary biology and German higher criticism. But, well before Darwin's views broke on to the scene, there had been a shift underway in terms of the metaphysics of nature.

A Mechanistic View of Creation, and Deism

Various ideas were being offered that would eventually move science and philosophy away from a dualistic view of reality (i.e., creation is made of both material and immaterial aspects) toward a more monistic, materialist view. For example, the French philosopher Descartes (1596–1650) believed that humans are a combination of a material body and a rational (intellectual) soul, but it seems that only humans have such an immaterial dimension.[39] Moreover, he thought the body and soul were united through the brain's pineal gland. However, that view is vulnerable to the *interaction objection*, according to which it is hard to understand how the soul could interact causally with a physical body, particularly if (as was being thought) physical entities are subject to mechanistic laws of causation.

However, already there were moves underway that would undermine a dualistic view of creation. The rise of nominalism via Ockham had implications along these lines. First, Plato's universals were thought to be metaphysically abstract entities; that is, they themselves are not located in space and time. Nominalism, however, denies the existence of such things.

36. Marsden, *UFE*, 135.

37. Marsden, *UFE*, 123.

38. Marsden, *UFE*, 124.

39. See, for instance, Hatfield, "René Descartes."

Instead, *all things in creation are located in space and time.* This has implications for what we would think exists and for what we would think we can know. For if things are spatially and temporally located, we would think they are empirically knowable. Thus, on a consistent nominalism, people would not tend to admit immaterial "things" into what they believe exists.

Second, the Scientific Revolution picked up this embrace of nominalism and linked it with mechanical philosophy and atomism. In the sixteenth and seventeenth centuries, the Revolution rejected Aristotelianism, which had been embraced deeply by the Scholastics. Aristotelianism had stressed strongly metaphysics, including universal, immaterial qualities.[40] In this view, universals have essences, as I discussed before. Drawing upon this paradigm, Scholastics utilized a more logical, *a priori* principled approach to doing science, deducing what must be the case.[41]

The natural philosophers of the Scientific Revolution, however, embraced a more observational approach. Pierre Gassendi (1592–1655) and Thomas Hobbes (1588–1679), both of whom were nominalists, endorsed *mechanical* philosophy, on which the universe is a large-scale machine. Gassendi and others also put to use Greek *atomism*. On that view, the material world is atoms in the void, and atoms are ultimate. Together, the *mechanical atomism* of that time had followers such as Francis Bacon, Galileo Galilei, Robert Boyle, and Isaac Newton, in addition to Hobbes and Gassendi.[42]

Another key distinction was introduced via scientists such as Galileo and Boyle. For them, matter has only "primary" qualities, things like quantity, size, location, and shape. On the other hand, "secondary" qualities (for example, odors, tastes, or colors) are not properties of matter. Instead, for Galileo, they are merely names or words that people used according to linguistic conventions (which is a common nominalist move today), or they are just subjective qualities of a perceiver.[43] Similarly, Boyle thought Aristotelian universals and secondary qualities are unintelligible due to how he conceived of the nature of what is real in the material world.[44]

---

40. Del Soldato, "Natural Philosophy in the Renaissance," 9; Klein, "Francis Bacon," 5.

41. Del Soldato, "Natural Philosophy in the Renaissance," 6, 9.

42. Even so, the mechanical atomists of this time tended to separate a "spiritual" world from their atomism. So, these people posited that minds, souls, angels, and God would belong to that "world" (Chalmers, "Atomism from the 17th to the 20th Century," 2). Boyle, a Christian, thought our spiritual faculties should be exempted because we cannot explain them by mechanical atomism.

43. Galilei, "*Il Saggistore*," 274.

44. Chalmers, "Atomism from the 17th to the 20th Century," 4.

Eventually, Aristotelianism was rejected. Instead, the new scientific methodology endorsed empirical observation of material, concrete particulars. Since these particulars were thought to be made of matter, they would not have universals or essences. This new method was a significant development in its stress upon empirical observation in science, for some important empirical problems have arisen for Aristotelianism, which fostered an over-reliance upon metaphysical theories.

So, particularly through the rise of Ockham's nominalism and the Scientific Revolution, nominalism came to ascendancy, and along with it, a belief that only particular, individual qualities or objects exist in creation. Moreover, if universals do not exist, then what we can know is limited to the particular as well, though we can strive to develop theories that can be generalized.

Now I will begin to explore how these key views had impacts in other areas of thought. In 1652, Hobbes published *Leviathan*. Though God was still in the picture for him, and though he wrote about Christianity in England during its civil war, he situated such discussions in his mechanical, atomist, and nominalist view of creation. Humans are aggregates of atoms, and he explained their desires for things in terms of physical motions toward some object. Hobbes described such motions toward things as what is good. Aversions were motions away from something, which he described as what is bad. Thus he shifted away from the broad medieval and ancient views of morals as immaterial kinds of things. Similarly, though he appealed to moral "natural laws," these too had to fit now in his materialist framework. Thus, Hobbes had no room for immaterial essences, or universals, unlike Plato and many others since his time.

Hobbes embodied the Enlightenment confidence in human reason, too, for he embraced *rationalism*, which involves the high confidence to know universal truths, apart from special revelation. He also utilized an *empiricist* epistemology, which is the view that *all* knowledge comes by way of the five senses.[45] Hobbes's use of an empirical approach to knowledge makes sense if all that is real (except God, at least) is material, for that would be empirically knowable. Coupled with a high confidence in human reason, special revelation is not really needed for knowledge.

Furthermore, people developed, utilized, and interpreted Newton's views along mechanistic lines, which supported a more deistic view of God in relationship with creation. Thus, God would be needed only to start the machine. Our inherited idea of "Newtonian" physics, however, has moved

---

45. *Empiricism* is not to be confused with *empirical* knowledge, i.e., knowledge gained by the five senses. Empiricism is an ideology that limits all knowledge to that one type.

further away from Newton's own views about God to a more deterministic, materialistic system.[46]

Marsden also notes that the Puritans embraced the seventeenth century's "new science." They valued highly providential interpretations of nature, and so these newer scientific readings might have created a tension in their views. But, as he observes, "the Puritans were so preoccupied with their understanding of God as an orderly lawgiver that they welcomed and fostered investigation of that orderliness."[47]

But, by the eighteenth century, the developing view of nature led to practical effects upon all Protestants. If the universe is basically a machine that runs by natural laws, then that position fits well with deism. Thus, Marsden suggests that "probably it is safe to say that even many of those who were theologically orthodox adopted a worldview that, in effect, had Deist tendencies. They viewed the universe as a machine run by natural laws, and *in practice* distanced the Creator from their understandings of the everyday operations of creation,"[48] although Jonathan Edwards was a key exception.

Now, this more mechanistic, deistic mind-set also led to a sharper distinction between what is natural and supernatural. Previously, people tended to think that God's routine, sustaining activity was behind the forces of nature. But now, under the influence of this mechanistic view, the forces of nature were being reinterpreted along more mechanistic principles that God had established. However, now God lets them operate on their own. Therefore, it seems that God's supernatural works would have to be more clearly identifiable than before, to distinguish them from the operation of natural laws. The result was the development of a complementary, two-tiered view of "natural" events. Since God is the author of the books of nature and special revelation, and his revelations would be consistent, these two books' principles *would harmonize*. Bishop Butler's and William Paley's works served to underscore their unity, yet diversity. Thus, on this view, empirical science and the natural would not conflict with the claims of Scripture; rather, they would harmonize.[49] This two-tiered worldview, of nature and

---

46. For example, see Smith, "Newton's *Philosophiae Naturalis Principia Mathematica*": "The 'clockwork universe' aspect of the Newtonian world view, for example, is not to be found in the *Principia*; it was added by Laplace late in the eighteenth century, after the success of the theory of gravity in accounting for complex deviations from Keplerian motion became fully evident."

47. Marsden, *UFE*, 130.

48. Marsden, *UFE*, 130 (emphasis mine).

49. Marsden, *UFE*, 131.

its laws below and supernatural truths above, became widespread amongst Protestants in the States by the end of the seventeenth century.

Now, empiricism drove the distinction between these two tiers, and it had been developing first through British philosophers (Hobbes, Locke, Berkeley, and Hume) and then Kant in Germany. So, it is not the case that the other forms of the Enlightenment, especially that influenced by Hume's and Kant's empiricism, did not have any effect in the states.

Through approximately the American Civil War, this two-tiered view led to a bifurcation between theology and any other discipline. Still, that "division" was not seen as problematic. For example, Marsden observes that there were no distinctively Christian perspectives on the Revolutionary War. On such "mundane matters they assumed that political science was identical for the Christian and the non-Christian."[50] This was due to the CS mind-set that these truths could be discovered by science, confirmed by our common sense, and seen to harmonize with the Bible.

Since there was no felt need to develop a rigorous integration of theology with other disciplines, Christians allowed the various disciplines to develop autonomously. Therefore, evangelical Christians' own mind-set helped pave the way for the secularization of these disciplines.[51] Yet, shortly, evangelicals in American society would be caught unprepared when these disciplines would be seen as autonomous under the interpretive scheme of naturalism, fueled by empiricism, and the confidence in autonomous human reason.

So, despite explicitly affirming orthodox doctrines, evangelicals in the States had accepted a *functionally deistic* interpretation of reality. Since creation (including humans) was seen as mechanistic and run by natural laws that God had set in motion, it was easy for God to subtly become understood as distanced from his creation.

The Fact-Value Split

Another bifurcation was taking place in Europe that would affect life in the States as well. Science already was seen as the paradigmatic way to conduct any discipline. But, soon science was given even more prestige by way of some philosophical developments.

---

50. Marsden, *UFE*, 131–32. There, he discusses also topics such as the self-evidence of the injustice of taxation without representation.

51. Compare Marsden's comments about Martin Marty's thesis, that "secularization typically took place through a peaceful separation of 'religious areas' in American life from the secular and scientific" (Marsden, *UFE*, 133, referencing Marty, *Modern Schism*, 98.

The sciences had come to focus on empirical means to discover truths, in a context of the metaphysical shifts we already have surveyed. So, when empiricism became more accepted, it was not really a departure, but an accentuation and further development of these same emphases. Moreover, since empiricism limits all knowledge to what comes by the five senses, it fits closely with nominalism. For we cannot use our five senses to experience an immaterial, universal quality. But, through them, we can experience material, concrete particulars. However, there is a tension here: if empiricism is right, then *all* knowledge comes by way of the five senses. If so, can reason provide any knowledge?

Of the British empiricists, two who wrote as Christians were John Locke (1632–1704) and Bishop George Berkeley (1685–1753). Locke (a nominalist) wanted to hold on to knowledge of reality itself, and not just how it appeared to us.[52] Berkeley thought that God was needed for a mind-independent world.

But, David Hume (1711–1776), also a nominalist, strove for greater consistency in empiricism. Hume believed that we cannot know that souls, essences, God, moral virtues, or principles really exist, for they are not things we can know by the five senses. Hume used empiricism as a basis for his skepticism, to undercut peoples' claims to belief in such things. Thus, morality would not be based on reason or empirical science; instead, Hume based it in the sentiments, or passions. Thus, morals are not subject to reason; rather, reason serves the passions, which alone can move us to action.

With empiricism as the standard to assess what counts as factual, morals became a matter of one's own feelings, and not something objectively right or wrong. By the same criteria, religious claims appeared to be something we could not *know*, and they began to be objects of skepticism. Thus, Hume would use his skeptical arguments to rebut many natural theological arguments for God's existence as well as the rationality of our believing in any miracles.[53]

Now, Kant (1724–1804), who also was a nominalist, tried to rebut Hume. He realized how Hume's views could undermine our trust in reason. Hume had claimed that in experience, we do not sense whole things, like people, tables, or dogs. Instead, we experience a series of discrete sense impressions (orange color patches, several green ones, square shapes, etc.). Moreover, none of them are identical to each other. From this flux of sense

---

52. See my *In Search of Moral Knowledge*, 181.

53. Natural theology uses reason to argue for God's existence; some examples of such arguments would be the cosmological, teleological (design), and moral arguments, along with the argument from mind.

impressions, the mind *projects* an object. The mind does this by what he called "custom," which seems to be a habituated pattern.

Now, Hume's views can pose a problem for any knowledge of a real world. If he is right, it seems that there are no tables that exist apart from the mind's projection. Moreover, what is the mind that he claims is doing the projections? Why would it not also be just a projection? But, if this is so, then what projects *it*? And, how would we know that what it projects matches up with a real world? It seems we couldn't.[54]

In his response, Kant developed a Copernican-like "revolution" in epistemology, which he laid out in his *Critique of Pure Reason*. Unlike many who preceded him (and very unlike the confidence found in CS), he did not believe our minds were "adequate" to know their objects directly. Instead of conceiving of our mental lives in terms of *matching up* our experiences, thoughts, beliefs, etc., with their objects as they truly are, Kant conceived of our mental lives in terms of *activity* that generates knowledge.

Now, Kant was an empiricist. Since "all our knowledge begins with experience," what would be the place for reason in knowledge?[55] He answered by positing two realms: 1) the realm of things in themselves (the *noumena*); and 2) the realm of our daily lives, i.e., the realm of experience (the *phenomena*).[56] Kant thought a person cannot experience something directly. For example, we cannot directly see the words on this page. Put differently, we cannot know things "in themselves," i.e., as they really are. *We can know things only as they appear to us, or as we experience them.* That is the effect of his empiricism at work.

By using just our sensory experiences, we do not encounter immaterial things such as essences. Indeed, we cannot *know* such things exist *if* all knowledge begins with what is empirically knowable. Without essences, there are no knowable, universal, and necessary features to all our various experiences. Thus, all that we know empirically is contingent. So, we might expect Kant to be a relativist in ethics, for if there are no universal moral principles we encounter (empirically), then for all we know, there are none that are universally valid.

But, that is *not* what Kant argues. Instead, Kant begins with his conception of ethics as being "categorical imperatives," *absolute commands* that apply universally and always. But, if there are no real universal morals (e.g., as on Plato's view) that we can know, how do we come up with these absolutes?

---

54. Taken consistently, it seems Hume's empiricism also would undercut justification for us to have knowledge of the natural world by the sciences.

55. Kant, *Critique of Pure Reason*, 25.

56. Kant, *Critique of Pure Reason*, ch. 3.

Kant argues that each of us is to will that our plans of action should be universalized for everyone. We are to be "self-legislating" (*auto nomos*, the root for *autonomy*) these categorical imperatives. In his view, we would will that murder (or rape) should be wrong for all people. But, to stress, this is not from what we know from Scripture, common sense, or natural law.

Since morals are absolute and unchanging, it follows that they cannot be in the phenomenal realm, for in that realm, things are always changing.[57] Thus, for him, morals are part of the noumenal realm, which is unchanging and the realm of how things really are in themselves, and not just how we experience them or think about them. Nevertheless, Kant posited a few things that we cannot know empirically in order to make full sense of morality. So, first, he postulates that we have free will, so that we can will our maxims to be universalized. Second, he posited that we have souls so that can grow into having a truly "good will," one which wills all these morals to be universally binding without consideration of empirical factors, such as observable consequences. Third, he thought God is needed to make full sense of morality. We are to act *as if* these three things are so. For example, that God exists helps make ultimate sense of why there are universal moral truths that command us categorically, and why we truly have a duty to obey them.[58]

At least in morality, Kant thought there are universals, but it is unlike Plato's system, in which universals exist independently of our cognition of them, or our willing them to be universalized. But, if empiricism is right, then why *should* we act as if we have free will, or that God or souls exist, especially if we do not want to maintain beliefs in their existence? Moreover, how can we know there are universally valid morals in view of empiricism? Finally, on empiricism, why would Kant's starting point on the nature of morals (i.e., as absolute commands) be right, and Hume's be wrong?

57. After all, our experiences continually change, and we even experience ourselves as changing.

58. There are, however, significant developments and new understandings of Kant from studies in his philosophy of religion. Chris Firestone comments that "recent work on Kant's later philosophy suggests that Kant's theological leanings may be even more robust than the standard sketch can capture. . . . According to this 'new wave' of scholarship, reason has further questions that it must address (i.e., What may I hope? and What is man?) and thus perhaps more things, transcendentally speaking, that we must believe about God and immortality for rational stability. . . . The verdict is still out on these new developments in Kant studies, and it is not at all clear that this version of Kant gets us anywhere close (or close enough) to Christian orthodoxy. Nevertheless, what is clear is that Kant is not necessarily the all-destroyer he has been made out to be and is certainly not trying to eliminate religion from society." From Firestone, e-mail (used by permission). See also, e.g., Firestone and Jacobs, *In Defense of Kant's Religion*, and Hare, *Moral Gap*.

After Kant, empiricist (and nominalist) views continued to dominate, at least in ethics, such as with utilitarian views and then naturalistic ones, and knowledge was seen as coming from sensory experience. Historically, the sciences use such a method, and they came to be seen as giving us knowledge of the facts of reality. Such knowledge was seen as *publicly* available, to any who would use empirical means. But, in contrast, disciplines such as ethics, religion, and theology (not to mention the rest of the humanities) came to be seen as only *privately* available, giving us merely our personal values, opinions, and preferences.[59]

Moreover, in Europe, the Reformation served to undercut the power of the Roman Catholic Church over the state. But, in the Enlightenment, violent revolution, as in France, overthrew state-sanctioned religion. This factor also influenced how religion was coming to be seen in a more bifurcated way, as part of the realm of the private (which Francis Schaeffer called the "upper story").[60]

Now, in the States this fact-value split was yet to be widely experienced due to the strength of the evangelical synthesis of science and Christianity by way of CS. But there, too, religion already had come to be perceived as being separate from (though harmonious with) all other disciplines. Coupled with what was largely a mechanistic view of nature, it would not be a massive shift to the present-day version of this bifurcation, the current fact-value split which is dependent upon naturalism and empiricism.

So, while Western cultures passed through the Enlightenment and its effects, the Reformers did not have that experience. The cultural assumptions I have highlighted were deeply held, and the many historical and philosophical factors (including the different forms of the Enlightenment) helped condition their reception, particularly in the states. There, those assumptions were seen simply as part of the way Christians should live and think in order to be faithful to God in that era. But, as naturalism arose in science and philosophy, the American CS synthesis between science and Christianity would be attacked, and in Europe, religion would be further marginalized.

---

59. The effects of these aspects of the Enlightenment, found at first more in Europe, came to have a profound influence on the now deeply entrenched mind-set in the West that morals and religion are personal preferences and mere opinions, but not knowledge. Indeed, I think the fact-value split is so deeply seen as an axiomatic truth that it pervades Western cultures, even at the unconscious level.

60. See Schaeffer, *How Should We Then Live?*

The Rise of Naturalism

There were various responses to Kant's views that are pertinent to our story. For instance, one response wed the influences of Romanticism to Kant's implications for religion, by the German theologian Friedrich Schleiermacher (1768–1834). His theology stressed experience that would help pave the way for liberal (modern) Protestant theology. Nietzsche (1844–1900) aggressively argued against Kant for a naturalistic view of reality and the "death" (irrelevance) of God.

Kant also helped give even more prestige to science. His views influenced people to see science as the unique set of disciplines that give us knowledge of facts by their use of empirical methods. But, now it became even more deeply believed that *we could not have knowledge* of God, souls, angels, universals, souls, or other essential natures. If we think that knowledge of what exists comes uniquely by the five senses, then it is easy to think anything immaterial does not exist after all.

Of course, the mechanistic, even nominalist, view of nature, or creation, supported this same position. But, the ascendancy of Darwin's evolutionary theory provided academic credibility that naturalism is true, since Darwinian evolution was a "scientific" view and thus one that gives us knowledge. On this overall mind-set, even philosophy could be discounted as not giving us knowledge insofar as it did not use empirical means.

Others in philosophy also argued for naturalism, including Auguste Comte (1798–1857), Ludwig Feuerbach (1804–1872), and Karl Marx (1818–1883). In the early twentieth century, the "logical positivists" arose, who were both naturalists and empiricists. A key project of theirs was to "naturalize" meanings of authors and speakers by using the *verifiability criterion* of meaning. That is, a sentence is meaningful if and only if it is empirically verifiable. But, that entailed that sentences like "God exists" would be meaningless. Historically and philosophically, we were ready for the rise of *scientism* and the further marginalization of religion to just a private opinion. Thus, religious claims became seen as inappropriate for the public realm, where public reasons (i.e., scientifically credentialed ones) would be needed.

Darwin's theory of evolution by natural selection enabled scientists to offer explanations of origins of humans and the rest of nature without a need for God. *Therefore, in light of a) the deep respect for scientific views (and their empirically based method), and b) the view that nature is a mechanism without immaterial aspects (or universals, and thus is nominalist), it was not that much of a change (in terms of what is real) to simplify and drop God from the picture.* Additionally, at least in the States, science (and other disciplines) were permitted to develop on their own, due to the view that the findings of "good" science would harmonize with Scripture due to their having the same Author. Marsden puts it well: "Science had been allowed to operate on a *naturalistic basis* free from theological assumptions, except for the assumption that objective investigation of nature would confirm what was revealed in Scripture."[61]

But then that assumption of the authorship of nature was challenged. Evangelicals had synthesized Christianity with science on its older model, which depended on God's authorship of both revelatory books, and that nature was fixed due to the existence of essences. But, on the "new" science, the empirically knowable world always seems to be changing and contingent. And, without essences, now nature was understood as changing and developmental.

Evangelicals in the States were unprepared to rebut adequately the Darwinian challenges from the "new" science. They often responded that Darwinian "science" was not good science, for (in the older model) it used far too much speculation. To them, "good" science must limit itself to "rigorous observation of facts and demonstration of laws."[62] But, the paradigms had shifted to the developmental, evolutionary model, and the evangelicals were left flat-footed.

Other naturalistic challenges arose in theology and biblical studies. German higher criticism applied naturalistic thought to the biblical text. Critics attacked Scripture as not being God's infallible word; instead, they understood it as a record of peoples' experiences with God. Some modern scholars believed that Scripture would not be able to withstand scientific scrutiny; for example, D. F. Strauss questioned the historicity of Jesus' life as presented in the Gospels.[63]

These pressures came to bear upon educated evangelicals who had embraced the CS basis for synthesizing science and religion. They were committed to the objectivity of both science and religion, and that seemed to force a choice. On one hand, they could agree with Charles Hodge of Princeton, who believed Scripture's supernaturalism "was utterly incompatible with the naturalism that he saw as essential to Darwin's position."[64] On the other hand, they could opt for a "middle" position. For instance, Henry Ward Beecher had recommended that preachers aim for "sentimental goals,"

61. Marsden, *FAC*, 20 (emphasis added).

62. Marsden, *FAC*, 20.

63. Marsden, *FAC*, 17.

64. Marsden, *FAC*, 19.

to kindle the "nobility of a heart opened when God has touched it."[65] This second, "middle" position is, of course, a liberal one, which was influenced by Kant, Schleiermacher, and Albrecht Ritschl, on which religion is a matter of experience and the heart, the spiritual, and the moral. But it is *not* something capable of objective, factual knowledge and support, and thus it is an example of defining religion in light of the fact-value split and naturalism.[66]

A Rise of Religious Experience

We have already seen how liberals emphasized religious experience, as opposed to how evangelicals appealed to truth found in the propositions in Scripture as the foundation for knowledge.[67] But there were other sources for appeals to religious experience in this overall time frame. Mormonism appealed to Joseph Smith's religious experiences as validation of its claims of further revelation given in the Book of Mormon. Moreover, true seekers could know the truth of the Book of Mormon by a religious experience—a burning in the bosom.

Further, in the late 1800s and early 1900s, Pentecostals claimed experiencing spiritual gifts from God of tongues, prophetic words, and various miracles. Some, reflecting Methodist Holiness emphases, concluded that "tongues should still be the sign of a Pentecostal experience."[68] Others (e.g., Assemblies of God and Four Square Gospel churches) put more emphasis upon sanctification as a process of growth in the power of the Holy Spirit. However, other revivalist preachers of the times who did not seek tongues were embarrassed by these claims to tongues and other revelations.[69] Additionally, some perceived these experiences as a threat to the authority of Scripture because they did not appeal to the strong evangelical emphasis upon objective truth that could be found in the Scriptures, which themselves could be known empirically.

Considered together, these perceived challenges to biblical authority from religious experiences helped foster distrust amongst evangelicals to many claims of religious experience. While liberal theology's appeal to

65. Beecher, "The Mission of the Pulpit," 395, cited in Marsden, *FAC*, 21.

66. Marsden, *FAC*, 21.

67. According to J. P. Moreland, a proposition is the content "expressed in declarative sentences and contained in people's minds when they are thinking. Propositions are also the things that are either true or false and that can be related to each other by means of the laws of logic (e.g., 'if, then,' 'if and only if')." See Moreland and Craig, *Philosophical Foundations for a Christian Worldview*, 184. See also 135.

68. Marsden, *FAC*, 93.

69. Marsden, *FAC*, 94.

religious experience posed the major challenge to evangelical Christianity, evangelicals were also concerned by Pentecostal appeals to further words from God, which seemed to challenge the Reformation principle of *sola Scriptura* and the closure of the canon of Scripture. That is, if God is allegedly still giving words of revelation to people today, would they not extend the canon? And, would they not also help introduce confusion? To help ward off these concerns, evangelicals appealed to the doctrine of cessationism (i.e., the "miraculous" spiritual gifts, e.g., prophecy, ability to do miracles, and speaking in tongues, had ceased with the passing of the apostles).

More recently, another, similar position has developed, called "open but cautious," according to which such adherents officially are open to God's giving more words of guidance to his people today, yet they are cautious about any such claims.[70] On this view, Scripture is our objective, inerrant, God-given revelation, and believers need to test any putative, further words most of all against Scripture, then also in prayer, and in the community of Christians who are walking with and obeying the Lord. Yet, on this view, we should not expect God to work in such ways today as he did in the early church, since God primarily uses Scripture through the empowered life of the believer. This belief can raise a concern, however, for, as proponent Robert Saucy notes, a "denial that the same phenomena of the apostolic era are normal for today naturally reduces the expectation of miracles, which may be no expectation at all."[71]

While this is a large-scale, detailed debate within Christian circles that is impossible to settle in this short space, nonetheless it might be interesting to observe a couple of possible, practical outworkings of the cessationist and open but cautious positions. For one, I believe they rightly seek to preserve the completeness of the canon of Scripture. Yet, it also could seem to some that all that God has to say to us is located in a book. If so, that can feel like even though God says he loves us, and has proven his love for us through the cross of Christ (Rom 5:8), nonetheless, relationally, God is distant. He doesn't personalize his love for us. For another, it seems to me that while we preach that God does miracles, and we pray for them, yet all too often we don't *really* expect God to show up in our midst. Yes, we rightly preach the resurrection of Jesus as the major example of God's miraculous work, but it still seems that all too often we discount his acting in miraculous power today.[72] Still, there is a large biblical and theological debate to be engaged. But,

---

70. For a detailed treatment of this and other such views, see Grudem, ed., *Are Miraculous Gifts for Today?*

71. Saucy, "An Open but Cautious View," 145.

72. See the discussion in Moreland, *Kingdom Triangle*, ch. 7.

whether or not these two positions are correct, I think it is interesting that these two implications of cessationism and the open but cautious positions tend toward similar practical effects as other, more naturalistic factors we have examined. Now, I will turn to a more detailed examination of practical effects of these various factors.[73]

Practical Implications

If we put some "shoe leather" to these various historical, cultural, and philosophical factors, we can observe some practical implications and effects, ones which I think we also will see are quite naturalistic. Now, in general, we should realize that all of us are shaped and influenced by our *sitz im leben*, or life setting (context). This context includes many factors, such as family upbringing, ethnicity, historical and geographic location, economic status, and much more, including (for this discussion) the ideas that we have been examining.

With the benefit of hindsight, we can see that there is a story with a common thread (the de-supernaturalization of Christianity) that helps explain several factors that helped shape perceptions of Christianity in the West, and especially in the United States. *But, these insights should help us realize how our evangelical predecessors did not perceive the significance of how their own conceptual framework (paradigm, "lenses") for interpreting reality shaped their own thought and actions.* Under the influence of CS, they believed it was simply common sense that they could intuit and know the truths of Scripture, or nature, politics, etc., without any need to consider to what extent their own paradigm was historically, culturally, and philosophically shaped. This was a serious mistake, and it blinded them to the need to integrate theology and science, or any other discipline, or to do rigorous philosophical work. Instead, they were lulled into thinking they really did not need to do such hard tasks.

But, had they done such work, they could have been better prepared to engage with Darwinian, naturalistic claims on their terms. That is, they could have developed rigorous engagement with naturalistic claims, and they could have drawn from good philosophical resources from the past that supported biblical positions. Instead, what actually happened was that they "bet the farm" on their belief in the authority of Scripture, but at the same time had little else to say to other disciplines and why they too should acknowledge what Scripture teaches. *There is nothing wrong with holding*

73. In my *In Fullness of Spirit and Truth* (tentative title; forthcoming), I examine these positions and their arguments in much more detail.

fast to the authority of Scripture, but in effect they left the culture to its own devices and thought.

Following that pattern, we will not be able to help grow mature disciples, since they are involved in many disciplines, professions, and kinds of employment. Moreover, today they are influenced greatly by education and media, which often are dominated by secular, naturalistic viewpoints. What then are some of these kinds of more practical effects?

First, by thinking we should approach any given subject scientifically, subtly we may reinforce the modern emphasis upon cataloguing all knowledge as objective facts (such as in an encyclopedia). But, that approach likewise suggests the Bible is a storehouse of God's facts written in propositional form. Just as with reading an entry in an encyclopedia, this mind-set could tend to lead us to treat the parts of the Bible apart from the context in which they were written. As such, they can be treated atomistically, as proof texts for a particular need.

Second, the Christian life's focus becomes one of knowledge and what is rational to believe. Now, of course, there is nothing wrong with a Christian growing in knowledge; Scripture commands and encourages it. For instance, we are to keep on growing in the grace and knowledge of Jesus (2 Pet 1:2–8). Plus, we are to have our minds renewed (Rom 12:2). And, Paul writes that we are to grow in true knowledge of God's mystery, Christ himself, and that in him are hidden all the treasures of wisdom and knowledge (Col 2:2–3).

But, unlike modernity, Scripture does not demonstrate the same high confidence in our own human abilities, apart from special revelation, to have knowledge of truth. Nor does it have the same high confidence in empirical knowledge. On the one hand, Scripture does not dismiss or devalue empirical knowledge, but on the other, it does not treat an empirical methodology as the best approach to gain knowledge. Rather, it treats empirical knowledge appropriately, as a key way to know empirically observable realities.

Nevertheless, stressing a scientific approach subtly, yet strongly, reinforces the idea that empirical observation is the main way we should know things. Coupled with nominalism and a materialist view of what is real, such a methodology focuses our knowledge on what is sense perceptible, and thus material. With empiricism, it even excludes in principle knowledge of immaterial things or persons. An empirical focus also can exclude in practice knowledge of the immaterial by how we have been habituated via the scientific method to pay attention to the sense perceptible.

With the high emphasis placed upon empirical knowledge found in our cultural and philosophical history, we might well expect to find a high emphasis placed by evangelicals on the empirically observable, written word of God. And, indeed, that is what we do find. Marsden notes this pattern in the Puritans and then the dispensationalists, who were "strongly oriented toward the printed word, eschewing the mysterious in both exposition and worship."[74] This fits with the Baconian-CS mindset of the times, that people could make observations of Scripture, and then inductively derive facts from those presented therein.

However, an empirical focus, coupled with mechanistic and nominalist views of creation, also can lead us to not take seriously the reality of the immaterial, such as our souls, or demons. Indeed, in my church, which on the whole is a highly educated congregation (many have graduate degrees, including many in medicine), I think there remains much confusion over just what is the soul. Though the Bible speaks of it as real, and we may say our souls will be with the Lord when we die, are these just "faith posits," yet not something we can *know* to be true? Is "soul" just an outdated, nonscientific way of talking, since science, and some post-evangelical theologians and philosophers, basically tell us we are just physical things?[75]

Third, if the universe operates mechanistically and is causally closed, then that strongly suggests that God should be understood to operate in a *functionally deistic* way. For even if God has all the attributes according to orthodox Christianity, and we still affirm all its core doctrines officially, nevertheless, God practically still chooses to operate in a way that distances himself from creation. It is easy, then, to conceive of God's relationship to creation mainly as the Initiator and Sustainer, which he does via laws he established. Yet, it is hard to see how God would be very personal and intimate with believers.

Fourth, for the same kinds of reasons, we would not expect God to act miraculously today, even though God *could* do that (since he is God). So, miracles should be rather rare. Instead of acting supernaturally in many places and with many people, it seems we would expect that God would use natural processes and laws to accomplish things, such as healings. Moreover, it seems we should not expect God to communicate with his people in intimate, personalized ways (i.e., in addition to Scripture).

Fifth, it seems we also would tend to view what Scripture describes as the demons in a more "naturalized" way. For instance, it would be hard to imagine how immaterial beings could interact with a physical creation, including ourselves. That has implications for their influences upon us, for how could they tempt us with distortions of truth, appeals to pride, etc.?

74. Marsden, *FAC*, 60–61.

75. See, e.g., Murphy, *Bodies and Souls, or Spirited Bodies?*

Instead, it seems more likely that we would tend to think of them as the vestiges of a prescientific view of the world, and not literally real.

Sixth, from CS and the overall high, Enlightenment confidence in humans' abilities to know truth (which Marsden calls a slight "astigmatism" from the fall), we should expect that people can read Scripture and make sense of it. Indeed, this expectation may seem to fit with the doctrine of the perspicuity of Scripture. However, this high confidence in our abilities to know and discern truth can lead subtly and easily into our thinking we do not need to rely self-consciously on the Holy Spirit to lead and guide us into all truth. If our abilities to reason are quite good in many respects, then this overconfidence in ourselves can deceive us to think we do not need to depend utterly upon the Holy Spirit for wisdom and understanding—despite Jesus' warning that apart from him, we can do nothing (John 15:5; cf. Prov 3:5–6).

Seventh, when such a mind-set is coupled with the inherited fact-value split, the various academic disciplines, and our professions and jobs, can develop autonomously apart from self-conscious dependence upon good theology, Scripture, and the mind and voice of Christ. Now, that suggests that God does not really care about how we conceive of our disciplines, unless what we propose clearly opposes Scripture. But, if there are some (or even many) aspects of our disciplines that he intentionally allows not to be under his lordship, that does not fit with the biblical admonition to take every thought captive to the obedience of Christ (2 Cor 10:5). It also does not fit with Colossians 2:3, that in Christ are hidden all the treasures of wisdom and knowledge. Instead, it helps promote a bifurcated worldview, leaving us as being people who are double-minded, who on the one hand are to listen to the Lord with our hearts and minds, and yet also can listen to what seems best to us.

However, to pursue integration between Scripture and our disciplines or professions as seems best to us is deeply misguided. Scripture never tells us to do anything in our own strength, or according primarily to *our* insights. That is "fleshly" living, in which Scripture warns not to put our confidence.[76]

---

76. Now, Christians might reply that, yes, what the Bible tells us is true and counts as knowledge. But they could go further and maintain that all else (in science, business, philosophy, etc.) is inferior knowledge, or just our opinions. In other words, they could appeal to a different kind of fact-value split, one that turns modernity's version on its head. But that approach would still leave all other disciplines or professions to operate autonomously apart from being subservient to and integrated with Scripture, and such a view is not of God.

Eighth, the fact-value split also affected perceptions of religion along male-female lines, in conjunction with head-and-heart lines. Consider Great Britain's Victorian period: men were viewed as being rational, and that meant they should be disposed toward thinking scientifically. Rationality was associated with the "head," or intellect. But, religion was seen as something personal and private, and a matter of the heart (here, the sentiments). Thus, women, who were seen as living more from their hearts, came to be seen as the ones who would be religious. Of course, this is not really the biblical view of men or women, or the heart as that from which we truly live, choose, and reason.[77]

Of course, this "head"-"heart" distinction lives on. But, for Western Christians today, it is easy to read the Scriptures with that same kind of template, believing that to love God with all our hearts means with all our feelings. But, somehow it is quite another matter altogether to love him with all our minds if being rational means we should believe what modern science tells us is true and reasonable.

Ninth, with the ascendancy and prestige of naturalism, both in academia and government, evangelicals reacted defensively to protect the Bible. Higher criticism had challenged the received, high view of Scripture by attacking its historicity, its miracle claims, and its claims to the truth of Christian orthodoxy. So, responses were needed, for Scripture was under assault. This need became very important after the perceived fallout from the Scopes trial.

The rise of naturalism has created other perceptions, too. God has become marginalized in naturalistically shaped societies. As Craig Gay explains, God becomes irrelevant in a practical atheism that flows from modern thought.[78] Moreover, the fact-value split bifurcates science from religion and ethics, relegating the latter two to an "upper story" of mere opinion and nonrational preference. Of course, that directly challenges the evangelical conviction that the Bible presents objective truth about ultimate reality and morals.

Overall, the modern period's proud, high confidence in human abilities to discern truths and follow them morally has led directly to an elevation of the human mind over God's own mind amongst believers and unbelievers. For non-Christians, the modern era has led to an abundance of confidence in our own minds to know reality, and even define it. We can see this in thinking that God is remote due to creation's being mechanistic, or he does not exist, period, under naturalism. For Christians, the period

77. For example, see Brown, *The Death of Christian Britain*.
78. Gay, *The Way of the (Modern) World*.

helped elevate their hearts so that they easily did not really see an utter need to trust in the Lord with all our hearts and minds, and so they could easily lean (to various extents) on their own understanding. But that misplaced trust in themselves betrays a heart that lives out its fleshly desires—to elevate itself over God and define reality as it sees best.

This breakdown of the Christian consensus (at least in America) also led to a breakdown of the threefold cord God uses to bind us to himself. In 2 Timothy 1:7, we see that God has given us a spirit of power, love, and a sound mind.[79] Scripturally, a sound, *healthy* mind abides in God's word and in deep unity with God's mind. That mind is being renewed by his Spirit's work through Scripture. Power comes only from the Spirit of Christ in us, whether it is power to live as Christ lived, to see God do miracles through us, etc., for apart from him, we can do *nothing*. And love is from God himself, who is love. We can abide in his love as we obey him, which again requires abiding in his Spirit, and his word abiding in us. His love binds our hearts to his heart. So, here we can see a significant set of factors, or a *threefold cord*, that God uses to bind us to him, each of which is designed by him to overcome the heart and mind bifurcation we have experienced from the effects of the fall. And yet, the effects we have been studying have served to divide our hearts and minds from living in deep unity with God.

In summary, then:

Practical Effects of these Cultural, Historical, and Philosophical Factors on Evangelical Christianity
Very high confidence in human reason, especially in light of the general Enlightenment mind-set, and in particular CS philosophy
Bible is seen as an encyclopedia, a perfect collection of objective facts
Distrust, discount experience in theology (too subjective) and rationality
Such a strong emphasis upon the mind that the heart (understood in terms of the emotions) is discounted
Disciplines develop autonomously; little need to integrate
God is distant (functional deism); God doesn't give personal communication other than in Scripture; little expectation of miracles, or of demonic activity
Universe is seen as mechanistic and closed; we too are seen as mechanisms

79. The NASB renders the third quality to be "discipline," or "sound judgment." The Amplified Bible also adds a "well-balanced mind."

I am *not* trying to say that all these effects were self-consciously undertaken; some of these are quite subtle and may not have been foreseen. Nevertheless, ideas have consequences; sooner or later, how we conceive of reality (and how we think we can know it) will have practical results.

Christians and Naturalism

I have been trying to show how, through a series of factors, there were major shifts away from the Christian worldview to a more naturalistic one. Moreover, while these shifts have major impacts on broader Western societies, and the States in particular, they have also impacted the church. So, it is important that we realize that naturalism is not *just* the philosophical thesis that only the natural exists; there is no supernatural (and so God would not exist). Obviously, someone cannot be a naturalist in that sense and still be a Christian.

But, there are other senses, or forms, of naturalism, and it is possible for Christians to be influenced by, or even embrace, them. Consider first the way science often is practiced today, which is called *methodological naturalism*. In that view, scientists should confine their explanations of physical events to the realm of nature. Thus, they should set aside appeals to a nonnatural agent (such as God, or human souls) or entities. For instance, Wilfrid Sellars, who was a naturalist philosopher, asserted that in "describing and explaining the world, science is the measure of all things, of what is that it is, and of what is not that it is not."[80] Therefore, for science, God is irrelevant. Yet, one could be a Christian and still practice science according to methodological naturalism.

I think there is another, more subtle form of naturalism, too. The famous German atheist philosopher Friedrich Nietzsche claimed that God is dead.[81] But, by that he did not mean that God ceased to exist. Instead, he meant that "the belief in the Christian God has become unbelievable."[82] That is, God had become *irrelevant for modern life.*

If lived out, that attitude has many implications. For one, it suggests that people can go beyond any "limitations" on their authority and freedom. Second, it steals believers' *focus* from God's authority, love, and power. Third, it seems to distance us from God. Fourth, it seems to be a denial of God's *personal* investment in each heart, soul, and mind. Thus, this form of naturalism seems to be captured by the attitude in Genesis 3:5: we can

80. Sellars, *Science, Perception, and Reality*, 173.
81. Nietzsche, *The Gay Science*, book 3, §125.
82. Nietzsche, *The Gay Science*, book 5, §343.

become like God, know (define and choose) for ourselves what is good and evil, and even define reality itself. We could take over God's throne. I think these attitudes and endeavors have marked humans ever since then.

Clearly, this form of naturalism is something from which Christians are not immune. One term for it might be *preternaturalism.* That is, while there are occurrences beyond the typical patterns in the nature, at the same time it *denies (or does not seek)* the true God as the source of true power. Quite accurately, therefore, this kind of Christianity has been de-supernaturalized.

Now, for those who do not embrace orthodoxy, God could exist, yet they would not seek him as the one, true God. Moreover, for evangelicals who hold onto orthodox doctrine, yet have been shaped by preternaturalism, they may hold officially to believe in the Bible and the Christian God's existence. Still, they would not tend to seek him for his power in their lives. Therefore, in either case, we have a people who live largely in their own strength, wisdom, and power, and not in what the living God would supply.

Clearly, though, Scripture calls such living "fleshly"; i.e., we live out of our sinful propensities. Thus, we cannot please God (Rom 8:8). Moreover, both types of Christians seem to be lack "sight," knowledge, or power beyond themselves. To the degree that Christians live in these ways, they will produce fruit in accordance with their "flesh," which will make Christianity look like just a human endeavor.

This is a good place to note that by "flesh" in this context, I do not mean the physical body. Paul distinguishes two Greek terms. First is *sarx*, the word used for the unregenerate human, as in Romans 7:18: "I know that nothing good dwells in me, that is, in my flesh." Here, by "flesh," Paul means the sinful propensities, the "old man," still present in every believer, even though the Holy Spirit indwells them. Second is *soma*, which is used for the human body. Now, God made the body, and what God makes is good, even if it is affected by sin. So, Paul is *not* a gnostic, and neither should we be gnostic.

Unfortunately, I think that in far too many ways, too many evangelicals in the West today, especially in the States, are living fleshly lives. Though this will vary by churches and individuals, it seems that too many evangelicals do not seem to be known for (and marked by) Jesus' promised power and presence (e.g., Matt 28:20, Acts 1:8, Eph 3:19). Though Christ lives in us (and I am writing as an evangelical), we do not seem to be a people who are known for bearing the fruit of the Spirit (Gal 5:22–23). Instead, we seem to be lacking the *fullness* of the Spirit of Christ. Similarly, though we preach the truth of Scripture, we seem to be missing the *fullness* of truth. If so, then it seems clear that something has gone terribly wrong with evangelicalism as practiced in the West, and America in particular. How could this be?

It seems straightforward from our historical "tour": evangelicals have been shaped profoundly by naturalism.

I think the Lord has important things to say in Revelation 2 and 3 about this situation amongst all too many evangelical churches in the West. The first example is the church at Ephesus (Rev 2:1–5). Jesus recognizes it for its many strengths: it resisted wickedness, and tested carefully and exposed false apostles. But, *it had lost is first love—the utter devotion to Jesus.* I am afraid that too many evangelical churches, at least in America, are like that church. Though they seek to hold onto the truth in the Bible, I am afraid it is still easy for them to not be living in a deep heart and mind unity with his. And, subtly, I am afraid they often may not live as though John 15:5 is really true—that apart from him, they can do *nothing.*

Second, like many American churches, the church at Laodicea (Rev 3:14–22) was materially well-off. But, it also had become self-satisfied, indifferent (lukewarm), and therefore, disgusting. These Christians had become half-hearted. Moreover, they did not see these as serious problems. Similarly, we have seen how today's Western, American evangelicals can become half-hearted, not living in the fullness of the Spirit and truth or in deep unity with God's heart and mind. Sadly, they can rely more upon what they think is true. Thus, they can become neither salt nor light to those around them. Plus, they don't really build up their fellow Christians. Such Christians have a form of Christianity, but they lack its real substance—the fullness of the power and presence of the Lord.

Going Onward

It is striking to me that the emergents' critiques of the practice of "modern" Christianity bear such close similarities to my own. I have come to realize that *to an even greater extent than I understood in 2005, emergents were much more perceptive and on target with their criticisms of the practice of Christianity by Westernized evangelicals.* In fact, many times while studying, I have noticed that in those criticisms *they are basically right: the evangelical churches in the West today have been shaped deeply by the modern era, having passed through the Enlightenment and its profoundly shaping influences.* Thus, I think they would agree with many of my observations that many evangelical churches tend to:

1. Be very knowledge-focused (i.e., as mental assent), with a very high confidence in human reason, such that experience becomes discounted;

2. Treat the Bible like a perfect encyclopedia of knowledge, facts;

3. Treat the Christian life as mechanistic, with an input-output methodology for sanctification; and

4. Practically act as if God is distant and not intimately involved in our lives.

To underscore these and other key observations, they would concur that all too many evangelical Christians are living *inauthentically*.

But, I think that attributing the problems of contemporary, Western evangelical Christianity mainly to modernity and the Enlightenment can obscure and even hide a more specific factor—namely, that these effects are due largely to the influences specifically of naturalism upon the church and broader society. Importantly, then, it may not be sufficient merely to ask if these emergents' proposals figure out how to live "faithfully" in postmodern times. As we turn to assess their criticisms of the received interpretation of the gospel story and its related ethical framework, and their suggested interpretation, we will also need to ask: to what extent do their proposals address how naturalism has deeply affected Christianity in the West, including evangelicals in America? Or, do they perhaps perpetuate it, too? I will start with several of their contributions.

3

Some Key Contributions by Emergents

In chapter 1, I tried to survey the main ethical (and related theological and philosophical) contours of the more developed recommendations of Brian McLaren, Rob Bell, Tony Jones, and Doug Pagitt for a Christian orthopraxis. We examined several foci in their writings, such as the stress upon relational intimacy, with both God and other humans; the need to reframe the gospel story so that it can be liberated from its captivity to the conventional version of that story we have inherited; and more. Now it is time to try to assess the various strengths and weaknesses of their proposals.

Initial Contributions

Positively, I will start with some initial contributions and briefly remark on them. Then, I will discuss some more substantive ones. First, McLaren is right to call our attention to how systems and groups (even of Christians) can perpetuate and foster injustice. It is easy for evangelical Christians to focus on individuals' sins, rather than carefully examine and expose injustices that systems can foster. Also, we can be blind to other harmful consequences that can result from narrow stresses on evangelism and discipleship.

To illustrate, let me tell a couple stories; the first one I have heard, and the second is one I have lived. First, in the days of the civil rights movement in the United States, Martin Luther King Jr. took many courageous stands against systemic evils that were being practiced, especially in the southern states, even though the days of slavery officially had ended about a century before. But what was troubling to a friend of mine was the experience he had as a student at a highly respected evangelical seminary in the South at that time. There, he experienced the attitude that "good" Christians were not to support King publicly in his fight against these injustices. Now, as we look back at such attitudes and inactions, we can see plainly that the attitudes of these Christians (well-meaning ones, I assume) were horribly wrong by effectively supporting these racial injustices.

Second, in the 1980s I experienced a mind-set amongst several fellow evangelicals in a parachurch organization. They questioned the need for a particular "ministry" that had been established in that organization to help educate Christians and develop in them a biblical worldview, so that they would understand cultural, philosophical, and other trends and be able to help preserve American society's core values. After all, they'd ask, since our primary responsibility as Christians is to share the gospel and make disciples, why do we need to preserve America, its values, and its institutions by stopping abortion, affirming the sanctity of life, preserving the separation of powers in government, and more? I recall hearing fellow employees say then that they would keep doing their primary task as Christians even if the American government was overthrown by the Soviet Union. So, why should Christians put their efforts into preserving America? Wasn't that a secondary endeavor at best and a sidetrack at worst?

But that mind-set is very shortsighted and naïve, I think. All we need to do is look at other countries with oppressive governments that have restricted or forbidden evangelism, or outlawed being a Christian. Just from a practical standpoint, the freedom to share the gospel and make disciples has been greatly hindered in such areas, with much attendant injustices, such as persecution and death. Also, many missionaries are supported financially by people in America; without that ability, those missionaries' work would be greatly hindered. Moreover, if for no other reason, it is worth working for the good of people so they would not be butchered, degraded, and oppressed under regimes like that of the former Soviet Union.

As a second contribution from McLaren, it has been easy for evangelicals not to give the attention due to the ethical issues of environmental protection, even though arguably we have the best basis as responsible stewards for such an ethic. It is wrong to rape and pillage the earth, for God has called us to be wise stewards (not owners) of his creation (Gen 1:26–28), and to him we will give an account. So, McLaren rightly calls our attention to this important issue.

Third, in discussions of the Pharisees, McLaren shines when he calls for our need to look at the heart level in order to deal with sin. He is right to stress the need for a pure heart before God and others. Repeatedly, God stresses the importance of a pure heart. It is from what fills the heart that we speak and write (Matt 12:34), and all kinds of evil come from what is in it (Matt 15:18–19). It is the heart that is more deceitful than all else and is desperately sick (Jer 17:9).

Fourth, McLaren is right to emphasize the need for being a disciple of Jesus *now*, with implications for how we live our lives now to impact the kingdom. Rightly he counters misguided understandings of the gospel that place all the emphasis upon "going" to heaven when we die, in order to avoid hell. Biblically, this seems straightforward enough, for why else would Jesus command us to make disciples (learners, apprentices of him) as opposed to mere converts? Furthermore, God has not changed in character, and the same God who cared deeply about justice in the Old Testament still cares now. Jesus calls us to live for him now; as but a couple examples, just imagine what history would have been like if William Wilberforce had not been driven by his convictions before God to bring an end to the British slave trade? Or if Martin Luther King Jr. had not spoken and stood up bravely against racial discrimination and civil rights abuses in the 1960s? So, what contemporary injustices might Christians be overlooking, or even be blind to noticing, due to their emphases?

In addition, McLaren, Bell, and Pagitt are not the only ones to emphasize that on the received, conventional version of the gospel, evangelicals have tended to emphasize preparing people to die, rather than to live. That flows from a focus on needing to be forgiven by Christ's atoning work so we will go to heaven when we die, but we can miss out on the joy and power of living with him today. Dallas Willard has also made this observation when he discusses the gospel of *sin management*, in which we focus primarily on keeping sin under control, rather than living for Christ *now*.[1]

More Substantial Contributions

Evangelicals Can be Coercive and Controlling

Now, let's probe what I think are some more substantial contributions from McLaren, Pagitt, Jones, and Bell. To begin, God does not coerce us to follow him. McLaren is right; God wants us to follow him in a loving relationship, so that we would desire from our hearts what is on his. In making us more and more like his son, God wants our hearts and minds to be in a deep unity with those of the Father, just as is the case with Jesus. Jesus always does what pleases his Father, out of his deep love and obedience, and also his knowledge of the beauty and fulfillment of abiding in the Father's love.

1. For instance, see his *Divine Conspiracy*, ch. 2.

But, why would God's being coercive, even violent, be such a dominant concern for McLaren and these other authors? It could be just a matter of an intellectual assent to pacifism. But, over and over, McLaren returns to the view that God *could not* be violent, and he reserves some of his choicest words for such a view. I am not sure of all the factors that move him (almost in revulsion) to recoil from such a view, but here might be a time to explore some possibilities that can be found amongst evangelicals, a group that also tends to receive his most pointed comments.

As we have seen, in some of his earlier books, McLaren clearly identifies evangelicals as ones who have been deeply influenced by modernity's paradigm. In *A New Kind of Christianity*, it seems that they now are seen by him as embracing the older, more encompassing Greco-Roman narrative. Now, I have noted in chapter 6 of *Truth* some good insights he has offered from some of his earlier books.[2] But here, I want to focus on ways that, perhaps subtly, evangelicals *can* be coercive, manipulative, and therefore perhaps violent.[3]

I think McLaren has put his finger on some key issues with evangelicals, and the way they (sometimes?) act can betray a mind-set that they can be violent and coercive, or manipulative. But that seems to reflect upon their view of the God they serve, for we all tend to become like the God (or god(s)) we worship. If we even give the impression in evangelism that our aim is to win a debate with someone, we convey (even if unintentionally) that we don't really care about the person him- or herself. In turn, this attitude can be manipulative; for instance, when we want to get the person to pray a prayer over and above the first priority, which is to genuinely care for the person. I think of Jesus' honest interaction with, and respectful treatment of, the Samaritan woman in John 4. He cared for her, even just by talking with her. God surely cares for and loves us, which is why we should be sharing the gospel in the first place.

These aspects of Christ's character remind me of another important contribution from McLaren. As Burson rightly notes, McLaren comes across with a charitable, gentle spirit, which I have observed firsthand. In his summation, Burson thinks that the *most* important lesson evangelicals can learn from McLaren is his generosity and kindness, which Burson says flows

2. Smith, *Truth*, ch. 6. There, I discuss, for example, these needs of the church: to be authentic; to live out our faith in community; to contextualize the gospel; to appeal to stories, to help communicate truths to postmodern people; and to help postmodern people experience God in his transcendence, and to find ourselves in wonder and awe over who God is.

3. As I have pointed out, Burson observes that McLaren points out other issues, particularly from five-point Calvinism.

from McLaren's "deep and abiding belief in the goodness of God."[4] There have been scathing responses by all too many evangelicals against McLaren, both in terms of his works and his person, and while his works need to be assessed, ad hominem remarks are uncalled for. But, as the theologian John Franke remarked, "one of the lessons evangelicals could and should learn from Brian McLaren is the value of a generous and charitable spirit. Brian has won a lot of supporters because of his demeanor. In my opinion, evangelicals lose support where they might not have because of their lack of graciousness and generosity. Even Hannibal Lecter despised rudeness!"[5]

Moreover, as I discussed earlier, subtly I think evangelicals can be prone to a tendency to elevate the use of their own reason to the place of authority in understanding and living out Scripture, such that they do not truly depend upon the Spirit with all their hearts and minds. That implies that Christians would get skilled at living "out of their heads," without really paying attention to their hearts' attitudes and condition.[6] Instead, they can lean too much on their own understanding.

Saul's actions as king of Israel illustrate this mind-set. God had chosen him and given him a new heart. He had also experienced the power of the Spirit upon his life (1 Sam 9–11). Today, he would make a highly marketable candidate for public office, for he was the tallest and most handsome man in Israel (1 Sam 9:2). Even so, he also was insecure (1 Sam 10:21–22). So, when he was faced with a tense situation, he acted foolishly and disobediently, relying on himself. As God's prophet, Samuel had told Saul to wait seven days for him to come, to offer sacrifices to God and tell him what should be done (1 Sam 10:8). But Samuel didn't come to him right when Saul expected. In the meantime, the Philistine army was gathering in numbers to fight, and a large number of his own men defected, leaving him with only 600 out of the original 2,000 men. Instead of waiting for Samuel, he took action, but he didn't even pray and ask God what he should do. Instead, he commanded that the people bring the burnt offerings and peace offerings to him, so that he may offer them. But as soon as he does this, Samuel arrives.

In this, Saul acted presumptuously by taking on a role reserved only for the priests, of which he was not one. Though moved by his insecurities, fear of being overwhelmed, and a deep sense of needing to do something, in effect his actions said that he not only did not trust God to bring Samuel in time, but also that he could worship God in the way he deemed best. But

4. Burson, *Brian McLaren in Focus*, 269.

5. John Franke, from e-mail to Burson, cited in Burson, *Brian McLaren in Focus*, 268.

6. My thanks to Joe Gorra for this suggestion.

that is *never* approved of in the Old or New Testaments. People are always to worship God in the ways he prescribes. So, Saul is a cautionary example of how easy it is, even for God's people, to be manipulative.[7]

Additionally, people in evangelical institutions can develop controlling leadership styles, whether more subtle ("light") or overt ("heavy"). I have experienced situations where employees were expected to submit to their leadership like unto Christ (i.e., as the one who placed them in positions of leadership over them). So, how will various members in a church or Christian organization know that God indeed is directing their leaders in their chosen courses of action? For instance, how do we know that God is speaking to the leaders to start a building campaign, or a new ministry emphasis? Unfortunately, it has not always been God's will to do what some leaders believed and pushed to be the case. In such situations, the expectation to submit to and follow the leaders can become manipulative and controlling, which no one appreciates.

In a further way, I think evangelicals can harm and perhaps even manipulate themselves and their brothers and sisters by teaching them to live out of their "heads," by placing an imbalanced emphasis upon the intellect at the expense of the heart (especially the will and the feelings). I think this can happen, even unintentionally, through well-meaning teachings that emphasize we should put our trust in truths given in Scripture, and then the feelings come along thereafter. We are told we should not live by our feelings, for they can be unreliable guides to truth. Moreover, the power to live the Christian life comes by faith in Christ, which involves primarily the intellect (knowledge of the Scriptures) and a choice to assent to them.

Now, since I have experienced strong feelings of anxiety and fears of rejection, I know that I do not want to live just by my feelings. But, at the same time, I also know what it is like when I have tried to ignore (or "stuff") my feelings and focus my mind mainly (or solely) on scriptural truths. My fears have deep origins, from my early years at home, and so they are deeply rooted in me. The result was that when something came along to trigger my fears of being rejected, I had some horrible times trying to get them to "follow along after" my intellectual beliefs and volitional choices. But in my case, it was through my being able to embrace my "little boy's" fears, along with the truths in Scripture, that I could experience the comfort that I needed.

Just as Pagitt says, I needed God to be down and in with me, a God who knows my pain and yet loves and is intimate with me. But, if instead I

7. Consider also the example of the actions of King Uzziah, who thought he could offer incense to the Lord, only to find that God struck him with leprosy for his defiance (2 Kgs 26:16–21).

had just kept trying to live "out of my head," I would have been stuck in an unlivable situation. I would have been left with a deep split in my life, knowing on the one hand the truth that God loves me, for the Bible tells me so, yet on the other not experiencing that, still living with fears and anxieties that if I wasn't perfect, oh no, God might reject me! So, this type of focus on living the Christian life from the intellect can shut us up in a prison that never allows wounded people (which all of us are, to some degree or other) to get the help they need at the emotional level. On the other hand, this approach to the Christian life also tends to downplay the deep joy that can come from the Lord's presence, and his meeting us in tender, merciful, and loving ways.

But God wants us to live in a deep heart and mind unity with him, to *taste* and *see* that he is good, and delight in him. Surely those involve deep feelings in our experiences with and of him! Also, his healing at my heart level has enlarged greatly my capacity to be united with his heart and mind.[8] This unity with him, and within ourselves, helps make us whole persons.[9]

Now, my mind and heart are much more in sync with each other, so that I can embrace with all my heart the truths found in God's word, including those about who I am in Christ. I also now can enter into the lived experience of the Spirit's crying in my heart, "Abba, Father!" And my heart's zeal for the Lord has been set free, having been freed up from so many fears of having to be perfect, such that I am much more willing to take bold steps and stand up for the Lord and what is good and right. Combined with the reasons I have learned about the truth and reliability of Scripture, along with other evidences I have studied for the truth of the faith, I have much greater boldness for the Lord now, as well as confidence in him. But, by stressing that we are to live out of our heads, we can inflict a kind of violence upon fellow Christians by keeping their own hearts and minds disconnected, "short-circuiting" them from enjoying a deep heart and mind unity with the Lord, not to mention within themselves and with others.

Moreover, as we have seen, *if we are living primarily out of our intellects, but not a deep heart and mind unity with the Lord, we can tend to listen to the deliverances of our own minds and the cognitive content of the Bible.* As good as that might seem, it still misses another vital piece. *For it is not just that the mind needs to know, but the heart also needs to bow before our great God.* To the extent that we live out of our *own minds* and *our interpretations* of Scripture, we will tend to be like the Corinthian Christians in 1 Corinthians

---

8. It also helped sever a vicious tool of the evil one, who loved to keep pressing those old anxiety triggers of my "little boy," to leave me bound up in fear.

9. This is a very good point that Pagitt makes, too, in *Flipped*, 188. There, he expresses our need to be healthy, well-functioning, integrated, whole people. I will elaborate more on this need in chapter 6.

2 and 3, who, though believers, still were living fleshly lives because they were not living in deep unity with, and dependence upon, the Spirit of God.

That said, evangelicals are right to stress the importance of knowing truth; after all, Jesus says true worshippers are to worship God in spirit and truth (John 4:23). *Nevertheless, truth can be used as a weapon in various ways, especially if it is not united with compassion.* And in so doing, we can be violent toward the "sheep" entrusted to us in our "flocks." It is good, for instance, to focus upon the mind's needs for truth, but at the same time, if we forsake the cries of the hearts of those given to us to shepherd, in effect we send them to look outside the body of Christ for the love they need, which is where the evil one's affections will overtake them. They will not see the love of God in us in such cases, and then knowledge becomes a weapon against their fullness of a future and hope. *Feeding knowledge above compassion encourages disobedience, which repeats the Eden experience.*

For instance, McLaren is on to something when he points out that too many Christians expect that they should never have any struggles in their faith. This mind-set seems to teach that there are only two sources of problems in life—spiritual problems (which are treated as though they can be reduced to the effects of *our* sin), and physical problems. So, if they do struggle, woe to them! They must simply lack faith, and they need to confess their sin and just believe the truth. But too many Christians have been wounded by more sources, such as others' sins against us, the general effects of the fall in the world, and the pain that can come from these actions which may have devastating, lasting effects. This brokenness is something with which Bell and Pagitt also seem very familiar and are right to emphasize.

So, they see the disconnection in evangelicals' lives of truth preached, but not embodied. Instead, truth needs to be united with God's grace and love in our lives and our deeds. Since Jesus embodied these qualities, so should we. This leads us to a second, major contribution.

The Lack of Father-Shepherds

God wants to shepherd us, and one thing I am becoming very convinced is deeply on his heart now is that he wants to turn the hearts of the "fathers" (including dads, leaders in churches, professors, and more) to the hearts of the "children" (including, kids, youth, young adults, and all those in need of shepherding), *and* the hearts of the children to the fathers (maybe even as a response to the hearts of the fathers being drawn in genuine love to the children).

In many ways, I get the impression that McLaren and others are crying out about the lack of good father figures as shepherds in evangelical churches. In too many cases, I am afraid they are right on the money in that complaint. Instead of being shepherded with compassion, grace, and truth, which should help unite them with the heart and mind of God, too many believers have not had God's heart and care modeled for, and extended to, them. I think a key reason for this might simply be that too many father-shepherds are not living in a deep heart-and-mind unity with the Lord, as I discussed earlier.

One key example of this is the all-too-common experience of many believers in evangelical circles: they feel they cannot ask their questions of their pastors and teachers. Perhaps these stem from their struggles with some aspect of the faith in light of (a) their lived experiences (perhaps a lived experience with evil, like the deaths of precious loved ones); (b) how to make sense of some teaching (maybe how Christ is both fully God and fully man); (c) some challenge they encountered to the evidence for their faith (maybe a challenge from someone like Bart Ehrman on the reliability of the Gospels);[10] or others. But, regrettably, too often believers feel they cannot ask their questions. If we preach and teach with tones of self-assurance and certainty, then someone else who is struggling in some areas with trusting God, or in his or her walk with him, likely will feel embarrassed and intimidated to even ask their questions, or admit their doubts.

Not long ago, I heard a sad story from a class in a church, in which a woman pulled the teacher aside and asked if she could ask questions in that class. Apparently, she had not been given that permission before, or had been denied it, so that she needed to see if it was okay (safe?) for her to do that in this class. I know of another person in another church who raised what sounded like good questions to me, only to be rebuffed by her teacher (who was also an elder) that he just would not go there and even consider her ideas.

There are messages we communicate when we do this, implicitly or explicitly. In effect, we tell people to shut up, just take *the* biblical teaching (which, on some topics, *may* really just be our own strongly held opinions) at face value as fact and accept it *by faith*, as though that by itself is a virtue. But biblical faith is not a blind leap; it involves knowledge—that God has spoken and is trustworthy.

When we act this way toward other believers, it has a further, chilling effect: *that Christianity doesn't really have the answers to hard questions, so that it really isn't about the way things truly are.* That is, we have to just accept

10. For example, see his *Forged*.

the Bible's teachings on faith, without any further evidence, as though religion and morality are not areas in which we can have knowledge of truth. But if Jesus is the truth embodied, and the Bible is God's inspired, even inerrant, word (positions I believe the evidence well supports), then Christianity can survive and handle tough, honest, and (perhaps most of all) heartfelt questions.

For too many, another effect of telling people to just accept the leaders' teachings because they are the authority figures is to create suspicion in the listeners' hearts, for we have all seen (or read of) too many cases of spiritual (and other kinds of) abuse. It also can communicate a condescending attitude: "Who are *you* to question *me*?" as though we are the ones who are high and lifted up. If we have hearts that are puffed up, our youth and postmodern people will detect that in a heartbeat. Indeed, if we are tending to live out of our minds and not in vital connection with the Lord in both heart and mind, we will not be living in fullness of Spirit and truth. Yet, to the extent that we (even unconsciously, subtly) keep attempting to live out of our own minds and resources, and thus not God's, to that extent we will be living out of our flesh, and the fruit of that will include *arrogance—the very factor so many are detecting amongst evangelicals today.*

By shutting people down from asking their questions, we also can belie an insecurity, such that as father-shepherds we want to appear to have it all together, yet we are not allowing questions because we may not know all the answers. But, whoever said we had to be know-it-alls? *We are not the saving grace; only the Lord is.* Besides, if we live out of our insecurities, we will tend to live like King Saul, and that drove him to acts of disobedience and self-will to try to keep power and not lose the kingdom to David. Are we trying to keep our own positions of power and prestige by not letting the people in our "flocks" ask their questions? Besides, admitting that I do not know the answer to some question may be liberating for both me and some others, to see that I can admit that I don't know it all, and yet I can still have ample, good reasons why I should trust God.

McLaren and Pagitt both recognize this problem. Even a major heading on the back cover of *A New Kind of Christianity* identifies this as a core issue: "What would Christianity look like if we weren't afraid to ask questions?" (Maybe we should add for evangelical father-shepherds: "What if we weren't afraid *to be asked* questions?")

We also need to keep in mind that well-meaning evangelicals are not immune to being overtaken by evil, in that even subtly they too can elevate their thoughts above the Lord's, even when trying to defend the truth. Those who have the truth, and are truly in Christ, can still live out of their hearts' default, fleshly condition, and to that extent they become arrogant and engage in the worship of their own minds. For instance, I think it is a temptation for apologists to rely on a particular kind of reasoning (e.g., philosophical), rather than humbling ourselves and submitting all our thoughts, ways, and hearts to the Lord, letting him assess our ideas, especially before proclaiming them as truth. Evangelicals who do not humble themselves before the Lord set themselves up for being influenced by their flesh and even by demonic forces, perhaps by speaking "truth" as if they created it, and in authoritative tones that put others in submission. Just as much as anyone else, evangelicals can become arrogant, perhaps by proclaiming that their place to stand is without question. This attitude feeds into another which I think McLaren has pinpointed.

The Temptation to Rely on Ourselves

Evangelicals can succumb to a temptation to live as though all they need to do is rely on information (such as what is found in the Bible), themselves, and even the (good) grammatical-historical method of interpretation, *but not really on God Himself.* Here's how McLaren puts it in his "paraphrase" of Jesus' words to Thomas in John 14:6–7: "You simply need to trust me . . . *I'm not trying to give you information or instructions so you no longer need me.*"[11] This attitude can be very subtle and hard to diagnose, I think, for evangelicals rightly claim that the Bible is God's inscripturated revelation.

Yet, as I tried to show earlier, that alone does not mean that evangelicals are immune from tendencies we all have, to elevate our own hearts and minds over the Lord's and not live in a deep heart, soul, and mind unity with him. If we do lean into that temptation, then we can all too easily end up thinking of *ourselves* as the answer, the truth, and the saving grace, rather than seeing the Lord as the only one who can meet these needs. And though we have been given the mind of Christ (1 Cor 2:16), we will not be able to benefit from that gift unless we abide in him. For we cannot know the things of God unless we draw upon his Spirit (1 Cor 2:11–12); otherwise, to the extent we do not, we will be living out of our fleshly minds. In that light, Jesus' blunt statement from John 15:5 needs to be taken to heart: "I am the vine, you are the branches; he who abides in Me, and I in him, he bears much fruit; for apart from me you can do *nothing*" (emphasis mine). That is a sobering caution to anyone that we must depend upon him through his Spirit, even when we come to interpret passages using good tools we have been taught and given. For he is the Author of Scripture, and if we want to know what the Author had in mind, ultimately we need to go the

11. McLaren, *A New Kind of Christianity*, 221 (emphasis mine).

Author and receive from him, even when we use good tools and principles of interpretation.

Overall, McLaren nails this attitude; in a discussion of how Jesus needs to be the answer, as opposed to Christianity, he remarks that Christianity can help, "but only if it doesn't see itself as the answer."[12] Instead, the Lord needs to be the One we go to for the answers, even in interpreting Scripture. Clearly, that applies to all of us.

Overall, then, I think people like McLaren, Bell, Jones, and Pagitt have put their fingers on many real, serious problems with the received version of Christianity. And, I have probably glossed over or missed completely other points which they have identified ably. *They are on target in more key ways than I realized when I wrote* Truth.

Now, their many diagnoses align very closely with the ones we have already surfaced in chapter 2 of this book. But, what about the root cause(s)? I have argued there that the crucial problem with the evangelical churches in the West is that to a very deep, even unexamined, extent, they have been shaped by naturalism, a worldview and mind-set that is antithetical to Christianity. But McLaren, Pagitt, Bell, and Jones seem to end with the conclusion that evangelical Christians have been co-opted by modernity, or the larger Greco-Roman version of Christianity we have inherited. They do not seem to consider naturalism as a factor.[13]

So, as we now turn to engage critically with several of their views, not only should we assess them on their own merits, but we also might see to what extent their recommendations might be naturalistic too. And, if they are, then those points are not real solutions, for they would only perpetuate a serious problem, albeit perhaps in different clothing.

---

12. McLaren, *A New Kind of Christianity*, 255.

13. That is, it does not seem that they take it to be much of a factor, if one at all. Explicitly, that topic just doesn't seem to surface in their writings.

4

Assessment of the Emergents' Thought, Part 1

Areas for Assessment

I will start by focusing on McLaren's Greco-Roman story and his claims that we have read the gospel in its light. Pagitt of course makes very similar claims. Then, I will consider McLaren's idea that in the Bible we see an evolution of interpretations of God's character. Following these points, we will explore the recurring themes that God cannot be violent; humans are not inheritors of original sin; that Jesus' atoning work was not a penal substitutionary offering for our sin; and that people of other religions will be in heaven, too, while God will not consign people to hell for eternal, conscious torment. Throughout, we will explore two types of issues McLaren and others raise: (1) are there really inherent dualisms, such as body versus soul, in Scripture? And, (2) is God separated from us due to our sin? Overall, my hope is to get a better glimpse into what God really is like for McLaren, Pagitt, Bell, and Jones, and draw out some implications.

But to help set an appropriate backdrop, I would like to remind us of a few key things, such as the role of orthopraxis vis-à-vis orthodoxy, and why these authors have made their particular moves. For them, *orthopraxis is the point of orthodoxy*. Compared to the conventional way of approaching Christianity, it seems very reasonable to say that on their views, orthopraxis is the new *given*. Each of these authors and many others are suggesting that we question traditional, received evangelical understandings of Scripture and doctrines. We have already seen several reasons why they think we should do this, including that they have seen "modern" Christians stress knowledge and truth so much that they end up living primarily out of their "heads," but not also their hearts, which leads to abstractions in teaching and little of the Christian life actually being practiced (for instance, a lack of importance being placed upon embodiment).[1]

Their solutions seem to come back repeatedly to a stress upon relationships, which are cashed out theologically in terms of connection and integration, and metaphysically in terms of holism (or holistic connection), the latter of which seems to reflect the "turn to relationality." So, their focus seems to have shifted from what they see as a more "modern," "received" view of having right doctrines as the given, which are to result in good, or right, behavioral outcomes, to one of having the behavioral outcome as the new given on which to base our *doxa*, or beliefs. We could diagram these two patterns as follows:

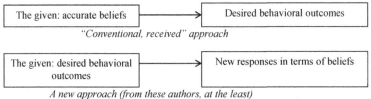

| The given: accurate beliefs | ⟶ | Desired behavioral outcomes |

"Conventional, received" approach

| The given: desired behavioral outcomes | ⟶ | New responses in terms of beliefs |

A new approach (from these authors, at the least)

With these reminders in place, let us now turn to the first area for assessment.

The Greco-Roman Narrative and Its Influence

From his reading of Plato and Aristotle, McLaren contends Christians today have become accustomed to understand Eden before the fall as a perfect state in which there was no becoming, no development, and so no story, which to him is not only inaccurate, but also undesirable. The human story is one of evolutionary development, with God also working with us to develop and mature. Indeed, for McLaren, the narrative focus is justified, for it is an important genre since our lives are best told as enacted stories—it fits reality as our being embodied, living humans on this earth.

---

1. They also hear several "moderns" emphasizing God's utter sovereignty, such that he must exhaustively determine all things. But if so, then isn't God the ultimate cause of evil? And, they see Christians living under the conventional view as just trying to manage sin, rather than living in the fullness and joyfulness of life that Jesus promised, even before we die.

Overall, like others, McLaren seems to bemoan the idea that it was Greek philosophy that introduced a plethora of unwelcome, destructive, and especially non-Hebraic dualisms into Christianity. It was this non-Jewish story that polluted the holistic emphasis found in the Hebraic scriptures and led Christianity astray from its true roots. By taking this path, McLaren tries to explain the emphasis of many Christians upon saving the soul so it goes to heaven when the body dies by connecting it to the (supposed) Platonic emphasis upon the inherent superiority of the immaterial over the material. Similarly, he seems to think he can explain the inherited, firm distinction between Creator and creation. He also tries to explain Christian exclusiveness by linking it with Roman imperialism, and Christian intolerance and arrogance (since Christians uniquely have the truth) with Roman views of the superiority of their way of life over and against barbarians, as well as with colonialism.

Misunderstanding Plato and Aristotle

It is notable, then, that McLaren seems to badly misunderstand Plato himself, not to mention Aristotle. To explore this, I will try to describe briefly Plato's ethical ideas. His ethics do utilize a metaphysical dualism, including universals (which are immaterial essences or forms) and particulars. An example would be various apples, all of which would have in common an apple essence (a universal property which we might call *appleness*), which makes them all members of that same species.

Utilizing this dualism, Plato's ethics focuses around two realms that can be described variously:

The Intelligible: the realm of the "forms"—the "upper" realm:	The eternal	The true, the good, the beautiful	Universals (*the one*): things in themselves (e.g., triangularity or appleness itself; essences)	Known by the intellect, through reason
The Sensible/Visible: the empirical world—the "lower" realm:	The temporal, spatial, finite	Particular examples of truth, goodness, and beauty	Particulars (*the many*): examples of particular triangles, or apples	Known by experience

The above diagram illustrates that the intelligible realm is that of the *forms*, which are immaterial. These are things in themselves; e.g., this is the realm

of triangleness, which is the essence of being a triangle. It is the realm of
the essence of being human, or humanness. Each of these is *one kind* of
thing. The realm of the intelligible is understandable by the intellect. It is
characterized by permanence and the infinite, and it also includes what is
truly good and truly beautiful. To put it differently, it is the realm of what is
essentially good (i.e., intrinsically good, or good in its very nature).

By contrast, the sensible realm is the realm of the *many*, in which there
are many particular apples, triangles, humans, etc. The sensible (or visible)
realm is that of the potential or the concrete, in which change takes place.
It is the realm of the spatial, temporal, and finite. It is where we live our
day-to-day activities.

Plato thought that essential goodness exists, and so that he had fundamentally a moral basis for the universe. Morals themselves are objectively
real entities, which exist as forms. The realm of the forms includes things
like goodness, truth, and beauty themselves, which are really the same, and
they, like essences of triangles, apples, and humans, are universals. For him,
these truths are known *a priori*, by reason.

In contrast, he thought we know truths of the sensible realm by experience. In it, we have particular virtuous people who have cultivated the different virtues, who have the virtues present in them. We also have instances
of rectangles, as well as people living in the *polis*, the Greek city-state.

Now, virtues are grounded in the good, and they are appropriate for us,
due to our essential nature. Part of our true end, our *telos*, is to try to have
a fundamental balance of the true, the good, and the beautiful. As I noted,
for Plato, the good is the true, which is also the beautiful. However, we may
analytically distinguish between them, or so it seems. Also, in his view, no
one is really fulfilled until he or she participates in being itself. To put it
differently, people are not really fulfilled until they have reached their *telos*,
which is their true end. So Plato is trying to find what the ideal is—what
it is we should strive after, to try to be like, and how people in *any* society
should live.

Does this mean that Plato thought reality is unchanging? Yes, in the
sense that essences (such as humanness, goodness, and beauty) *themselves*
do not change. But what happens when the form (universal) humanness
is instantiated in a particular human? J. P. Moreland explains that "when
a universal is exemplified, the universal is modified and constitutes the essence of its instances, which, in turn, are complex, dependent particulars."[2]
So, when the universal humanness *itself* is predicated of (or exemplified by)
a particular human, that human has a soul—which is his or her *particular*

2. Moreland, *Universals*, 99.

essence. So, the universal is modified and becomes that person's essence (or soul), and so it is with other humans too. Humanness fits the criterion of being a *one* in *many*.

But, to say that what is in the material realm is all illusion is incorrect. McLaren says that these are like images, shadows appearing on "the wall of a dark cave."[3] But for Plato, human beings are not mere shadows of a higher reality; they are ensouled beings who are to live out their lives developing their virtues in service of their community, the Greeks' *polis*. So, *they are anything but static*; they can develop and grow, such that change is part of their lived experience. Indeed, change and growth presuppose sameness of the person throughout those changes.

Moreover, on McLaren's Greco-Roman story, God would be a perfect Platonic being, a pure essence, and thus (to be consistent) static. But the view of God as Theos that McLaren rejects with disgust is hardly a static being. After Adam and Eve's disobedience, Theos flies off the handle at the resulting imperfection and overreacts with violence and hatred. This alone seems to be an inconsistency on McLaren's part in his portrayal of what God is like (i.e., like Theos) in the evangelical, Greco-Romanized version of Christianity.

But perhaps I have been unfair. McLaren says that he appeals to Plotinus's more Neoplatonic interpretation and adaptation of Plato, and not Plato himself, as being the most formative of the Greco-Roman narrative. And, Augustine was influenced by the Neoplatonism of the Manicheans, influencing him to think of matter (and thus the body) as bad and something from which the soul should flee.

However, suppose we grant his appeal to Plotinus's interpretation of Plato for sake of argument; then what about McLaren's treatment of Aristotle? For example, McLaren describes Aristotle as affirming that the changing, material world (e.g., chairs, people, etc.) is real. The words "chair" and "people" are unchanging, which we impose on those things. So reality is "a collection of material things," and these are inherently changeable.[4] He even claims this is what Raphael portrayed Aristotle as meaning in his painting, "The School of Athens."[5] But this is a serious misunderstanding of Aristotle. Let me try to explain Aristotle's basic ideas and how they are used in his ethics.

In terms of knowledge, Plato uses speculative reason, and the highest form of knowledge is of the ideal, or the forms. He therefore tends to deduce

3. McLaren, *A New Kind of Christianity*, 37.

4. McLaren, *A New Kind of Christianity*, 37.

5. McLaren, *A New Kind of Christianity*, 265, note 6.

particulars from the ideal. On the other hand, while Aristotle uses reason, he works from particular examples of different people and different kinds of cases, and then he proceeds inductively to arrive at generalizations.

The very terminology Aristotle uses in his *Nicomachean Ethics* shows a strong reliance upon his *Metaphysics,* where he had developed his views about the reality of immaterial aspects of reality, such as souls (the essence of human beings), the principle of life of each other kind of living thing, virtues, and more.[6] As our nature, the soul sets the boundaries for the kinds of changes we can undergo, as well as what is appropriate or normative for us, all of which is due to the kind of thing we are. There are certain kinds of things that would be appropriate for a human's essential nature that would not be so for a dog's nature. For example, there are certain moral qualities I ought to have, but dogs shouldn't. Also, in his view, plants have essences (or their principle of life) within them. In general, the respective natures of living things mark off the boundary conditions for what is appropriate for them if they are to grow into a full-blown kind of human, dog, oak tree, etc.[7]

Now, in his view, we are a unity of body and soul, which means his view, traditionally understood, is a kind of *substance dualism.* It is not like Descartes's view, however, in which the body and soul are "connected" only via the pineal gland in the brain. That leaves Descartes with a view in which there is a radical dichotomy between body and soul, such that it is hard to see how they could interact with each other. Instead, for Aristotle, the body is "rooted" ultimately in the soul, thus developing a deep unity between them. The body parts humans have are appropriate for them due to their nature, while the same would be true for animals and plants and their respective natures.

Similarly, there are certain kinds of character qualities (or moral virtues) that will be appropriate for us due to our nature. Aristotle focused on what we know as the *cardinal* virtues—justice, temperance, courage, and prudence. The capacities for these virtues exist in all our souls, but once developed, they are realized properties in given individuals. Importantly, they are *not* physical. They are soulish traits that have been cultivated and developed through habituation in manners appropriate to the kind of thing they are. And, on the traditional interpretation of his views, Aristotle held

6. And, all humans (as primary, individuated substances) have predicated of them humanness (a secondary substance) as their essential nature.

7. Aristotle, *Metaphysics,* Book VII, parts 3–4; Book V, 8. This should be no surprise to McLaren, either, for Aristotle's biological classification system, which was replaced by the Darwinian evolutionary scheme, was based on the *existence* of natural *kinds.*

that the virtues are objectively real, universally valid, and intrinsically good for all people.[8] They are not our cultural, or individual, products.

As for Plato, there is a proper order to the soul and the virtues. However, Aristotle develops his ideas in more detail. This ordering involves the idea that our souls, as our essential nature, come complete with a hierarchically arranged set of ultimate capacities. That is, even at the initial stage of a fertilized ovum, all humans have a complete set of lower- or higher-order capacities.

Now, Aristotle realizes that our ability to grow presupposes a fundamental sameness to human persons, and yet is such that we can change. How can we best account for these twin features about us? His answer lies in what the soul is, and two kinds of change which he distinguishes. The soul is a person's set of essential properties and ultimate capacities. It defines the limits to the kinds of changes we can undergo; without the soul, we would cease to exist. That is, we cannot undergo *essential change* and still exist. So, essentially, we each can remain the same person through time and change due to sameness of our souls. That is how I am still the same person I am now as I was when I was, say, twenty-one.

Even so, many things have changed since then. I married my wife in 1984, graduated with my PhD in 2000, and became a father at age forty-four. These examples are *accidental (i.e., nonessential, contingent) changes*, as Aristotle would call them. They are not necessary traits for me to be me. On the other hand, I am still Scott Smith. There is something that makes me *me*, the very same person, through all those and other changes, which Aristotle would maintain is my soul.[9]

These two Aristotelian concepts of change help us understand his virtue ethics. The capacities for the virtues exist in our souls, but a given person may or may not realize them.[10] The development of a virtue is, strictly speaking, a nonessential kind of change, even though ethically they are normative for us. That very development presupposes there is something about me now that makes me the same person as I was before I developed the virtue, and even during that process. Otherwise, there could not be any growth in my character. In addition, in a fundamental way, I *have* that virtue *exemplified*, or present, in me.

These concepts also fit together with his teleological view of human nature. That is, Aristotle thought that becoming virtuous is important for reaching our *telos* as humans. In one sense, goodness in itself is our *telos*,

---

8. See my *In Search of Moral Knowledge*, 49–50.

9. Aristotle, *Metaphysics*, Book V, 9.

10. Aristotle, *Nicomachean Ethics*, Book II, 1.

the goal toward which all of life should aim. This goodness is happiness (*eudaimonia*), or well-being, in contrast to an American sense of it as feelings of pleasure that can be fleeting.[11] In another sense, reaching our *telos* is the function of a human being, and that function is directly tied to our nature.

So change (especially amongst living things) is well developed in Aristotle's views. Change trades upon something that remains the same, which is our essence. Without that basis for literal sameness, there would not be any continuity of *personal identity* for myself or anyone else as we change, for good or bad. *Change presupposes sameness.* Instead, there would be only a succession of different person-stages with replacements by subsequent (and different) person-stages, but no sameness of person throughout.[12]

So McLaren's treatment of Aristotle seems deeply misguided, in particular his claim that what is really unchanging are words we use for things. Nor is he correct that on Aristotle's views, reality is made up of changing material stuff. Moreover, when Aquinas synthesizes Aristotle's philosophy with Augustine's theology, the result is not what McLaren should seem to expect. He acknowledges that Aquinas's synthesis helped restore a more "dynamic tension in Christian intellectual life" against Neoplatonic influences, and that fits with his understanding of Aristotle's emphasis being upon material, particular things.[13] But that is not the view Aquinas develops; he picks up much the same metaphysical dualism I discussed above from Aristotle's own works, in which each given human is a deep unity of body and soul, with the soul as the individual, particular essence, which is an instance of the universal humanness.

This metaphysical basis for Roman Catholic theology will endure long past Aquinas, and it still lives in the Catholic emphasis upon natural law. Moreover, the Reformers did not repudiate Aristotle on this count. On the one hand, Luther firmly rejected Aristotle insofar as Aquinas used him to acquire the virtues by habits, which establishes the believers' own righteousness and allows them to grow in merit. Yet, on the other, he agreed with Aristotle that justice, temperance, and courage are virtues. In addition, Luther accepted a natural law basis for civil law. Yet, neither he nor Calvin rejected Aristotle's dualist metaphysics of humans.

11. Aristotle, *Nicomachean Ethics*, Book I. See also my *In Search of Moral Knowledge*, 53.

12. I have also addressed Alasdair MacIntyre's attempt to reappropriate Aristotle's virtue ethics today by drawing upon the unity of one's narrative instead of one's soul, all in an attempt to ground personal identity through change. I argue that this move will utterly fail to achieve that goal. See ch. 6 in my *Virtue Ethics and Moral Knowledge*, and ch. 11 in *In Search of Moral Knowledge*.

13. McLaren, *A New Kind of Christianity*, 264, note 3.

What then are some implications for McLaren's Greco-Roman narrative and how it has (supposedly) distorted Christianity? McLaren relies upon his treatment of Aristotle to explain the fall in his Greco-Roman narrative. We have fallen into Aristotelian becoming, a world of matter that is not in a perfect, unchanging state.

But, if this were so, it seems we would find that the views about Aristotle in particular that have been passed down from this Greco-Roman narrative would have persisted and remained largely the same (i.e., they would have been consistent). *But, that is not what we find*; it is *not* the view about Aristotle that was passed down through Aquinas and the Reformers. Even today, Alasdair MacIntyre realizes that when he wants to reappropriate Aristotle's ethics in our contemporary age, he must jettison Aristotle's "metaphysical biology," which must be a reference to Aristotle's view of essences.[14] For McLaren to stake the treatment of the fall (according to the Greco-Roman narrative) on his version of Aristotle is to undermine that crucial stage of that narrative, *for those are not Aristotle's views*, nor are they the ones that have been handed down and used through the centuries, even by Christians.

For Aristotle, it is *not* the case that it is bad we develop and live in a world that is changing. Nor is matter bad, nor is the body something from which we should flee. Moreover, for him, the very basis for us to be able to change is that something about us remains the same (essentially). So, in a key sense, our respective, individual souls, as our set of ultimate capacities, are unchanging; however, we can develop (or lose already realized) intellectual abilities, body parts, or virtues. As such, these can and do change, and they are rooted in the soul. For Aristotle, these qualities and our souls are *very real* in his view, and they are *not* mere shadows or words we use.

Moreover, contrary to McLaren's Greco-Roman narrative, on Aristotle's own views it is far from being bad that things change. Rather, change is needed so that we can realize our true goal (*telos*). So, it is not the case that by embracing (even if implicitly) Aristotle's metaphysics, Christians down through the centuries have bought into a view that is somehow negative or bad. Aristotle's metaphysical views can also be used to explain life *before* the fall, in terms of how Adam and Eve could live, develop, and grow, and yet remain the same. After all, Adam *grew* both in his knowledge of, and experience with, the various species of animals, as well as in his relationship with Eve. Something else is needed to explain the fall in McLaren's Greco-Roman version of Christianity, for it cannot work on his treatment of Aristotle.

14. MacIntyre, *After Virtue*, 162.

Even so, McLaren, Pagitt, and others are very intent on showing that Christianity has been distorted by Greek philosophy. Why? *What does this move do for them, or allow them to try to preserve?* Actually, several things; in general, it allows them to maintain that the many dualisms we have inherited are not intrinsic to the Bible's main story line, but instead are interpretations drawn from a different framing story that corrupts the main biblical focus on holism and integration. Also, it allows them to reject body-soul dualism, as opposed to a (supposedly) Hebraic holism and deep unity of human persons.[15] And, it allows them to reject universals in favor of particulars (i.e., nominalism).

Our Personal Identity and the Hope of the Resurrection

So, let's consider more implications of their metaphysical position. Change (of whatever sort) does seem to presuppose a fundamental sameness, lest there not be change to some (one and the same) thing, but that thing is simply succeeded and replaced by something else. This consideration pushes us to look at the nature of *identity*. Leibniz's law of the *indiscernibility of identicals* maintains that "everything is identical to itself and thus shares all properties in common within itself."[16] So, for two things to be identical, they have to have all their properties in common. If so, there are not really two separate things, but just one and the same thing. We have already seen how Aristotle can account for the literal sameness of our personal identity through time and change because our essential set of properties do not change, but our contingent ones can and do.

Practically, if we do not have souls (i.e., as our essence), what would that imply for us? At any given time, I would be identical with the set of properties that just is *me*. And, if there are no universals, but nominalism is true, then those properties are just particulars. "We" are just a bundle of discrete qualities. But, over time, those properties change; e.g., my hair color is changing from brown to gray, and I have less hair as I get older. I have been married since 1984, and I became a father in 2001. So, the set of properties would no longer be identical through time. Thus, I cannot be the same person now who married Debbie Hubbard on October 27, 1984, or became Anna's dad at age forty-four. Nor should someone who murdered another person in 2014 be held responsible today for that evil action, because that

15. In his e-mail dated February 28, 2006, Tony Jones remarked to me that he thought Nancey Murphy's nonreductive physicalism is the best explanation for the Old Testament's emphasis upon the unity of persons.

16. See Moreland and Craig, *Philosophical Foundations*, 194.

murderer has ceased to exist and a new person has taken his or her place. Nor could any of us sustain interpersonal relationships with others, even with God, it seems, for that too presupposes a continuity of persons through time.

Here's another crucial implication, especially for the hope of the resurrection: I could not be the same person who trusted Christ at age twenty, had his sins forgiven, and was adopted into God's family, yet who will die one day and be resurrected to life. My resurrected body will not be literally identical to the one I now have, nor is it the same in all respects to the one I had at age twenty. So, it seems that I cannot realize the promise of life after my death.

Now, in a physicalist (and nominalist) view, we do not have a soul as our essence; each of us is just a bundle, or set, of physical properties at any given time. So, there are practical implications of a physicalist view of human persons for Jesus and his resurrection. In such a view, when his body died, *Jesus the human person also died* (i.e., ceased to exist).[17] Now, if humans are physical things, then the Jesus who died is not identical with the Jesus who was raised, for their respective bodies had different properties. That implies that Jesus did not survive his death on the cross, regardless of how we may think of him as the same person.[18]

Obviously, this result has major implications, for it seems we too cannot survive our deaths and be resurrected. However, perhaps there are a couple ways that McLaren and others could respond, to try to preserve our sameness, so that we are the ones who will be raised from the dead. Let's consider two similar suggestions, one made by McLaren, and the other made by Joel Green, a New Testament exegetical scholar. McLaren has suggested in one of his earlier works that God remembers us: "All the momentary members of our life story . . . will be re-membered, reunited, in God's memory."[19] As he puts it, we will be *reconstituted* in God.

Similarly, in *Body, Soul, and Human Life,* Joel Green thinks that our identity "is formed and found in self-conscious *relationality* with its neural correlates and embodied *narrativity* or formative histories."[20] Green has

17. Jones claims in *A Better Atonement* that in the crucifixion, "God really died" (locations 316–19). Now, Jones clearly affirms that Jesus is fully God and fully human. But this quoted portion is stated imprecisely. Though Jesus died (his body died), did God, the second Person of the Trinity, die, i.e., cease to exist? Certainly not.

18. See my *In Search of Moral Knowledge,* 275. See also my earlier chapter, "The Presuppositions of the Self," in my *Virtue Ethics and Moral Knowledge.*

19. McLaren, *Story,* 153.

20. Green, *Body, Soul, and Human Life,* 179. Green also argues that our traditional interpretation of Scripture as requiring that we are a dualistic unity of a body and soul

embraced a kind of physicalism, which he thinks is compatible with biblical exegesis, and he believes "our personhood . . . is inextricably bound up in our physicality."[21] Green appeals to our stories as the basis for a "narrative unity" of the self.[22]

Green realizes that if we are physical beings, then at death, not only does the person die, that person's narrative also "fades." However, God re-embodies us at the resurrection, which "provides the basis for relational and narrative continuity of the self."[23] Green partly appeals to "mystery" as the basis for our personal identity, but he also appeals to a relational ontology he finds in Paul. That is, our personhood is preserved *in* Christ, or *with* Christ. For Green, this "suggests that the relationality and narrativity that constitute who I am are able to exist apart from neural correlates and embodiment only insofar as they are preserved in God's own being, in anticipation of new creation."[24]

So, both McLaren and Green appeal (at least in part) to the narratives of our lives as the basis for preserving our sameness of person, even after death and the resurrection. But, will this move secure their desired outcome? I do not believe it will; consider what a narrative is. On a view in which essences have been either marginalized or have no place, it seems a narrative is just a group of sentences about one's life. Unfortunately, though, one's narrative is changing continually; my life story at age twenty did not include having graduate degrees, or being married. At age forty-three, it did not include being a father. At age fifty, it did not include my being a full professor. What then makes the narrative the same through change? It seems like one's narrative needs something to make it identical through change, too. But, if so, then narratives themselves cannot serve as the basis for our sameness/personal identity through change. Their sameness trades upon something deeper that allows them to be about the same person, and, again, Aristotle's view of the soul as our essential nature meets that need. But, without a basis in reality for preserving our sameness, it seems we will not survive death.

---

is mistaken. Instead, he defends the thesis that it is plausible to interpret Scripture as being open to a monistic interpretation of human beings (that is, we are made up of one kind of thing, not two, which is physical). For a longer treatment of his thought therein, see my "Joel Green's Anthropological Monism."

21. Green, *Body, Soul, and Human Life*, 179.

22. Two more examples of an appeal to the narrative unity of the self are found in MacIntyre's *After Virtue*, 204–25, and Hauerwas, *A Community of Character*, 144.

23. Green, *Body, Soul, and Human Life*, 179.

24. Green, *Body, Soul, and Human Life*, 180.

The same problems will apply to Bell's "enduring patterns" as what grounds our sameness through change. This too will fail, for what *is* an "enduring pattern" but something made of matter/energy that we conceive of as being a pattern? Intrinsically, it does not have an essential nature. Moreover, if ontologically we are but physical, then no change is possible. So, all their appeals to growth and development of any kind (including moral, relational, social, intellectual, etc.) *cannot* happen.

On the Very Possibility of Having Interpersonal Relationships

Now, if creation is mechanistic, and if we are just physical things, then it becomes hard to see how God can have a *personal* relationship with us. For on such a view, suppose God is immaterial, as traditionally conceived. Yet, we are just physical beings. How then could God interact with us? Nancey Murphy, a Christian who maintains that people are physical beings, suggests that God can interact with us by acting in the quantum level of our brains.[25]

Now, my having personal relationships requires my having thoughts, beliefs, experiences, and more about a person, as well as about me. To know my wife means I need to be able to experience her richly. Knowing her involves my forming thoughts and then beliefs about what she likes, what she values, what communicates love to her, and more. It also requires that I can observe her and see how she responds to various situations, such as if she seems to like receiving gifts of cookies (which I often supplied while dating), or if she liked riding in my sports car with the convertible top removed (which she did not).

Now, such "mental" states as beliefs, thoughts, desires, experiences, and others seem to have a special quality—almost every single one of them is *of* or *about* something, a quality known as *intentionality*.[26] It is *not* the same thing as an *intention*, like my intention to finish this chapter's draft today. There, my goal is *about* something—finishing this chapter. So, intentions are one kind of mental state, and virtually all mental states have intentionality.

But, if we are physical things, I don't think this will work to have genuine communication with us, which is essential to any healthy relationship. Importantly, intentionality defies being explained as just a physical kind of thing.[27] Physicalists (even Christian ones) and naturalists try to explain

25. Murphy, *Bodies and Souls, or Spirited Bodies?*, 131–32.

26. Yet, some experiences, such as a pain, may not be of or about something. J. P. Moreland suggested this to me in conversation.

27. This is a major thrust of my book *Naturalism and Our Knowledge of Reality*.

intentionality in one of two main ways. First, it is just a causal correlation between a brain state configuration and some physical object.[28] That is, the external object causes that brain state to occur, due to the physical causal chain that exists between that object and my brain, such as when light waves bounce off the object, travel to my optic nerve, and physical states travel to the brain, causing that last state.

But, there are two main problems with this view. Suppose I see a red ball. First, if a series of physical states stands between me and the ball, I can never transcend the chain of those states and arrive at the ball itself. All I have access to is the last state in the chain. How then can I know the ball I take my experience to be of actually *is* the thing that is causing the brain state in me? Second, I can have thoughts about things that do not exist, such as of Pegasus. Yet, that cannot be so in the physical, causal chain view. Whatever the physical object is that is causing the series of physical states, it needs to exist, or else there will be no such experiences (i.e., brain states) of the ball in me. But, plainly, we can think about things that do not obtain in reality; scientists do this all the time when they develop hypotheses, test them, and find them to be inaccurate. So, these states cannot be physical; they must be nonphysical.

The second main way physicalists try to address intentionality is illustrated by the naturalist Daniel Dennett. If we take the Darwinian, naturalistic story seriously, Dennett claims that all that really exists are physical forces and patterns, and brains that process the physical inputs of our senses. There are no real immaterial things, like souls, beliefs, or intentionality. Moreover, natural selection is a completely *blind* process: there are no intentions, plans, or goals—no representing something to be a certain way.

Dennett proposes that humans (and computers, aliens, robots, and more) are "intentional systems," which are anything "amenable to analysis by a certain tactic," which he calls the *intentional stance*.[29] In turn, the intentional stance is "the tactic of interpreting an entity by adopting the presupposition that is an approximation of the ideal of an optimally designed (i.e., rational) self-regarding agent."[30] For example, by adopting that tactic, when we are observing two chess players competing in a tournament, we can *interpret* their moves (or, behaviors) as their "desiring," or "intending" to try to checkmate their opponent. Moreover, we can predict their moves in order to accomplish their "goals."

---

28. For example, consider the views of Tye, *Ten Problems of Consciousness*, 96–102.

29. Dennett, "Dennett, Daniel C.," 239.

30. Dennett, "Dennett, Daniel C.," 239.

But, are there really such desires, intentions, beliefs, or intentionality at work here? Not for Dennett; all we are doing is making interpretations of their behaviors and predicting what they will do by *attributing* to them these qualities, when there really are none. Intentionality is *not* real in this view; it is just a useful way of speaking to help us predict behavior.

Now, apply these findings to God's being in a personal relationship with us. Though God can have thoughts, desires, beliefs, experiences, and intentions about us, we could never *know* them. Why? If we are just physical stuff, we will be unable to have any mental states with their intentionality, for they are immaterial. But without such mental states, I could not have a relationship with my wife, much less with God. Nor could I ever know God's intended meaning (or application) in a passage of Scripture, for that requires my having God's intention present in my mind too.

Yet, if we pay attention to what is before our minds in conscious aware-ness, we can notice that *we have* desires, beliefs, and more, and *we use them* to move us to action, even to communicate with others in our relationships. But that seems to require that there is something that *has*, or *owns*, these mental states (with their intentionality), which often people have assumed is the mind, or soul. But, there is no such thing on this kind of view. Plus, if a physicalist suggests that the brain is that owner, then that person faces the interaction objection; how can a physical brain "own," much less use, these mental states?

So, treating ourselves as somehow being mechanisms actually serves to distance God from us in several respects. It makes it impossible to have a personal relationship with him. To the extent that Christians start to really act as though that is true, they will tend to not truly listen to God through Scripture. Nor could they hear his voice. But, at the least, *functionally* God is distanced from us *in practice,* as One who may have created all nature and humans, but who now is more remote, despite official doctrinal teaching to the contrary. We might call this a *functional deism.* Thus, there would be a disconnection between doctrine and practical implications.

But, couldn't someone (perhaps McLaren) object and say that even though we do not have souls as our essence, nonetheless these mental quali-ties, along with their intentionality, emerge from the brain at given stages in its development? He has suggested that "from the integration of the faculties of the body and mind, the soul emerges with an ethical and aesthetical and relational dimension—the person whose story includes a body and mind, but is not limited to a body and mind."[31] So on such a view, there could be room for real, emergent mental states with real intentionality.

31. McLaren, *Generous Orthodoxy*, 281.

Notice that this option allows for a "pluralistic physicalism," in which we basically are physical beings. Yet, there is room for emergence of higher-level, even genuinely mental, properties. Suppose we grant for the sake of argument that such immaterial states can emerge from, and depend for their existence upon, the physical brain. Even so, their mere existence will not suffice for our being able to have interpersonal relationships. For we are not like a mere collection of immaterial "inputs" (mental states) into a physical processing system (the brain). If we pay attention to what is before our minds when we are interacting with someone, we can be consciously aware not only of our particular thoughts, feelings, etc., but also that *we have them*. Our usual experience is not that of the existence of a jumble of such states, but that they have an owner, a subject who has them, who can ponder them, draw inferences, consider how to act in light of them, consider them in light of that one's overall history, and much more. But what *is* such a possessor? If the answer is the brain, then the physicalists have begged the question at hand. They need to supply an answer as to how it can use these states and perform such things, for it is physical, but these states are not. Moreover, without an essence to the person, the brain is just a bundle of biological, physical properties. How then can it own these mental properties?

So, all these necessary qualities for relationships seem to evaporate if we are but physical beings, or even if our mental states emerge from the physical but there is no immaterial soul that owns, compares, and uses them. There is something incredibly sad and disappointing about this result. Instead of truly being able to live in community and thrive therein by embracing the "one anothers" in Scripture, *we simply will not have any interpersonal relationships whatsoever.* We would be utterly isolated, solitary individuals. (I would add that we would be utterly alone, except we would not feel lonely, because we couldn't have any feelings whatsoever.)

But, in terms of an interpersonal, intimate relationship with God, we are hopeless . . . and it is due to how God has made us, or allowed us to evolve. While I empathize greatly with Pagitt's desire for a down-and-in (i.e., intimate) God, *this view of what we are actually distances us from God.* Without the reality of what is needed for us to have interpersonal relationships, we will not be able to experience his deep groanings and cries within our hearts that we are the Father's adopted children, and that he is our Abba, Daddy. So, the Father will be separated from us, for there is *no possibility of intimacy with him.* On this view, we are not the kinds of beings that *can* have personal relationships. Thus, we cannot receive the Father's love, which he would pour out within our hearts through his Spirit given to us. But this tragic result simply guts the Christian gospel of its beauty and hopefulness, as well as the desire of our hearts to love, and be loved by, God. On this view, God is incredibly distant in the ways that count the very most, and it would not be different even if Christ was standing right here and trying to talk with us.

There is a further problem in the emergents' views for having an intimate relationship with God, and this time, the problem is with God. By rejecting essences, it seems God will not have an essential nature either. Thus, there is nothing about God that will enable God to be the same being, or have the same character, through time and change. This result is contrary to McLaren's belief that God's being does not evolve ontologically. Indeed, the problem gets worse—without any basis for maintaining God's sameness through time and change, God will not be able to endure at all. God will cease to exist, and (evidently) some other being we call God would come into existence.

But, if we take nonreductive physicalism about creation seriously, yet have a God who is not physical, we have the interaction problem that physicalists themselves raise against dualism. How could God interact with, much less be personal with, a physical creation? However, take, for instance, Bell's and Pagitt's sweeping statements about reality, that *all* reality is energy flow, that matter is energy, etc. It seems that God is also matter/energy.

Now, all the problems we have seen about humans (if physical) being able to have interpersonal relationships return in force, but now applied to God. For God could not have interpersonal relationships, either, nor could God have thoughts, beliefs, desires, or experiences. There would not be any callings from God to us into the future, which seem to presuppose God has thoughts, dreams, and goals. But, when our authors portray God as having such things, and as being personal, it seems plain that they are engaging in *anthropomorphisms*, only here applied to God.[32]

But to even do that seems impossible if we do not have any real abilities to have thoughts, beliefs, experiences, and so forth. Instead, I think we have been taught for a very long time that we can be physical beings and yet have these kinds of abilities, and by now people have taken that belief for granted. So, it often does not seem troublesome to us to offer such theories. Nevertheless, if we are merely physical beings, we cannot have interpersonal relationships, and God cannot either.

It therefore seems that there is a devastatingly high cost for embracing their proposal. One of their central motivations for embracing physicalism and panentheism is to have God be immanent with us. And that is a good goal—due to its shaping influences, evangelicalism can leave us with a God

---

32. Scripture has much to say about that mind-set, though, for we are trying to make God in our own image, thereby defining reality, including him (Gen 3:5).

who can seem distant, and not intimate. But, this is not the way to solve that problem. Indeed, I will discuss in chapter 6 how we can truly experience God's nearness and intimacy, yet without having to embrace physicalism or panentheism.

There is one last point to consider before pressing onward—free will. If we are but physical beings in a physical creation, then it seems we will be subject to the laws of physics. So, free will, which at least McLaren, Bell, and Pagitt all value highly, would seem to be an illusion, or just wishful thinking. On the other hand, if we are essentially embodied souls, then it seems that as such, our souls themselves would not be subject to the laws of physics, since they would consist of immaterial "stuff."

Now, it will not seem to help to appeal to higher levels of causation as a way to secure free will. For even in that view, there is nothing new ontologically. There are only physical properties to draw from, and therefore there will not be any thoughts, beliefs, experiences, desires, purposes, etc. (nor, as we have seen, any owner of them that can then compare, think through, and then use them). But the ability to will something seems to presuppose these things exist. Moreover, the exercise of free will seems to require an active agent that can do these things and then act. But there are no such things on their kinds of nonreductive physicalism, and so free will seems to be a pipe dream. And, even more damaging, even God will not have any such ability.

Sin, Evil, and God

This fundamental metaphysical position also poses serious problems for God in relation to evil and sin. Our authors do not deny the reality of sin, but they do deny inherited, original sin. If we are basically physical things, then original sin just doesn't fit well in such an anthropology, as Jones realizes. Moreover, it becomes hard to understand how we could be "dead in our sins" in relation to God, for in their view, if our bodies are alive, then quite simply we are alive. And since we already are "embedded" in God, or at least in relationship with him, then quite simply we are not separated from God.

But, there are several problems with this view. If we are basically physical things, it becomes much harder to understand sin in much of any meaningful way. Sin is not simply a matter of movements of body parts or behavior. Fundamentally, it is a matter of what is in our hearts, as Jesus taught. For instance, it is from the heart that all sorts of evil, defiling things spring (Matt 15:18–19). From the heart, we will and desire, both of which are mental kinds of things with their intentional qualities.

Moreover, this God does not seem to be holy. Whatever else sin and sinful acts are on this view, they are connected to, and even "embedded" in, God.[33] So, God would not seem to be separated from sin; rather, sin is related to, and even in, God. But, perhaps a rebuttal might be that when Jesus lived among us, he was not separated from being amongst sin or sinners; indeed, he came to save sinners (1 Tim 1:15). Of course, that is quite right, but his being present with us and dealing with our sin did not require that he himself would have sin related to him, in his being. As our High Priest, Jesus is separated from sinners (Heb 7:26), but this must mean that he himself is undefiled by sin. But how can God avoid being defiled by sin in this holistic, integrated view?

If that's the case, then our God is *not* truly holy, and that has vast implications for the rest of God's character. God's holiness entails that he is morally perfect, and so to be holy, God is truly just, and truly good. But if God is defiled by sin (by having sin be related to, and even be "in" him), then it means he is not truly good or just. But then, why should we trust God? These implications work to undermine his being truly worthy of our worship, since he would be finite and deficient.

It seems then that this suggested, holistic version of the gospel story offers little to humble us before God, so that we would seek him out of deep need for being delivered from sin, even its power and penalty. That would not be our real need. Instead, in this "new" version of the gospel story, the human spirit seems adequate to transform us morally. How so? We are not dead to God; we are already in relationship with him and need to grow in that by following the way of Jesus. Nor does this "gospel" offer us the ability to truly be in an intimate relationship with God, much less others. It cannot deliver on its most attractive points.

Before we move to a second set of concerns, regarding McLaren's "Jewish" story, the Bible, and its evolving interpretations, perhaps we should take a step back and gain a larger perspective from what we have examined thus far.

We have already considered that on these views, we are working with a new "given," that orthopraxis, understood roughly as *faithful living as Christians in our context*, is the *new given*, and beliefs flow from that. And, faithful living is ethical living, yet it seems to be done in our own strength, and not from being deeply united with God's heart, mind, and Spirit. The importance

---

33. Indeed, if creation is basically physical stuff, then what makes something evil, or good? Those are not intrinsic properties of matter or energy. Are they therefore human constructs—simply how we interpret matter or behavior? But, surely some acts, such as murder or rape, are wrong in themselves, and not simply due to our interpreting them as such.

of relationships and ethical living (which our authors rightly stress) seem to be their basis for suggesting fullness of life, as they perceive it, as opposed to what they perceive as a "wooden" orthodoxy as being practiced on the "conventional," "received" view by too many evangelicals and others.

Their stress upon holism in human beings leads us to see that they think humans are not to be bifurcated into body and soul. Instead, they are to be conceived of as a deep unity of mainly one kind of thing. With their stress upon embodiment as necessary for relationships, and the charge that essences (and souls) are static and therefore cannot enter into relationships, it is a natural conclusion that they would tend (at the least) to distance themselves from body-soul dualism and, in its place, embrace metaphysical holism, which most likely would be a form of physicalism.

So, in sum, there are three "strands" needed for their thought thus far considered:

(1) the priority of living in relationships as the given;

(2) metaphysical holism and embodiment in our anthropology, along with the turn to relationality; and

(3) a rejection of essences (souls).

But I have given several reasons why these moves are deeply problematic.

Our authors have started with a new, behavioral given that suggests to them fullness of life, especially in light of the failures they have seen, and I have surfaced earlier, too. Then, in that light, they seem to be questioning if God really meant that we are made of body and soul, to raise doubts about that position—e.g., is it really biblically faithful? This seems to be an intellectual kind of appeal. To help answer that, they seem to be looking at their experiences of how the "received" view has been misused, leading, for instance, to misguided views that the *body* is bad and therefore must be escaped.

Having started with this new given, as well as their questioning the received view about our being a unity of body and soul, and then considering their experiences with how that has been lived out, they seem to be ready to embrace a third appeal, one of suspicion. Here, it manifests itself as their suspicion toward the received view that we are a unity of body and soul. Their suspicion is also directed at "modern" evangelical Christian leaders, whom they think are trying to exercise power and control over Christians by using an exceedingly powerful, *humanly constructed* dualism—the prospects of eternal reward in heaven, or the dread of eternal conscious torment in hell.[34]

34. After all, in Pagitt's and McLaren's views, these dualisms—and their paradigm's concepts too—are just human constructs that are historically contingent.

However, the sad result of their views—that they do incredible violence to our being able to have a relationship with God and other people —is suspicious itself, and not as just an intellectual mistake. For there seems to be a pattern to this kind of thinking. It seems much like what we see in Genesis 3. There is a questioning of what God intended and said, and of what the truth is, in order to doubt what we have received. There seems to be a slight twist to that truth, too: embodiment, while utterly important and even essential for life on earth, nonetheless (we are told) makes most sense on a monistic understanding of humans—even though a monism of physical stuff results in the problems we have seen. There is an appeal to experience, too, to help support and even drive the desire for the new given. And then there is the attempt to cast suspicion, that this doctrine of humans being both body and soul is based upon a power move, to control them. Finally, the unintended result (from the peoples' perspective) is the same: separation from God. In Genesis, that line of questioning and thinking is attributed to a given character: the serpent, or the devil (cf. Rev 12:9, 20:2). At the least, it is interesting and perhaps suggestive to note that these two patterns seem to fit closely. It also is interesting to note that this view fits with a naturalized kind of Christianity, in which Satan and demons are not thought to exist or are basically disregarded.

Before ending this chapter, let me raise one more line of consideration regarding McLaren's proposed three-line narrative. Burson suggests that McLaren's claims actually serve to undermine our confidence in God: "to accept McLaren's hypothesis—that the majority of the Christian church for the past seventeen hundred years has believed a 'barbarous' and 'hideous' false gospel narrative—raises several new vexing questions. For instance, what are the implications for divine providence, Holy Spirit guidance, and Christ's concern for the church?"[35] But, this kind of claim is in line what many others have suggested in history, including Joseph Smith, Mary Baker Eddy, and others. If indeed most Christians have radically misunderstood the gospel, then it seems the God is not very good at communicating his message, or leading and guiding the church in the truth.

Now, to what extent are McLaren's, Pagitt's, and others' suggestions about how we should perceive the biblical story a faithful interpretation of Scripture and its story line? Is their depiction of the Bible accurate? We will turn now to this main question, with its various sub-issues.

---

35. Burson, *Brian McLaren in Focus,* 241.

5

Assessment of the Emergents' Thought, Part 2

Having considered the emergents' depiction of the Greco-Roman narrative and several issues with it, now I will look at two more major claims: that in the Bible, we see evolving interpretations of God's character, and that everything is interpretation.

The Bible and its Evolving Interpretations of God's Character

McLaren claims that we have distorted the Bible's story line by reading it "backwards" through the lens of the Greco-Roman narrative, and that instead if we read it "forwards," through the lens of his self-styled "Jewish" narrative, we will come to a very different understanding of its story line. Of course, Pagitt too thinks we have distorted the gospel by reading it through the lens of a Greco-Roman framing story. So, let's read the Bible forward, to see what we find, and in that process, let's examine McLaren's version of the "Jewish" story, to see to what extent we should accept it. Let us see if his story of the God of Abraham, Isaac, Jacob, David, the prophets, and Jesus is the one portrayed by a faithful, forward reading.

Genesis, Exodus, Isaiah, and Our Holy, Loving God

To begin, McLaren is right that in Genesis, creation is not portrayed as some stale, sterile, utterly static Platonic realm of essences. It is not a perfect world in *that* sense; rather, it is a good creation, and all that God has made is good. Yes, creation takes place in stages (days one to six), such that (clearly, obviously) there is room for reproduction, relationships, and stories to be told about these, even from the beginning to the end. And, God is intimately involved with his creation, in particular with Adam and Eve, as he walks in the garden with them, without fear on their part.

But just because there is room for stories in the beginning, before the fall, it does not mean that there had to be an ontological shift from a perfect Platonic state to story (McLaren's Greco-Romanized version of the fall). Not at all; there is room for story from the get-go because God has made his creation and humans, in particular, with the abilities to grow and develop in their qualities (and, for us, as image-bearers). This fits with our being made as a deep unity of body and soul, as Aristotle realized. He knew that there is no change whatsoever (which would apply even in a prelapsarian world[1]) without sameness, which requires essences.

Now, McLaren depicts God's reaction to the sin by Adam and Eve as not giving (explicitly, at least) "a furious promise of eternal condemnation."[2] Instead, he sees it as a coming-of-age story, much like a father with a daughter who has come of age, yet acts foolishly with the gift of a new car.[3] The father gave her proper instruction and guidelines for safe driving, yet she foolishly crashed the car. He responds with a stern lecture, then a second, "starter" car. Yet again, she acts foolishly and needs to be rescued. Each time, he doesn't allow her full privileges, but still provides an alternative, such as a bicycle. And even when she crashes again and breaks her arm, he cares for her by rushing her to the hospital. The father doesn't disown or condemn her.

Similarly, in Genesis, God repeatedly and "patiently bears with a rebellious and foolish humanity."[4] So this is what McLaren's God is like: though we act foolishly with new opportunities and freedoms, God does not disown us because we are in his "family," so to speak. This corresponds with Bell's claim that *God has reconciled everyone to himself*. He cares for us when we get harmed (by ourselves or others) and need rescuing. Yet, he will not let

---

1. Prelapsarian simply refers to creation before the fall.

2. McLaren, *A New Kind of Christianity*, 48.

3. To be explicit, McLaren does not think the story of the fall should be read literally. See McLaren, *A New Kind of Christianity*, 48.

4. McLaren, *A New Kind of Christianity*, 49.

our freedoms run wild; he restricts what we can do sometimes by limiting our freedoms and letting natural consequences take their effect, so we learn and grow.

So, in this story, as humanity develops socioeconomically and technologically, often faster than morally, we "fall" into sin, not just personally but also by these social, or group, dynamics. It is as we develop too fast that we can fall into all sorts of heinous group sins, ones we might never conceive as possible as individuals (for example, how so much of Germany was swept up in the Nazis' agenda). It is the social dynamic of empire-building, for instance, that grieves God's heart, whether in the case of the Egyptians, Babylonians, Solomon's kingdom, or the colonialism of Western countries, including the United States.

Both Jones and McLaren also appeal to René Girard's use of mimetic desire to help explain sin. As Jones puts it, mimetic desire "is not bad; it is a deep, anthropological truth, rooted in our evolutionary history."[5] But, that desire "inevitably leads to violence. Exhibit A: Cain and Abel."[6]

Is this a faithful telling of the biblical authors' understanding of sin? While I will try to sketch such a view in more detail in the last chapter, here I will observe that biblical authors consistently portray the heart as more deceitful than all else and desperately sick (Jer 17:9). As depicted in Genesis 3, but then reiterated and lived out over and over again in other passages (and even our own lives, I might add), our default heart-attitude is to usurp God, to take his place and be like God ourselves, defining good and evil, right and wrong (Gen 3:5). Our need is not a mere moral transformation, because we have hearts that are bent on dethroning God, however subtly we may try to do that.

But, McLaren observes that God does not react by killing Adam and Eve, or Cain. Though they do die eventually, God is gracious and compassionate to them, unlike Theos would have been. Instead, Genesis presents a story about "the downside of 'progress'"; it is a story about God's faithfulness in spite of our folly and irresponsibility.[7] In it, people intend evil, yet God creatively and nonviolently overcomes evil with good. McLaren cites Joseph's story as a prime example, in which he overcomes the evil of his brothers by creating a good outcome.

This appeal to Joseph's life allows McLaren to claim that we are truly free, that the future is unscripted, so that God does not exhaustively

---

5. Jones, *A Better Atonement*, locations 533–35. For Girard on mimetic desire, see Girard, *Things Hidden*.

6. Jones, *A Better Atonement*, locations 533–35.

7. McLaren, *A New Kind of Christianity*, 54.

determine the future. Now, I realize that there is room for debate between well-meaning believers who affirm a high view of Scripture, yet at the same time hold different views about God's sovereignty and our freedom. McLaren has major bones to pick with *exhaustive determinists*, on whose view God is causally responsible for every event. On that view, we do not have true freedom in a libertarian sense. Yet, McLaren seems to swing to the opposite stance, that we are free and the future is genuinely open, so that we can coauthor with God the future's story.[8] Now, proponents of open theism still affirm that God is omniscient, yet some future events are unknowable in principle, even to God, such as the freely chosen acts by free creatures (e.g., us).

Yet, McLaren does not address another position, known as *middle knowledge*, in which God knows not only all future free actions that *will* be made by his creatures—he also knows all *possible* actions they might take in any situation they *might* face, even if they don't make a particular choice. In their decision-making, they are free in a libertarian sense and responsible; yet, God is also sovereign and omniscient, and he works all things together for good for those who love him (Rom 8:28). This position has been defended extensively by William Lane Craig and others, so that McLaren *should* consider it in his deliberations and recommendations.[9]

Now, it is interesting when McLaren shifts to a discussion of Exodus, and how God sides with the oppressed against the oppressors, that he discusses some of the plagues the text says God sent on Egypt. Instead of God acting coercively or violently, McLaren claims that the "miracle" of the Nile turning to blood was more likely the result of a red tide, which turned the color of the water to red.[10] His telling of the plague that killed the firstborn

---

8. Sometime I wonder, though, for McLaren just how much of an active agent God is. He keeps emphasizing the importance of *our* working to extend the kingdom. If we fail, e.g., in preserving the environment, then God's dream for his "sacred ecosystem" might fail after all. Sometimes I get the impression from McLaren that God is weak and really needs us to do his work, or that he is cheering us on toward the fulfillment of his dream, yet he is dependent upon us to realize it. Perhaps McLaren can come across with that view because he does not want God to be forcing his story on creation. Still, by his emphasis upon our work to extend the kingdom, sometimes McLaren reminds me of postmillenialists, in that they seem to share that same emphasis on *our* bringing in the kingdom.

9. For example, see Craig, "God Directs All Things." In addition, there is a third position on free will, also known as soft determinism, or compatibilism. McLaren does not distinguish hard determinism from the softer variety, which at least tries to preserve free will, but in a different sense than on the libertarian view. For more, see Burson, *Brian McLaren in Focus,* 215–18, as well as Moreland and Craig, *Philosophical Foundations,* 267–83.

10. Burson nuances McLaren's view about miracles. McLaren does not try to

says nothing about God's instrumentality behind it. Remarkably, then, while he claims correctly that God was amazingly patient with Pharaoh, nonetheless he didn't force Pharaoh to comply.[11] I think this is true in the sense that God gave Pharaoh (and us) free will and does not exhaustively determine all events; otherwise, it is hard to me to see how God would not ultimately be the author of evil. Exodus says that, yes, God hardened Pharaoh's heart, but also that Pharaoh hardened his own heart (for instance, 9:34) and was responsible for that.

Nevertheless, McLaren goes further, claiming that God works *only* "indirectly," through people (Moses, Aaron) or natural phenomena. Thus, "the so-called supernatural . . . seems remarkably natural."[12] This telling of the story is not what the text says, and while McLaren could reply that he does not take this story literally, still, the text does ascribe these actions to God, and not merely as the course of natural events. The Egyptians had been murdering the male Hebrew babies, besides treating the Hebrews harshly as slaves. So the text uses language to say that God pronounces judgment upon Pharaoh and Egypt in many ways and places; for instance, the Nile's water turning into blood by his command (7:17), and his command of the frogs (8:2), gnats (which the magicians could not duplicate, 8:17–19), and many other plagues.

It is amazing then that McLaren does not even address the apparent problems for his view in the Passover story. God requires each household amongst the Israelites to slaughter a lamb (a violent act, to be sure) as a substitute for them and wipe its blood over their doorposts. The story says that when God sees the blood, *he* will pass over the household, "so no plague will befall you to destroy you when I strike the land of Egypt" (11:13). It is God who says *he* kills any who are not covered by the substitute's blood, and this is what delivers the crushing blow to Pharaoh, so that he lets Israel go.

But then, at the crossing of the Red Sea, the text says that God used *his* great power against the Egyptian army and Pharaoh (14:31) to destroy them in the Red Sea. And the examples continue to multiply. Here is just a brief sampling: the destruction (by God's hand or command) of Israelites who were disobedient, such as with the worship of the golden calf (Exod 32); the forging of a nation through God's commanding his holiness code (Leviticus), which involved the sacrificial system and the death of a multitude of animals; God's sending Jehu via Elisha to destroy the house of Ahab from

demythologize miraculous events in Scripture, nor does he deny their existence. He believes in Christ's resurrection. At the same time, he does not try to emphasize miracles. See Burson, *Brian McLaren in Focus,* 167–68.

11. McLaren, *A New Kind of Christianity,* 58.

12. McLaren, *A New Kind of Christianity,* 58.

Israel (2 Kgs 9:1–10), who had done "more to provoke the LORD God of Israel than all the kings of Israel who were before him"(1 Kgs 16:33); God's sending the Assyrians to remove Israel from their land due to their deep sin (2 Kgs 17:18, 22–23); and his sending the Babylonians to destroy Judah and send it into captivity (2 Kgs 21:10–15).

And, since McLaren specifically mentions the God of David as one who fits his faithful, forward reading, we should not forget that the texts say God told David to attack and smite the Philistines (1 Sam 23:2, and again in 2 Sam 5:23–25). David also experienced God's striking down of Uzzah for his irreverence, who touched the ark of God (2 Sam 6:6–7), and as a result, David, a man who knew God intimately, was angry and even afraid of God. Even David says that God executed vengeance for him on his enemies (2 Sam 22:48). He also saw God inflict a pestilence on Israel for his sin (2 Sam 24:1, 10, 15–17; cf. 1 Chr 21:1, where the author identifies Satan as the one who incited David to sin). Like the previously mentioned examples, these texts depict God as acting violently.

Now, McLaren focuses on the good news of the prophets of a peaceable kingdom, yet repeatedly in the texts that promised hope is couched clearly in the context of his *judgment* upon Israel and Judah. Consider McLaren's focus on the prophet Isaiah. In chapter 2, Isaiah writes of that future vision, in which people will hammer their swords into plowshares (v. 4). Yet, starting in v. 12, a stinging message of judgment and the coming terror of the Lord are prominent. Indeed, a theme running through Isaiah 1—8 (at least) is God's holiness, and because of the peoples' repeated, deep-seated rebellion, God will rise up and put them in dread of him: "It is the LORD of hosts whom you should regard as holy. And He shall be your fear, and He shall be your dread" (8:13). Isaiah also describes his vision of the Lord as holy, holy, holy, but he therefore sees himself as unclean and ruined. Yet God is merciful and provides atonement for his sin (6:1–7). God also declares that he has sent Assyria against Israel, literally, to "make them a trampled place" (Isa 10:6). The same applies to his call on Babylon to do his bidding against Judah, for it is the instrument "of His indignation, to destroy the whole land" (Isa 13:5).

The other prophets write similarly. Jeremiah weeps at the revelation of God's judgment upon his sinful people. Daniel is undone by some of the revelations he receives, both of how God will use various enemies and the destruction they will wreak. Amos reveals God's wrath against the horrific acts by Israel, Judah, and their surrounding nations. Though God declares through Micah that he requires us to do justice, love mercy, and walk humbly with him (6:8), that passage immediately continues to declare God's deep displeasure with injustice, lying, and deceit, so that he "will make you sick, striking you down, desolating you because of your sins" (6:13).

So, despite McLaren's claims about the "Jewish" story from his "forward" reading of the Bible, it does not seem to fit with the evidently consistent telling by many biblical authors over many years (and many social settings). What then might be a more faithful, forward telling of the Bible's story line? It seems to me that right from the beginning of Genesis and even to the end of Revelation, *God's great desire is to dwell with us, to live amongst us and be our God.* In Genesis, God creates Adam and Eve to enjoy his presence and experience intimate fellowship with him in the garden. This experience of his presence is much more than a cognitive assent to God being present everywhere, due to his omnipresence. Instead, it is a lived experience of intimacy with him being with them. But due to their sin, God must cast them out of the garden, away from his presence.

Through Abraham, God will bless all the families of the earth, and this will be by their common trust in God, like Abraham the believer (Gen 12:3; compare Paul in Rom 4:9–16). So God is making a people, and he shows us again through the lives of Abraham, Isaac, Jacob, and Joseph that he would be intimate with them. Yet, this God would not only turn evil actions and intentions for good for those who love him (e.g., Joseph), would but also punish evildoers (e.g., Gen 18:20 and chapter 19, with the destruction of Sodom and Gomorrah).

When God calls Moses from the burning bush, we get a clear statement about God's holiness, that Moses needed to humble himself and remove his sandals, for he was on holy ground (Exod 3:5). God makes them a nation when he delivers Israel from Egypt, and he does so through the Passover. It is noteworthy that God requires them to take an unblemished male lamb to be sacrificed, and its blood was to be painted above their doorposts, so that God would not destroy them along with the Egyptians (Exod 12:13). But, why would the text even say that God would consider destroying Israel, too, who had been the oppressed ones? Why not just Egypt?

The feast of unleavened bread helps answer this. It is a feast to be celebrated at the same time, in which all leaven shall be removed from their households for seven days. This is a feast that pictures the need to remove sin from our lives, as Paul explains in 1 Corinthians 5:6–8, and thereby be holy people, for God is holy. How that happens is through the sacrifice of Christ our Passover lamb. Peter echoes this, saying that he is a spotless and unblemished lamb (1 Pet 1:19).

The Passover helps depict a key principle: that which is redeemed by God belongs to him, and the Israelites were redeemed by the life of a substitute, the lamb that was sacrificed in the peoples' stead (an early indication of a penal substitutionary view of atonement). Similarly, after God gave the Ten Commandments and formed a covenant with Israel, and the people ratified it (Exod 24), God had Moses, Aaron, Nadab, Abihu, and seventy elders go up to Mount Sinai and eat in his presence, such that they "beheld God [which itself is amazing!], and they ate and drank" (24:11). God's plan continues to bring a people to himself and have fellowship with them.

But, before they even leave Mount Sinai, the people rebel (again) against God, even though they have seen his awesome acts to deliver them from Egypt, his daily provision of manna for food, and his miraculous provision of water. When they impatiently confront Aaron to make them a god (and he then makes the golden calf), they proceed to engage in a sexual orgy, which was an imitation of the acts of their "god"—a bull, which was a symbol of fertility and power. Now, Aaron attaches God's name to the idol (Exod 34:4), thereby using God's name in vain. They worship an image that he made, although they were told explicitly not to do any such thing. And, they were not to have any other gods before him; yet, here they clearly violated that commandment.

Why does God pronounce judgment and then act to slay those who sinned? The text says it is because they have "corrupted themselves," "turned aside" from God's commands, and worshipped a false god of their own making. Their deep, spiritual unfaithfulness offended a holy God. And without Moses' intervention as a mediator, he would have destroyed them. Even Moses offers himself as a substitute for them, to die that their sin may be covered (Exod 32:32).

This is similar to the Levitical system of sacrificial offerings, which were deeply embedded in Jewish culture, from the time Israel became a nation all the way up to (and including) Jesus' time. As clear acts of violence, many offerings required the death of animals for the people. The arrangements and procedures for the sacrifices in the tabernacle required separation and *distance* from a holy God.

However, at the same time, they provided a way for a holy God to dwell in the midst of sinful people. People could bring their offerings to the entrance of the tent of meeting, but the priests would then need to take a sacrificed animal's blood and sprinkle it on the altar (Lev 17:1–6), and the priests also had to offer sacrifices for their own guilt and sin. The priests could enter the outer part of the tabernacle (the holy place). But only the high priest could enter the most holy place (the "holy of holies," which was veiled off and separated from the rest of the tabernacle) once a year, going into the presence of God, and only under the conditions that God prescribed, with a substitute offering of blood to atone for his sins and those of the people (Heb 9:7). Even so, despite this sense of distance and separation from him due to their sin, God had Israel set up the tabernacle right in the midst of the tribes. Why? So, out of his love, our holy God could dwell in the midst of Israel, his people. There is no inconsistency here, unlike what Pagitt suggests, between a Hebrew "love" God and a "blood" God.

That system required a mediator (the priests) between the people and God. It also required the blood of animal substitutes (Lev 17:10–11) on the peoples' behalf. But Jeremiah looked forward to a time when God would *not just cover over* their sins temporarily, as with the Levitical offerings, which had to be offered repeatedly. He would make a better, new covenant, in which he would write his laws on their hearts, and they would be his people, which is the same objective as we have seen before. And, he would forgive their sin and *not remember it any more* (Jer 31:31–34). So when the fullness of time came and God sent forth his Messiah, John says that Jesus, the Word, "became flesh and dwelt among us" (John 1:14). Another way to translate "dwelt" is "tabernacled," such that we might say today he "moved into our neighborhood." In John 14:21, Jesus expounds on this idea, that those who have his commands and keep them are the ones who truly love him. They also shall be loved by his Father, and he and the Father shall come to them and make their dwelling with them. And those who abide in him will have the presence of his Spirit living, or dwelling, in them, making them a temple (or tabernacle) of the living God (John 14:16–17; 1 Cor 3:16).[13]

Here we have this overarching theme repeated again: God seeks out a people to be his own, to dwell among them and be their God, and they his people. It is repeated and extended at the end of the Bible, in Revelation 21: "Behold, the tabernacle of God is among men, and He shall dwell among them, and they shall be His people, and God Himself shall be among them, and He shall wipe away every tear from their eyes; and there shall no longer be any death; there shall no longer be any mourning, or crying, or pain; the first things have passed away" (Rev 21:3–4).

Throughout the Bible, then, we have these big-picture themes, of God seeking out a people to be his own. Yet, that cannot take place on any terms other than his, for he will not accept worship of false gods, nor tolerate the making of images of himself. Why? Is he just intolerant or prone to fits of rage, like McLaren's Theos? *No; it is because while God is love and is good, he also is holy*, which works hand-in-hand with his goodness. When God gives his own self-description to Moses, who had found favor in God's sight, he uses the following language: "The LORD, the LORD God, compassionate and gracious, slow to anger, and abounding in loving-kindness and truth; who

13. Compare also 1 Corinthians 6:19–20, which indicates that God owns the believers' bodies, so that they should glorify him with their bodies—a highly significant statement that our bodies matter to God and thus should to us as well.

keeps loving-kindness for thousands, who forgives iniquity, transgression and sin; yet He will by no means leave the guilty unpunished . . ." (Exod 34:6–7).

Those verses portray a God like the One McLaren depicts, except for the last clause: the God of Exodus (and, I'd argue, throughout the Bible) will by no means leave the guilty unpunished. This is because God is purely holy and just, and to be purely good, God has to be truly holy. Otherwise, he could allow evil to be in his presence and go unaddressed. But that is not the God we see portrayed in the tabernacle worship; in the prophets (e.g., Isa 6:3–7); in David, who had a healthy "fear" of (reverence and awe for) God; and Moses, too, whom the author of Hebrews tells us was full of fear and trembling at God's awesome display on Mount Sinai (Deut 9:19; cf. Heb 12:20–21). Indeed, God's purpose in coming down on the mountain with fire, lightning, and earthquakes was to make the people revere him (see Exod 19).

And, lest we forget, there is a consistent pattern between the Old and New Testaments in recognizing God as a *consuming fire*. Having just drawn all the parallels between the Levitical and Mosaic system and sacrifices with Christ's superiority (especially as high priest and in his sacrifice), the writer of Hebrews goes on to remind his mainly *Jewish* readers that, just as they had learned in a *truly faithful* telling of the biblical story, God still is a consuming fire, just as he was on Sinai (Heb 12:29; cf. Deut 4:24, 9:3; Isa 33:14).

The "Jewish story" includes much prophecy about the Messiah, so we should take its content into account, too. Zechariah wrote that "they shall look on Him whom they pierced" (Zech 12:10, quoted in John 19:37). He was to have his hands and feet pierced (Ps 22:16), and he would feel forsaken by God (v. 1; cf. Mark 15:14). He was to be a suffering servant, as Isaiah foretold, to be pierced through for our transgressions (Isa 53:5), for *God* would cause the iniquity of us all to fall on him (v. 6). He would render himself a guilt offering (v. 10), and he bore the sin of many (v. 12). As a guilt offering, the death of a ram was required in place of the worshipper, who unintentionally sinned by doing what was forbidden in any of the Lord's commands (see Lev 5:14–19). So here, too, Christ, as our guilt offering, had to die in our place.

What then should we think? To me, this seems to be a more faithful rendering of the "Jewish" story in the Bible. *McLaren's telling of the "Jewish" narrative from the Old Testament reveals a highly selective reading, choosing to bring certain emphases to light while ignoring or dismissing others, in particular that God must punish sin, due to his being holy.* Indeed, McLaren's interpretation seems to privilege a controlling belief that is *not* to be found in the story's many texts, that God cannot be violent. And this core position then serves to guide how he interprets the Bible.

Yet, perhaps he might reply that all I have done is appeal to what the Bible says. But, as he has indicated, he does not take the Bible to be inerrant Scripture, including a record of literal history in all its narrations (such as the garden of Eden). Rather, it is a series of human interpretations that witness to the God whose character we see emerging over time. Yet, my point is that there is not an evolution of views about God's character in Scripture; instead, there is a highly consistent portrait of God's character, right from the start, and it is *not* the one privileged by McLaren. While we do see developments in terms of the degree of revelation that God is giving to humans ("progressive revelation"), we do not see an evolving series of views of God's character. Also, it seems clear that *God's requirement of sacrifices was not an evolutionary development.*

So far, I have focused on problems with McLaren's claims about a faithful, forward reading of the Bible, and the kind of God that reveals. Contrary to his claims (or Pagitt's), God is depicted therein as One who must punish sin, and it is not due to his anger management problems. Rather, he is morally perfect (though not a static, unable-to-be-personal Being), and thus he must judge sin. But there are other inferences we might surface from a more philosophical assessment of McLaren's views, as well as that of Jones in particular.

An Arbitrary God? Philosophical Explorations

As before, so here, too, it seems there are three "strands" involved in our authors' thought:

1. The priority is on living in relationships; orthopraxis is the new given.

2. God essentially is both loving and good, and love is essential to good relationships.

3. Violence (e.g., with punishment of sin) is incompatible with God's character as good and loving, and with good relationships and love.

Let us begin by considering the third strand, McLaren's ethical principle that violence, coercion, and cruelty are wrong, period. His position reminds me of the *logical problem of evil*, as used by atheists. I wonder if McLaren's view of God might succumb to this argument. The argument goes something like this, directed against the "O-3" God of Christianity:

1. If God is all powerful (*omnipotent*), he *could destroy* evil.

2. If he is all knowing (*omniscient*), he *would know how* to do this.

3. If he is all good (*omnibenevolent*), he *would deal* with evil.

4. But, evil exists.

5. Therefore, the O-3 God (the God of Christianity) does not exist.

Now, I think McLaren could reply that God, as he understands him, could meet the requirements of dealing with the logical problem of evil. Indeed, he has dealt with evil by Jesus' "absorbing" it into himself and then forgiving and forgetting it. And, though McLaren may not like the language of God's "destroying" evil, he could reply that God will *overcome* evil through his creative means to work out all things for good. Of course, Alvin Plantinga has offered a crucial rebuttal against the logical problem of evil, so it need not be a defeater of belief for the Christian.[14] But, I think we can extend the logical problem of evil for McLaren's view by explicitly introducing the attributes of God's justice and holiness: *if God is truly just and holy, he would hate evil and exact punishment for it.* We then come to a crucial issue: while McLaren explicitly is deeply concerned (and *rightly* so) about God's goodness and justice being realized on earth as it is in heaven, he does not seem to have a view of God that can sustain his *character* as being just and good. Why? My colleague Kevin Lewis puts it this way: if God hates sin necessarily, he necessarily will punish it. So, if punishment is optional for God, it is grounded in the operation of his will, not his nature of being absolutely holy.[15]

McLaren cannot choose the option that God's attribute of holiness is absolute, for that entails his acting retributively in justice. So, if God can choose not to punish sin (as McLaren apparently must maintain, and as Jones says), this seems to leaves us with two dismal, even disastrous options. On the one hand, God would be defective in his attributes of holiness and justice because, by his own nature, he would not necessarily be repulsed by evil. If so, then God could allow evil into his presence and tolerate it. But that view is anything but the biblical view of God. John says God not only is love (1 John 4:8), but also light, in whom there is no darkness at all (1 John 1:5). If sin could be present in God, then that would be a view that is flatly contradictory to Scripture. Moreover, it would make God unworthy of our worship and unable to save us from our sin.

14. For example, see his *God, Freedom, and Evil.* Briefly, Plantinga's defense tries to show that God's existence is not logically incompatible with evil. Only *free* agents can do moral good, but genuine freedom requires the possibility of their doing what is morally wrong. So, even God cannot create free moral agents who never *could* do wrong.

15. E-mail correspondence with Kevin Lewis, November 9, 2009.

On the other hand, if God can choose not to punish sin, then he would punish sin simply due to his own willing that to be right, rather than due to his character traits of justice and holiness necessitating that. If that were so, then we have arbitrariness in God's own ethical commands and requirements and even his character, which McLaren seems to presuppose to *not* be arbitrary. This situation surfaces the *Euthyphro dilemma*, an objection first developed by Plato and often used by atheists against Christians, who often appeal to divine command ethics. The dilemma can be phrased in terms of two "horns": *Is something good because God commands it, or does God command it because it is good?*

Take the first horn: If something is right *because* God commands it, then his commanding it *makes* it right. It would not be right in and of itself. Or, consider the second horn: If God commands it because it is right, then God seems subject to some external moral standards he must consult before commanding anything. These moral standards would exist apart from God's creative activity. Moreover, God's commanding something would seem redundant and unnecessary. If so, why should God bother to issue a commandment? Would we not know it already?

Now, the Euthyphro dilemma has been addressed in a number of places, so here I will mention only a few lines of reply. According to the first horn, theoretically God could command something that seems clearly wrong to us. Yet, because God commanded it, that would make it right. For instance, God could command people to fly airplanes into the infidel's buildings, and that command would make that act right. This view has been called *ethical voluntarism,* or *theistic subjectivism*—something is right simply because God willed it to be so. The concern here is that the reason why something would be morally right is arbitrary, depending on whatever God happens to will. But Christians have replied appropriately that God is not arbitrary in his ethical commands; rather, they are willed because they accord with his perfectly good character, and *that* is the basis for why they are right.[16]

What then can we say to the second horn? Just because God commands what is right, it does not follow that there is some external moral standard apart from God. God simply commands that which is in accordance with his perfectly good character. And, it does not follow that we automatically would *know* what would be right apart from God's commands. Even with God's character being clearly revealed through creation, people can suppress that knowledge (see Rom 1:18–20). Furthermore, though I think all

16. For more treatment of this dilemma, especially the first horn, see Alston, "What Euthyphro Should Have Said," 284. Alston acknowledges that he is following and developing the work of Robert Adams.

people know that murder is wrong, they may fail to see certain cases as incidents of murder. The Sawi people of whom Don Richardson wrote come to mind; they invited neighboring tribes for dinner, but after they fattened them up, they would slaughter and eat their guests! They did not see that behavior as wrong, but I still suspect that if, say, a Sawi man decided to kill another Sawi and take his wife as his own, the rest of the Sawi would see that act as wrong because it is an example of murder.[17]

So, in general, Christians have good answers to both horns of the Euthyphro dilemma.[18] But what about McLaren's views? Since God would base his ethical requirements in his willing something to be moral, rather than on the basis of his character, there is no real reason why God could not change his mind and will that which seems clearly wrong to us (or even to McLaren). In that case, suppose God willed that it is moral to send people to hell for eternity; if so, who would McLaren be to complain? He seems left with a God who is arbitrary. McLaren has no resort to appealing to God's essential nature as a way out of the Euthyphro dilemma.

Thus, it seems obvious that McLaren has privileged a certain interpretive scheme for reading the whole of Scripture, one that precludes even his reading of Christ's second coming in Revelation as being literally in power and justice. Also, he must reinterpret (or reject perhaps as erroneous?) many Old Testament passages that speak, for instance, of God's killing those priests who do not revere him in their offerings (like Hophni and Phinehas), or his punishing Israel, Judah, and Gentile nations for their sin. McLaren says his basis for interpreting Jesus' second coming and these kinds of passages is that "I believe Jesus is the ultimate revelation of God . . . so I don't form my idea of God from Deuteronomy 7, etc., and then fit Jesus into it.[19] I form my view of God from Jesus, arising from within the Jewish narrative."[20]

But, is this a fair reading of Scripture? I do not think so. I already have touched on reasons for my belief, including that the Jewish narrative into which Jesus was born included the long history of the slaughter of animals that were sacrificed as offerings. Moreover, while McLaren is right to (1) try to situate and interpret Jesus' words and the Gospels within their historical contexts, and (2) appeal to God's revelation in Jesus as ultimate, nonetheless we should pay attention to more of what Jesus himself taught. For instance, Jesus accepted the Law and the Prophets as Scripture. He said that Scripture

17. See Richardson's *Peace Child*.

18. See also my *In Search of Moral Knowledge*, ch. 1.

19. In Deuteronomy 7, God tells Israel that when he brings them into the promised land, they are to utterly destroy the nations currently therein because otherwise they will turn the Israelites' hearts away to other gods.

20. E-mail correspondence from McLaren, November 10, 2009.

cannot be broken, and that not one jot or tittle of the Law would pass away until all is accomplished (Matt 5:17–18). He also taught with authority, for example, in the Sermon on the Mount. Though they had heard it said, *he* gave the authoritative teaching and interpretation of the Law (e.g., Matt 5:21). And, he said he is Lord of the Sabbath (Mark 2:28). Now, God gave the commands and instituted the Sabbath, so he is indicating that he is the Lord who gave that Scripture.

Therefore, what did he affirm (or at least imply) regarding violence and coercion? Since he affirmed the Old Testament writings by his repeated appeals to its books as authoritative, we can look at what it teaches about God's use of violence and coercion. We have already touched on many examples, such as how God executes justice upon individuals and nations, and that the Law is full of examples of God requiring animal sacrifices. God brought plagues, even upon the Israelites, due to their sin. He pronounced punishment upon Gentile nations for their violence (e.g., Amos 1, 2). And, God prophesied and brought Babylon against Judah, so it would execute his wrath upon his people.

Even though it is apocalyptic literature, John still quotes Jesus in Revelation as saying in similar terms to the church in Thyatira that he will cast Jezebel on a bed of sickness, and that he will kill her children, so that "the churches will know that I am He who searches the minds and hearts" (2:23). But even in the Gospels, Jesus shows and speaks of violence. His cleansing of the temple of the money changers seems to be an act of violent fury, for zeal for his Father's house consumed him. And, when he says to them that it is written that "My house shall be called a house of prayer for all the nations," but "you have made it a robbers' den," he seems to be shouting this at them with fury (Mark 11:15–18).

Also, in many parables, he taught that God would use violence toward his enemies. In the parable of the marriage feast (Matt 22:1–14), he compares the kingdom of heaven to a king who punishes one who was improperly dressed at this feast (which seems to be a metaphor for being clothed in one's own sin; compare Zech 3:1–5). The same kind of fate awaits the worthless slave in the parable of the talents (Matt 25:14–30).

So far in this section I have focused on McLaren's view of God. But what about Jones? Jones uses the Orthodox position, that God is essentially love, to try to give room for God to be just and yet not have to punish sin. He claims that due to his view of God's freedom, God can do whatever he wants. Thus, God could forgive our sins in whatever way God would choose, such as requiring us to do penance; shrugging off our sins as "youthful exuberance" or old foolishness; winking at them; or anything, even if it seems to us to be totally unrelated to our sin; or nothing at all.

Here, it should be clear that Jones's view of God ends up like McLaren's; God is arbitrary in his justice. Nor must it be the case, as Jones suggests, that without such freedom, God might be subject to some external standard of morality.[21] The answer Christians have given to that claim has been that his character is the standard for morality.[22]

But this contention, that God's justice is not based in his character, but in his will, needs to be pressed even more. For, unlike McLaren, Pagitt, Jones, or Bell seem to realize, *such a God is not only not worthy of worship; this God is dangerous.* This is a "God" who could explode, for there are no intrinsic restraints on what he wills as justice. *How ironic, then, that the very kind of God they want us to reconceive ends up being like One from whom they recoil.* For their God is One who could blow up in unquenchable rage, abuse innocent victims, and needs therapy. Such a "God" isn't safe to be intimate with, because he isn't trustworthy.

The Partnership between Justice and Love

But, couldn't they reply that God's being love sets an intrinsic constraint on what he'd will as just? You would hope so, but that seems to apply only if God has the attribute (as an essential character trait) of being just. Moreover, if God is not intrinsically just, as part of his very nature, but just a matter of his will, then is God truly loving (even as to his nature)?

Love and justice are partners. Love *protects* what is good and cared for. A few years ago, while my daughter was still young, she and two of her close friends, their mom, and my wife and I held a joint yard sale. After it was over, we all were very tired, and we were trying to clean up. My daughter helped by bringing things to one of her friends. But then she just left them with her, telling *her* to pack them all up. Now, that didn't make her friend too happy, to say the least. So, we needed to help correct our daughter, to help her see that this was not a loving thing to do to her friend. Plus, she offended her friend, so she needed to apologize for her actions, to *make things right* with her and clear the air between them. That's what justice required, and it was also the loving thing to do. It was the loving thing to correct our daughter and help her see the need to make things right by giving to her friend what was due her—an apology and a change in my daughter's behavior.

God despises sin because it is an affront to his holiness, and also because it steals us away from loving him. God had Hosea take a harlot as his wife, as a sign to Israel how God was her husband, yet she had been faithless

21. Jones, *A Better Atonement*, locations 621–24.

22. See more in chapter 1 in my *In Search of Moral Knowledge*.

to him. A husband who loves his wife will guard their relationship with a godly jealousy. If he sees that someone else is trying to lure her heart away, he will step up and intervene for her sake and the sake of their relationship. If I see that someone is trying to seduce my daughter into sexual immorality, drugs, or ideas that will harm her (like, her body has to reflect a particular image, or else she won't really be lovable), I am going to protect her because I love her. Likewise, Scripture describes God as a jealous God in this same sense—he is jealous for us, his beloved, and he will intervene to protect his beloved from seductions, because they are not good for us.

We cannot separate God's love from his justice, properly understood. God cannot perform an action that is just *and yet* unloving, or loving *and yet* unjust; to do so would violate his absolutely good moral character. Justice requires more than just a fair distribution of goods and services (distributive justice). It also requires that God repays each *according to his or her due*, so that justice is met. And that standard of justice is not some abstraction; rather, it is God's own character that is just and thus the benchmark for justice. So, God executes his justice in proper proportion to the offense. He is perfect, complete (not lacking) in his justice, just as he is in his love. If we borrow Aristotle's virtue theory, we can see then that for God to be perfect in his justice, he will always be appropriate in his response to injustices, never extreme by shrinking back from proper punishment or discipline, as though he were *deficient* in the virtue of justice, as Aristotle would have said.[23] Nor would God be extreme by bursting into uncontrollable rage (as though he were *excessive* in justice—a vice, to be sure!).[24] Deuteronomy 32:4 says it well: "The "Rock! His work is perfect, for all His ways are just; a God of faithfulness and without injustice, righteous and upright is He."

Yet, today, many people have had their sense of justice deeply distorted. Consider how a Canadian appeals court overturned a mother's murder conviction for strangling her newborn infant:

> An Alberta judge has let a woman who strangled her newborn
> son walk free by arguing that Canada's absence of a law on

23. Compare David's lack of punishing his son Amnon for his rape of Tamar, or his son Absalom for his murder of Amnon, and the disasters that resulted (see 2 Sam 13–19).

24. Bell is right; it is hard to see how we could love a God like that. I had the fear that unless I had my life all under control, I might slip and have an accident for which my dad might flare up in sudden anger and slap me—which he did one time, for a minor accident I had in the yard. I have had to work hard emotionally to separate the fear I had as a child toward my dad (who otherwise was quite loving) from God, upon whom I projected that same fear—only I knew he is all powerful, so my fears were magnified with him.

abortion signals that Canadians "sympathize" with the mother

. . . .

Katrina Effert of Wetaskiwin, Alberta gave birth secretly in her parents' downstairs bathroom on April 13, 2005, and then later strangled the newborn and threw his body over a fence. She was 19 at the time.

She has been found guilty of second-degree murder by two juries, but both times the judgment was thrown out by the appeals court. In May, the Alberta Court of Appeal overturned her 2009 murder conviction and replaced it with the lesser charge of infanticide.

On Friday, Effert got a three-year suspended sentence from Justice Joanne Veit of the Alberta Court of Queen's Bench. As a result, she was able to walk out of court, though she will have to abide by certain conditions.

According to Justice Veit, Canada's lack of an abortion law indicates that "while many Canadians undoubtedly view abortion as a less than ideal solution to unprotected sex and unwanted pregnancy, they generally understand, accept and sympathize with the onerous demands pregnancy and childbirth exact from mothers, especially mothers without support."

"Naturally, Canadians are grieved by an infant's death, especially at the hands of the infant's mother, but Canadians also grieve for the mother," she added.[25]

In this case, justice has become deeply twisted, so that the infant, who deserved to be protected, could be killed by the mother, who yet could go unpunished. Is that really the loving thing to do?

Yet, God is a God of justice, and if he did not repay those who do evil according to their deeds, then he would not be just. Being just in retribution does not mean, however, that God would act irrationally or vindictively. Rather, he repays according to the true standards of justice (which, again, is part of his very character, not an arbitrary, capricious will): "Do not be deceived, God is not mocked; for whatever a man sows, this he will also reap" (Gal 6:7; compare also Hos 12:2, Matt 16:27, Prov 24:12, and 2 Tim 4:14).

Miroslav Volf also connects God's punishment of evil and how that is required by his love:

My last resistance to the idea of God's wrath was a casualty of the war in the former Yugoslavia, the region from which I come. According to some estimates, 200,000 people were killed and over 3,000,000 were displaced. *My* villages and cities were

25. Craine, "Shock: No jail time for woman who strangled newborn."

destroyed, *my* people shelled day in and day out, some of them brutalized beyond imagination, and I could not imagine God not being angry. Or think of Rwanda of the last decade of the past century, where 800,000 people were hacked to death in one hundred days! How did God react to the carnage? By doting on the perpetrators in a grandparently fashion? By refusing to condemn the bloodbath but instead affirming the perpetrators' basic goodness? Wasn't God fiercely angry with them? Though I used to complain about the indecency of the idea of God's wrath, I came to think that I would have to rebel against a God who *wasn't* wrathful at the sight of the world's evil. God isn't wrathful in spite of being love. God is wrathful *because* God is love.[26]

And Volf is far from being alone in such claims. C. S. Lewis agrees. My colleague Clay Jones concurs, for "if humans are basically good, God's judgment seems barbaric but once we understand how evil we are, God's wrath, as Lewis put it, appears 'inevitable, a mere corollary from God's goodness.'"[27]

McLaren, Pagitt, Jones, and Bell all want a God who is just—who will restore relationships, and establish economic, environmental, and racial justice, but they cannot stomach a God who could exact repayment as appropriate punishment for wrongs committed, especially if done with violence. But in trying to separate God's love from God's being able to be retributively just, they end up separating out a necessary part of God's very character. Sometimes I get the impression that they (unwittingly, in effect) end up, as Volf says, with a doting grandparent for God.[28]

As a brief aside, but a related note, I wonder how God could be just in a retributive sense (punishment for wrongs) without using something that surely some people would consider violent. Even if God uses a means that is just against our wills, couldn't that be considered violent by some, especially those to whom it would be happening? Who gets to say, after all, what counts as being violent—especially if everything is our interpretation?

Still, I think there is more at work here than mere intellectual mistakes. Truth has been altered, and God the Father has ended up largely absent.

---

26. Volf, *Free of Charge*, 139.

27. Lewis, *The Problem of Pain*, 52, quoted in Jones, "We Don't Take Human Evil Seriously," 14. I am indebted to the research Jones has done in this paper, assembling and surveying a massive amount of primary sources. See also his book, *Why Does God Allow Evil?*

28. And so it is interesting and perhaps suggestive that they have much to write about Jesus, and some here or there about the importance of the Spirit, but not much at all about the Father.

Look at the following quotes from Bell and the tone in which they are offered. First, at the moment of our deaths,

> A loving heavenly father who will go to extraordinary lengths to have a relationship with them would, in the blink of an eye, become a cruel, mean, vicious tormenter who would ensure that they had no escape from an endless future of agony.
>
> . . . If there was an actual human dad who was that volatile, we would contact child protection services immediately.
>
> If God can switch gears like that, switch entire modes of being that quickly, *that raises a thousand questions about whether a being like this could ever be trusted, let alone be good.*[29]

According to Bell, *this* God that so many have been taught is unlovable, for God can be loving but then turn right around and be cruel.[30]

Or, consider these comments from McLaren about the view of God from the "Greco-Roman" story. First, we have seen his reaction to the flood account in Gen 7–8, that a god who intentionally would commit an "unparalleled genocide" through a flood is not deserving of worship.[31] Next, in regards to the second coming of Christ in Revelation, McLaren claims that Jesus is not coming back in vengeance as the "Divine Terminator," but instead in the power of love, who "promises mercy to those who strike him" (cf. Luke 23:34).[32]

Make no mistake—McLaren is telling us that the "god" whom Christians have worshipped over the past fifteen hundred or so years is genocidal, could care less about life, and growls in thirst for our blood.[33] Yet, McLaren has also tried to emasculate God, having stripped his character of being retributively just and holy—and, ironically, thereby loving—by denying that he could exact a just punishment for wrongs committed. So, let us ponder this charge some more, in particular in regards to genocide.

God and Genocide

Genocide—a very powerful moral term that today immediately evokes powerful feelings and brings to mind all sorts of hideous examples. Indeed, that

29. Bell, *Love Wins*, 174 (emphasis mine).

30. Bell, *Love Wins*, 175.

31. McLaren, *A New Kind of Christianity*, 109 (emphasis mine).

32. McLaren, *A New Kind of Christianity*, 126.

33. To me, it is ironic, yet curious, too, that McLaren's description of the received view of God is very much like what Peter attributes to Satan, that he is prowling about like a roaring lion, seeking someone to devour (1 Pet 5:8).

it is seen as clearly, even *objectively*, wrong is one of the few moral truths (perhaps beside murder and rape) upon which most everyone in the West today would agree immediately. But before we go further, we had better try to be clear on what genocide is.

To begin, genocide is *not* simply the mass destruction of a large group of people. That could happen through a natural event, like the tsunami in northern Japan in 2011. Genocide, instead, is carried out by moral agents. Nor is it merely murder, which I take to be the intentional taking of innocent human life. According to the United Nations Convention in 1948, genocide "means any of the following acts committed with *intent to destroy, in whole or in part, a national, ethnical, racial or religious group, as such*: (a) killing members of the group; (b) causing serious bodily or mental harm to members of the group; (c) deliberately inflicting on the group conditions of life calculated to bring about its physical destruction in whole or in part; (d) imposing measures intended to prevent births within the group; (e) forcibly transferring children of the group to another group."[34] So, genocide is an intentional attempt to destroy a people group *because of* its nationality, ethnicity, race, or religion. As such, they would be *innocent* of any crime worthy of a death penalty.

As a prime example, many of us immediately think of the Holocaust and the Nazis' attempt to eliminate all Jewish people. They did succeed in massacring six million Jews. The stories of Nazi atrocities have been well documented; just to scratch the surface, we know of gassings, hideous medical experiments, and tortures. But we also know of the incredible number of *average* Germans it took to make the camp system work. Clay Jones says that 10,005 camps have been identified positively, and the major camps had many satellite ones. Dachau, for instance, had 174 satellites. Auschwitz had fifty satellites and 7,000 guards. At the satellites, prisoners provided slave labor for major corporations. As Jones observes, the corporation I. G. Farben "produced the Zyklon-B used [to exterminate prisoners] in the gas chambers. The Bayer Corporation was a subsidiary of I. G. Farben and sold Zyklon-B out of its sales office. Of course, countless administrators, typists, rail workers, policemen, truck drivers, and factory workers knew—and their families knew—what was going on."[35]

However, we also can think readily of all too many more examples, even if from just the twentieth century. The Soviets' reign of terror brutally murdered at least twenty to twenty-five million people, with another

---

34 "Convention on the Prevention and Punishment of the Crime of Genocide," Article II.

35. Jones, "We Don't Take Human Evil Seriously," 5 (insert mine).

estimate ranging as high as sixty-two million.[36] Included in these figures are the six million Ukrainians who were killed by Stalin's plan of forced starvation from 1932 to 1933. As R. J. Rummel observes, "no mercy was shown the starving peasants. During the famine, detachments of workers and activists were marshaled in the countryside to take every last bit of produce or grain. . . . To isolate the victims, the Ukrainian borders were sealed off to block the importation of food. . . . The peasants simply starved slowly to death throughout the Ukraine."[37]

The Chinese Communists provide another case, with the deaths of perhaps twenty million "counterrevolutionaries" in the prisons.[38] Also, the occupying Japanese army tortured and killed over 300,000 Chinese in Nanking, starting in December 1937. Iris Chang has documented the particularly horrific methods used:

> Chinese men were used for bayonet practice and in decapitation contests. An estimated 20,000–80,000 Chinese women were raped. Many soldiers went beyond rape to disembowel women, slice off their breasts, nail them alive to walls. Fathers were forced to rape their daughters, and sons their mothers, as other family members watched. Not only did live burials, castration, the carving of organs, and the roasting of people become routine, but more diabolical tortures were practiced, such as hanging people by their tongues on iron hooks or burying people to their waists and watching them get torn apart by German shepherds. So sickening was the spectacle that even the Nazis in the city were horrified, one proclaiming the massacre to be the work of "bestial machinery."[39]

Moreover, Pol Pot and the Khmer Rouge butchered between 1.7 to 2.2 million Cambodians from 1975 to 1979 in an effort "to remove foreign influence and intellectuals in an attempt to return to an agrarian culture."[40] Approximately 1.2 million Armenians died at the hands of Ottoman Turkey's Young Turks.[41] About 500,000 to 750,000 Tutsis were killed in the 1994

---

36. On these two lower estimates, see Courtois, "Introduction: The Crimes of Communism," 4, and Yakovlev, *A Century of Violence in Soviet Russia*, 234. The sixty-two million figure comes from Rummel, "Genocide."

37. Rummel, *Lethal Politics*, 87–88.

38. Margolin, "China," 463–64.

39. Chang, *The Rape of Nanking*, 6.

40. Jones, "We Don't Take Human Evil Seriously," 6. See also Etcheson, "Khmer Rouge Victim Numbers," 617.

41. See estimates cited by Balakian, "Armenians in the Ottoman Empire," 98.

Rwandan genocide.[42] And time will fail us if we also discuss the genocides of Sudanese in Darfur, the Kurds in Iraq, and the Baganda people in Uganda. Pakistani soldiers killed three million people in 1971 (and approximately ten million fled to India).[43] Guatemalans have targeted Mayans, and the Islamic State has murdered many Christians. And, well over fifty million unborn have been aborted in just the United States since *Roe v. Wade* in 1973.[44]

Two startling, even overwhelming, things immediately confront us even when we begin to examine cases of genocide. The first is the incredible inhumanity that is demonstrated in all the attitudes and means used by the perpetrators. The second, and *even more* sobering, fact is that consistently, scholars have found that these genocides were committed by *ordinary* people. They were not necessarily criminally insane, as we might tend to think, as though we could shrug off such actions and attitudes as just the products of a few people who belong in mental wards and maximum security prisons. Quite the contrary; consider the conclusion of historian George Kren and psychologist Leon Rappoport:

> What remains is a central, deadening sense of despair over the human species. Where can one find an affirmative meaning in life if human beings can do such things? Along with this despair there may also come a desperate new feeling of vulnerability attached to the fact that one *is* human. If one keeps at the Holocaust long enough, then sooner or later the ultimate truth begins to reveal itself: one knows, finally, that one might either do it, or be done to. If it could happen on such a massive scale elsewhere, then it can happen anywhere; it is all within the range of human possibility, and like it or not, Auschwitz expands the universe of consciousness no less than landings on the moon.[45]

Jones also concludes from his research that "every genocide researcher I read concluded that the perpetrators are ordinary people."[46] Former Soviet gulag prisoner Aleksandr Solzhenitsyn raises serious questions that point to the same conclusion:

42. Rummel, "Genocide."

43. Baxter, "Bangladesh/East Pakistan," 118, and Thorp, "Bangladesh, Genocide In," 115, cited in Jones, "We Don't Take Human Evil Seriously." 6.

44. As a general reference with links to other sources, see Jones, "We Don't Take Human Evil Seriously."

45. Kren and Rappoport, *Holocaust and the Crisis of Human Behavior*, 126.

46. Jones, "We Don't Take Human Evil Seriously," 11.

> Where did this wolf-tribe [i.e., officials who torture and mur-
> der] appear from among our people? Does it really stem from
> our own roots? Our own blood?
>
> It is our own.
>
> And just so we don't go around flaunting too proudly the
> white mantle of the just, let everyone ask himself: "If my life had
> turned out differently, might I myself not have become just such
> an executioner?"
>
> It is a dreadful question if one answers it honestly.[47]

So, how could ordinary people have done (and still do) such horrific things? McLaren seems to think that what we need is to have a change of "heart," i.e., a change of paradigms, such that we start to live the way of Jesus now. *But there is no deep need to be born from above (by the Spirit) for our authors,* for it does not seem that we are spiritually dead to God on this view and in dire need of being born from above, lest we never see the kingdom of God (John 3:3). *Rather, the spirit of human beings seems adequate to know and do good.*

However, we should consider the words of Langdon Gilkey, a teacher of English and philosophy at a college in China when the occupying Japanese army relocated him from Peking to an internment camp. He wrote in his memoir that before his experience in a Japanese prisoner of war camp, he believed in the inherent goodness of humans. Indeed, as he writes, "Nothing indicates so clearly the fixed belief in the innate goodness of humans as does this confidence that when the chips are down, and we are revealed for what we 'really are,' we will all be good to each other."[48] Yet, from his experiences there, he realized later that the opposite was really so: "*Nothing could be so totally in error.*"[49]

How then could people possibly have performed such deeply wicked, unthinkably evil acts? I think the answer is astonishingly simple, yet hard for many to accept, because it hits home. It is just as we saw earlier, in the biblical depiction of the human heart, how its default bent is to usurp God's rightful place, to become powerful over God and even *be* God—surely the most audacious (and foolish) attitude of all. Yet, the Bible often is remarkably matter-of-fact in how it presents this and other truths. One example is Genesis 6:5: "the wickedness of man was great on the earth, and that every intent of the thoughts of his heart was only evil continually." Jesus exposed this attitude in the scribes, elders, and chief priests in his parable of the

---

47. Solzhenitsyn, *Gulag Archipelago*, 160.
48. Gilkey, *Shantung Compound*, 92.
49. Gilkey, *Shantung Compound*, 92 (emphasis mine).

vine-growers, whom he knew even wanted to kill the owner's (God the Father) beloved son (Jesus).

Again, matter-of-factly, the Bible describes how this same attitude looks in practice:

> There is none righteous, not even one; there is none who understands, there is none who seeks for God; all have turned aside, together they have become useless; *there is none who does good, there is not even one.* Their throat is an open grave, with their tongues they keep deceiving, the poison of asps is under their lips; whose mouth is full of cursing and bitterness; their feet are *swift to shed blood, destruction and misery are in their paths,* and the path of peace they have not known. There is no fear of God before their eyes. (Rom 3:10b–18; emphases mine)

This passage describes the default attitude not just in perpetrators of genocide, *but in each of us,* something which I think is born out in our experience every day, around the world and even in our own hearts, if we are honest with ourselves. *This is the condition of our hearts, which apart from God's grace, is set only on evil continually. That each of us is capable of the most vile, gross intentions and behaviors cries out for an explanation! How can this be?*

I do not see any other explanation that even comes close to accounting for the empirically verifiable evil that fellow human beings perpetrate upon each other, let alone what they will in their hearts, but do not physically carry out. I think the best explanation of the phenomena of genocide is that we have a real, bloodthirsty enemy, who wants to steal, kill, and destroy, just like Jesus told us (John 10:10a), and since in our default condition we are united with him from our hearts and minds, we will tend to do his will.

With this backdrop, let us examine two alleged cases of genocide by God in the Bible. First, did God commit genocide by commanding the flood in Genesis 7? McLaren accuses God (or, at least, the Greco-Romanized "god") of this. But, in that story, God did not destroy everyone except Noah's family *because* of their nationality, ethnicity, race, or religion; instead, he slew them because of their *evil*—their deep immorality, which is an offense against the holiness and justice of God, which therefore merits God's acting in retribution. They were *not* innocents, and therefore this is not a case of genocide or a callous disregard of human life.

But, second, what about the Canaanite's destruction, which the Bible says God ordered? Did God command genocide?[50] Let us explore what the Bible has to say about this situation. Genesis 15:16 indicates that God foretold Abraham that his descendants would enter and possess a land where

---

50. I also address this issue in *In Search of Moral Knowledge,* 351–57.

the Amorites then lived. But, there would be a gap of time before God would remove the Amorites, for their sin wasn't yet "complete." In Exodus 23:20–23, God gave more revelation about this land and its present inhabitants, the Amorites, Hittites, Perizzites, Canaanites, Hivites, and Jebusites. There God declared that he would destroy them. Moreover, Israel was to "utterly overthrow them" (v. 23).

Who were these people, and what were their practices? According to Jones, the term "Canaanites" referred collectively to all these groups. They were mainly agrarian people, who worshipped the god Baʿal. Following Jones, a Canaanite epic myth tells us that Baʿal raped his virgin sister up to seventy times seven or even eighty times eight.[51] Moreover, Baʿal is the god most mentioned amongst the Canaanites, so he is the one they worshiped and were to be like.

Leviticus 18:19–23 further shows that the Canaanites' sin had been great, even to the extent that they committed child sacrifice by offering their children to the god Molech (v. 21). Deuteronomy 18:10 in turns warns the Israelites against the evil practices of the Canaanite peoples in the land, including making sons and daughters "pass through the fire" as offerings to please their gods (see Deut 12:31).

So, we should observe that the Scriptures state that they were destroyed because of their specific *actions*, and *not* because of *who* they were, nor for their having a different religion *per se*. Now, I think it should be clear that incest's morality is not relative to cultures or individuals. But, suppose someone still wants to challenge my claim. Nonetheless, it seems that rape is morally wrong universally. Additionally, child sacrifice is not morally neutral. If it were practiced today in the West, it would still be morally wrong. It seems it would be a form of murder.

If these same actions were performed today, people would rightly cry out for justice. Likewise, the Canaanites' actions also required justice. Since God's character is the ground for all objectively true moral principles and virtues, then God must be just.[52] Biblically, consider also the principle that God would not destroy good people (i.e., those who obey God) along with those who do evil. Thus, Abraham intercedes with God to spare Sodom and Gomorrah (along with his nephew, Lot, and his family) if there are even as few as ten righteous people there. Abraham appealed to God's justice: "Far be it from Thee to do such a thing, to slay the righteous with the wicked, so that the righteous and wicked are treated alike. Far be it from Thee!

51. See Jones, "We Don't Hate Sin," 64, note 47. Jones appeals to Smith, trans., *Ugaritic Narrative Poetry*, 148, and Albright, *Yahweh and the Gods of Canaan*, 128.

52. This is a major conclusion of my *In Search of Moral Knowledge*. For example, see 325.

Shall not the Judge of all the earth deal justly?" (Gen 18:25). God's answer underscores his justice: "I will not destroy it on account of the ten" (v. 32).

Now, we can know that rape and child sacrifice are morally wrong and deserving of punishment. Since God is perfect in his moral character, he also is truly just. Thus, he must not let the perpetrators of those evil actions go unpunished.

Still, we debate the morality of capital punishment versus life in prison, at least in the United States. Both positions raise important arguments, and I will focus on two from abolitionists. First, by executing a prisoner who actually is innocent, there is no possibility of making right that wrong. Second, in the United States, a large percentage of inmates on death row are from minorities, which raises serious concerns that racial prejudices have influenced their convictions. Again, if they are innocent but executed, there is no way to correct those injustices.

But consider now the case of the destruction of the Canaanites, in which God is omniscient and is truly just. God would not make such mistakes; nor would he be blinded by prejudices. Still, that does not mean that humans as instruments of justice would always interpret clearly and correctly God's moral decisions. For we have limits to our understanding, and we are influenced by our biases and particularity.

Nevertheless, consider Moses as leader over Israel and God's spokesperson. If Moses misrepresented (intentionally or unintentionally) God's decision regarding the Canaanites, God could have interposed readily. Scripture even includes just such an occasion. The people of Israel put God to the test by grumbling about a lack of water (Num 20:2–13). God then told Moses to speak to the rock, but instead Moses struck it out of anger, thus disobeying God. God then told him and his brother Aaron that there would be a consequence for not treating God as holy. Since God publicly corrected Moses as his representative on that kind of occasion, then surely he could have intervened and corrected him if he had misunderstood or distorted what God meant to do with the Canaanites. Moreover, since he is just, he would have wanted to intervene and do what was right.

Still, since we debate the morality of capital punishment today, condemning the Canaanites to death, even for their specific actions, could seem unjust to us. Here, I am not trying to give a definitive answer on the morality of capital punishment in our context. However, the actions of child sacrifice were morally wrong, and being unjust, they deserved punishment. If God did not punish them, then he would not be truly just.

But now, let's consider a further issue: would it be the case that all the Canaanites were guilty of these wrongs? For example, what about a person who never had a child and thus couldn't have sacrificed their own child? I am speculating, but it seems there had been a deeply established pattern of child sacrifice and rape in the broad Canaanite culture over hundreds of years. Now, in our context, we punish people for being accessories to murder. So, I suggest that similarly, these people arguably had been complicit in these child sacrifices, since it was deeply embedded even in their religious activities.

I also think the Canaanites should have known better than to commit rape and sacrifice their children. Evidently, though, like the Sawi tribe we looked at above, they did not see their sacrifices as instances of murder. But I think they should have. There seems to be in each of us a deep knowledge of some basic morals, including that rape and murder are wrong.

This is compounded by there being a large gap of more than 400 years between the time when God first told Abraham that his descendants would possess the Canaanites' land, but the sin of those people was not yet complete (Gen 15:16), and the time when Israel prepared to enter that land (Deut 18:9–10). If God is just, he would not hold people responsible for some moral actions they could not have known to be wrong. But God *does* hold them accountable for these actions. Since we all do seem to have a knowledge of some core moral truths, and God will not act unjustly, then it surely seems the Canaanites knew (or should have known) better than to commit these actions. Moreover, God gave them much time to stop committing them, but apparently they never did. So, when God's justice was executed, arguably, they were judged justly.

However, this patience raises a possible rebuttal. Was God unjust for giving them that much time, so that more people would be raped and burned as offerings? Was God unjust for allowing them the freedom to choose actions they should have known were horrific and wrong?

In reply, without freedom to choose what is good (or evil), we seem to lose what is necessary for us to be moral, loving beings. In addition, Scripture repeatedly declares that God is just, but also patient, for he takes no pleasure in the death of the wicked (Ezek 33:11). Jesus' death and resurrection also demonstrate God's justice and patient love. By Jesus' bearing the punishment for the wrongs committed by all people, past, present, or future (Rom 3:21–26), God provided a way to meet the requirements of his justice. Yet, his actions also show his love, by providing a way for people to have a relationship with God (Rom 5:8).

But God also ordered the killing of the Canaanite children. So, some object that this action would be unjust, for they were innocents, if they were too young to know what they were doing, or to be held accountable for aiding and abetting the acts of child sacrifice. What can we say in reply to this objection? Clearly, it is wrong to treat the innocent in the same way as the guilty (Gen 18:25).

However, suppose we know with *utter certainty* that in the future, Dave *will* murder his wife, Mary. If we could have such infallible knowledge, it seems we would be just in punishing Dave now to preventing that murder from happening. Of course, we are not infallible, but God is all knowing, even of all possible, future, freely chosen actions of free people, including those who have not yet been born. Since God is just, he will not destroy the innocent with the guilty, and since, due to his omniscience, he knows all future, even freely chosen events that will (or possibly will) happen, then it seems he would be just to act in a way that would prevent Dave from murdering Mary.[53]

Now, from our standpoint, without special revelation, it seems we would not know for certain how the Canaanite children would act when they grew up. But, suppose the Israelites spared the children and let them grow up in their midst. If we speculate, then I would think that as they grew up, they would want to know what happened to their families, and why. When the Israelites would reply that God commanded them to execute justice upon the Canaanites for their immoral actions, I would think that the Canaanite children could easily develop a deep-seated desire for revenge against the Israelites.

For two main reasons, then, God ordered Israel to destroy the Canaanites: for one, to bring judgment upon them; and for another, to protect Israel

---

53. But, further, why doesn't God intervene so as to prevent evils in all situations? This is a difficult question, and people may be motivated in asking it by personal suffering from evil. These people need much compassion and empathy.

But then, where would (or should) we draw the line on how much evil should be permitted? Should God only stop murder? What about rape, or what about fighting? If we answer that no evils should be permitted, then it seems our free will would be eliminated. But then we undermine moral responsibility.

Suppose God prevented all cases of evil from ever happening. If so, would we ever learn that these actions are wrong, even monstrously so? How would we learn the horrors of evils that we commit unless we are allowed to see just *how much* evil we inflict on one another?

It also seems we still would want to commit them. The only difference would be that we couldn't. But that alone would not change our hearts' desires. Instead, we likely would become deeply frustrated and angry at God for doing that, without any real change in our hearts' desires.

It seems we need to be able to form well-justified beliefs about the consequences of our actions if we are to make free and efficacious choices between what is right and wrong, and that seems to require regularity in our experiences, including of the results of actions. Finally, it also seems God has already limited the amount of evil in the world. For example, brutal murderers, like Hitler, Stalin, and others are dead and so cannot inflict more evil on others. Thanks to Clay Jones for suggestions on these points.

from their sin. Now, in light of God's command to kill the children, too, somehow it seems that that sin would be passed on if the children were allowed to live. If that is the case, it seems the children had also been impacted by the rest of the Canaanites' sin. In a key sense, they were carriers of that sin. Now, older children would have been morally responsible for their sin (even if just condoning it, versus acting it out). Even with little ones, before they are able to reason, they are imitators, and they would follow their examples from Canaan. So, they too would help transmit those sinful patterns. So, to preserve Israel from following in the Canaanites' sinful patterns, God commanded their destruction too.[54]

Additionally, God warned Israel not to let the Canaanites live amongst them because they would turn the Israelites' hearts after their immoral practices (Exod 23:33; Deut 7:4). And that is what happened when Israel did not utterly destroy them; eventually the Israelites also worshiped Ba'al and Molech and committed child sacrifices (e.g., Judg 2:11; 1 Kgs 16:29–31; 2 Chr 28:2, 3, and 33:6). So, quite arguably, God knew that if the Canaanites were allowed to live, they would hold to their old practices, which had been condemned justly. Since God is just and will not destroy the innocent along with the guilty, and if God knows all things, including all future, freely chosen actions people (even children) would make, then it seems that God would be just when he ordered the destruction of all the Canaanites.

Additionally, contrary to McLaren, God did not condemn the Canaanites out of some arbitrary preference for Israel, as though he were some biased, tribal god. Rather, God warned the northern ten tribes of Israel to not follow in the acts of the Canaanites, but they still did. As a result, God acted in judgment by eventually allowing Assyria to deport the tribes (Hos 10:1–6, 11:5; Amos 9:8), and the descendants have remained scattered abroad ever since.[55] When Judah sinned in like manner, eventually its people were conquered and exiled, too.

Might God act similarly today? That is, might God order another destruction of a people group today by his people? No; I think God himself has put the limitation on that possibility. In the Old Testament, Israel was under a theocracy. They literally were a people under the government of God, with the Law of Moses to govern the moral, ceremonial, and civil lives of that people. But, now, in the New Testament, the moral law's principles still apply, but not the civil or ceremonial laws. That is, there has been a change in how God has chosen to operate. *There is no place any longer for*

---

54. Even so, God would be merciful in deciding their eternal destiny of the children, for he knew their hearts.

55. "The Assyrians."

God's people (i.e., the church) to act as a nation under the government of God to execute justice upon other nations. Therefore, though I have argued God justly ordered the destruction of the Canaanites through a nation (Israel), after Jesus there is no room for such actions.

Moreover, we can now see that God was not careless of their lives, as McLaren charges would be the case with our received views. Nor was he unjust to take the Canaanites' lives. Rather, he was very patient, giving them time to repent, even though their horrific actions deserved punishment. But, without repentance, their just punishment was sure to come and finally did.

To help draw together the many parts of this section on God's being able to act violently in retribution upon evildoers, we have explored that God must punish sin and evil retributively in order to be truly holy and just, and that his justice cannot be separated from his loving-kindness. I have tried to rebut McLaren's and others' charges that on our received view of God, he is genocidal. We have looked at what genocide is, as well as examples of the depths of evil that have been carried out by humans upon one another, including through acts of genocide. Then we considered two biblical examples of alleged genocide commanded or carried out directly by God, yet in both cases we found that these were not true examples of genocide. Rather, they were examples of retributive justice being carried out upon guilty persons.

Now, it is time to address some more specifics in McLaren's notion of the Bible and its evolving interpretations.

Are Humans Really Depraved? Our Condition and Need

While we have touched on various subjects related to this theme, we still need to address this question specifically. For McLaren and our authors seem to deny that we are totally depraved, along with the related doctrine of original sin. First, let's clarify just what these doctrines mean on the traditional, evangelical view.

Traditionally, the doctrine of radical depravity has been linked with that of original sin, "which followed Adam's transgression and which now inheres in all his posterity, [which] embraces a) hereditary guilt (culpa hereditaria) and b) hereditary corruption (corruptio hereditaria)."[56] Radical depravity involves two components, one negative and the other positive. Negatively, it *does not* mean that people are as depraved as they can ever be, or that every person who does not know Christ will do every form of sin.

56. Mueller, *Christian Dogmatics*, 216 (bracketed insert mine).

Nor does it mean that as sinful people, we are incapable of doing morally good acts, or that we do not have a "conscience that discriminates between good and evil."[57] Positively, it *does* mean that the inherent corruption from original sin "extends to all aspects of man's nature"; there is no spiritual good a sinner can do in relation to God; and sinners utterly lack any ability to change their own corrupt human nature.[58]

Clearly, this received doctrine has been challenged by the emergents. As before, it seems there are three "strands" involved in their thinking:

1. The priority is on living in relationships, which is the new given (orthopraxis).

2. Sin damages and disrupts our relationships, including with God, but since (a) we already stand in relation to God, and (b) God is good and loving, we are not separated from God by our sin.

3. While humans are capable of gross evil, that is not due to a "radical depravity." Instead, we still are capable of great moral transformation by embracing the way of Jesus.

Related to the second point (2a) would be Jones's criticism that the doctrine of original sin trades upon a metaphysical view which few today would embrace. That is, original sin is something that is fundamentally soulish, yet on a view of humans as basically physical beings, such a doctrine simply must be reconsidered.

Yet, I have argued above that without our being a unity of body and soul, we lose completely any understanding of sin. For one, we lose intentionality on such a view. For another, what could sin be in a world that is made simply of matter? We also lose all the other important qualities needed for relationships, including thoughts, beliefs, experiences, and more.

But, consider original sin as a deep privation of the souls of Adam and Eve. No longer were they alive in him; they were dead to God, and his Spirit could no longer live in them. Though created in the image of God, they lost their relationship with him in terms of no longer having a unity of their hearts and minds with him. Instead, their hearts and minds were corrupted and became united with those of their "father," the devil. That is, they listened to and followed Satan's heart and mind.

What then could they pass along to their posterity? They could pass along only what they had, and so the human race inherited the corruption of their sin. But, what about Jones's appeal to Abelard, that it is unjust to

57. Lewis, "Hamartiology II."
58. Lewis, "Hamartiology II."

hold us guilty for their sin? Even if so, we *still* inherit a corrupt human nature that is dead to God that, as we grow up, results in sinful acts we have chosen. So, every aspect our being is affected by sin, and being dead to God and bent on defining reality and usurping God's throne, we cannot "be good *in terms of a relationship with God.*"[59]

Now, I just highlighted examples of some of the most horrendous evils committed by humans, and a key conclusion of those researchers is not that these were acts committed by particularly, extraordinarily vile people. Rather, they were perpetrated by ordinary, everyday people. Indeed, that evidence shouts loudly: human beings are *not* inherently good.

Now, McLaren, Pagitt, Jones, and Bell also have encountered many evils, whether directly or through people they have counseled, including those acts committed by other Christians. They are right to point out such actions (and patterns thereof), call for their rebuke, and urge us to repent of them. Moreover, they are right in that we can get caught up in our social conceptions of what's right and wrong, all the while missing the heart of what is truly good. The genocide examples underscore this point, as does the widespread mind-set of white Southerners in the United States toward slavery in the antebellum period. Indeed, my emphasizing these examples of genocide is not intended to minimize the evils the emergents are rightly calling to our attention.

But it is to say that they seem very mistaken about our own human natures' need primarily for a conceptual and moral transformation. They seem to be saying that we can be good enough if we follow the way of Jesus, without having to be born from above by God's Spirit coming into our lives when we trust Christ to save us from our sins. However, I think they are deeply mistaken. We have a *much* greater need. Though we can discern right from wrong, we still have a deep bent from the heart on rebelling against God. And for God to be who he is—purely just, holy, good, and loving—he must punish sin, and God will not be tainted by evil. Speaking anthropomorphically, Scripture says that God's "eyes" are too pure to look upon evil with approval (Hab 1:13).

Moreover, on this set of three strands, we lose God as being truly good, and we thereby lose God's truly being just. By misunderstanding and misrepresenting what sin is, we diminish the problems from sin and the depth of our need for a Savior. For instance, while McLaren's notion of repentance seems good in many respects, at least one key ingredient is missing: a repentance that truly is from the heart. How so? Though he uses "heart" language at times, and though he is very concerned with unethical behavior, McLaren

---

59. See Grudem, *Systematic Theology*, 497 (italics in original).

describes repentance more in terms of a "framing story" to be embraced, as though repentance is largely a matter of a paradigm shift in terms of how we understand (and therefore live in) reality. He is right to stress the importance of our "framing stories," and he realizes how deeply they shape us. Nevertheless, I think he misses the depths of the issues with sin.

For example, McLaren, Pagitt, and Jones treat the demonic and even Satan more as human evils than as actually existing fallen angels. This becomes evident in terms of McLaren's treatment of Jesus' predominant opposition from human systems and human evil, and also in terms of the solutions to the current crises we face. It is *our* work that brings in the kingdom, and though McLaren mentions the Spirit as God's gift, *there is virtually no discussion of our utter need for dependence upon him, even to live our daily lives, which is strikingly unlike the emphases of both Jesus and Paul.* Instead, McLaren seems to think that the human spirit is adequate for moral transformation. In stark contrast, consider Jesus' blunt statement that apart from him and his Spirit in us, we can do *nothing*—John 15:5. So, the Spirit seems largely unnecessary in his gospel, as would be Jesus' atoning work.

Moreover, if it is true that there exist actual demonic, nonhuman beings, then one of the deepest, most intransigent kinds of dualisms would be that there exist two kinds of moral beings: good ones, including God and his angels, and evil ones, namely, Satan and the demons. That deep dualism would strike a fundamental discord with the holism our authors want us to accept, for it reflects a deep bifurcation in reality, in that not all can be reconciled to, and integrated in, God, lest evil be present in him. It would also serve to undermine Bell's idea that all creation already has been reconciled to God through Christ. But on their kinds of views, our opposition is not against actually fallen angels (Paul's principalities and powers), but mainly against humans, *their* systems of evil, and their framing stories that blind us to evil. Hence, the need is mainly to deconstruct them and thereby expose injustices and evil, name them, and then reject them.[60]

Yet, the possibility of the existence of actual, fallen, immaterial angels is enhanced by the lines of evidence we have for the reality of a creation that is dualistic ontologically, particularly concerning human beings. For example, it is enhanced by the arguments I have raised against the turn to relationality and the related view of individual substances (individual humans' souls, for example) as static.[61] I do not know how to argue philosophi-

---

60. There also will be no real place for the reality of literal demons if creation is merely physical, or even if we are physical but they are not.

61. Here, of course, I am thinking of demons as having an essential nature, or "soul," of an angel, which God created good, but demons' souls are privated, or spoiled, and irredeemably so. There is no mention in Scripture of an opportunity for repentance

cally for the existence of actual demons, but there is considerable scriptural support for that. And one thing I think we should observe is the default bent of the human heart, which I have discussed earlier. I think that if we are honest with ourselves, we can see that over and over again, humans repeatedly live out the mind-set described by the serpent (Satan) in Genesis 3:5, that God has been holding back something good from us, but if we eat of the forbidden fruit (and disobey God), *we will be like God, knowing (deciding, choosing) good and evil.* Over and over again, throughout human history and across cultures, it seems humans want to *be* God and *define* what is moral, and even the rest of reality. The catch, of course, is that we did not become like God, but instead like Satan as the Bible describes him and his character— one who is out to usurp God's throne, define what is good, evil, and the rest of reality, too (compare John 10:10a).

Another line of evidence for the reality of real, fallen angels is the nature of many peoples' experiences with supernatural events. Now, I am not trying to suggest that all preternatural events are necessarily demon-based. They may have a human or natural explanation. Nor do I mean to imply that behind every evil human action is a demon *directly* inspiring a person to act. People can follow their own sinful propensities, or those that have been enculturated in socially acceptable ways.

Nevertheless, there is considerable literature devoted to exploring accounts of spirit possession and exorcism, including in contemporary settings. Craig Keener has provided detailed accounts and commentary on this subject in an appendix to his two-volume work, *Miracles,* including many accounts of power encounters with spirits.[62]

Let's return to McLaren's emphasis upon our need for a conceptual, moral transformation, so that we expose and name evil, and then reject it in its many forms. He is right in this; we do need to do these things, and it is hard to see some things as wrong or misguided due to how we have come to understand what the Christian life is to be like. Still, from what we can see in McLaren's writings, it seems he has set his heart on defining God according to his own understanding—and so we see a God who is love, in that he names and absorbs evil, but will not punish people for their sin. But, Jesus rightly said we speak, write, and live from what fills our hearts (Matt 12:34), so that perhaps it is unsurprising that God ends up being like McLaren, who himself comes across as very gentle and kind.

---

and salvation for them. This view of their souls as essentially angelic, yet fallen, follows Augustine's view of *metaphysical evil* (what evil *is*), that evil is not something positive that God created; rather, it is spoiled goodness.

62. Keener, *Miracles,* appendix b, also 843–56.

In McLaren's view, our problem is not that we are dead to God in our sins (Eph 2:1). *Instead, what we seem to need is education and therapy, both moral and conceptual (but not forgiveness via Christ's atoning sacrifice), with a change in how we understand and live our lives (e.g., in community), to help us get better.*[63] God seems to be the head of an educational and therapeutic ministry. This suggestion has numerous implications. Surely there is a need for education; not only do we need new hearts, but our minds need to be renewed (Rom 12:2), and we need practice in learning to live out our faith. In terms of therapy, there is no doubt that as pastors who have counseled many people, our authors have seen all manners of dysfunctional patterns. No doubt they have seen plenty of real abusers and victims who are caught up and ensnared in dysfunctional, even evil, patterns of behavior, such as alcoholism, sexual abuse, and much more. Dysfunctional, codependent patterns often are lived out at an unconscious level, but they reinforce the underlying root problems, rather than confronting them and "unraveling" the deeply enmeshed victims, enablers, and perpetrators.

I do not write abstractly here; I know from experience what codependent patterns are like. While I was growing up, it seems a pattern in my house was that the kids were to "take care" of Mom's anxieties, all the while living in an atmosphere in which it was explicitly taught that anger was sin, and implicitly that we were to be perfect and keep our emotions tightly under control. If not, we might not be perfect and keep all things steady, and if so, something bad might happen! So I learned how to enable my mom (and dad too) by being "fused" with her, to take good care of her and her anxieties, and at the same time keep my own feelings deeply under control (or suppressed in denial; it took me many years in therapy to allow myself to feel angry).

After my wife and I were married, we did not understand the emotions and behaviors that were surfacing in our relationship. For she too had anxieties, and unconsciously I went into my enablement mode. But, this time, in my marriage, this pattern did not "solve" the conflicts; it only exacerbated them. Since then, we have worked long and hard on our own "little boy" and

---

63. The emphasis upon therapy (which perhaps is what McLaren is trying to *do* to his readers) is similar to what we can see in Stanley Hauerwas's Christian ethics. Brad Kallenberg has explained that Hauerwas wants not just to perform conceptual therapy on his readers, but also a moral therapy, to get them to see life rightly (from under a particular aspect, like Wittgenstein) so that their stories are more in conformity with the story of Jesus. Such skill happens as we learn the language and behavior appropriate for the Christian community, and he and Kallenberg believe this will enable us to see the truthfulness of the Christian story. For an overview, see my *Truth*, chapter 2. See also Kallenberg, *Ethics as Grammar*, 51. This concept is the central (and very well-taken) argument of his second chapter. See also Hauerwas, *Dispatches from the Front*, 7.

"little girl" patterns, fears, and more, and we have been able to deal with the roots of how we were getting fused and living dysfunctionally.

As I experienced, enablers *absorb* the pain of others, and rather than helping to set them free from the roots of their own painful issues, enablers keep them ensnared in these same cycles of dysfunction and evil. By doing that, enablers get their own *felt* (yet twisted) needs met too, but in a perverse way. Some can even hold subtly a paternalistic attitude of superiority over those they are enabling, thinking (perhaps unconsciously) that they are the ones who will solve their problems.

I am afraid that McLaren's God seems to be an enabler. Like human ones, myself included, he *absorbs* others' pain, taking it all into himself. McLaren seems to think that God then turns to us with a smile on his face, and while he may name the person's sin, he doesn't act justly by punishing it. God seems like an enabler who does not hold alcoholics accountable for their destructive behaviors. Those involved in dysfunctional relationships usually have poor boundaries, and it seems that McLaren's God does as well. He does not really draw the line and hold people accountable for their destructive, rebellious, evil actions. Even good human parents do that with their children, so that they learn from their actions' consequences that those acts are wrong, hurtful, destructive, and will not be tolerated. But McLaren's God strikes me as an enabler with poor boundaries, who will let virtually anyone into his family.

We also should remember that enablers often have anger issues. Deep down, I was angry about feeling the need to enable others, and that surfaced rather surprisingly years ago against a former boss who was quite dysfunctional. I have seen others who have enabled people for years, "de-selfing" themselves in order to keep the peace, and yet suddenly erupting in anger or rage toward the one who was causing all the turmoil. And these back-and-forth patterns can continue for a lifetime.

To the extent McLaren's God is codependent with us, being our enabler in our sinful acts and patterns, several immediate implications present themselves. For one, God too will probably erupt in anger or rage against us at some time(s). Though he is love, love still needs to be moral, and eventually he would be aware that he too has been "de-selfing" himself. Coupled with a view that God can do anything, no holds barred, as Jones says, we then have a God of whom to be afraid, who likely will blow up in unquenchable rage.

No matter how good and helpful they may seem, enablers are not moral heroes. I was trying to be kind, compassionate, and caring during all my years of practice as an enabler, but in so doing I was not helping deal with root issues that had been perpetrated by our sin, or others' sin against us. I was no savior by trying to keep others feeling calm and secure by carrying their pain.

And so it would be with God. Indeed, I don't think we really want such a deficient God. Deep down, I think we want a God who is worthy of worship—who is perfect, not lacking in any good quality, pure in love, compassion, grace, and mercy, but also all-powerful, all-knowing, and holy, just, good, and in control, so that one day he will make right every wrong and deal decisively with, and even eradicate, evil. But McLaren's God cannot deal in any final way with evil. He simply allows evil to continue. Moreover, if there are actual, fallen angelic spirits (Satan and the demons), then by his not eradicating evil, God would allow evil beings to remain. The God who is revealed in Scripture is worthy of our worship, but McLaren's God does not seem to be.[64]

Now, I realize McLaren and our other authors know that codependent patterns are destructive, so I expect they would say that God would want to set us free from them. I also realize McLaren wants a God who is good, loving, and just. But McLaren also seems to feel a need to control God, and not just evangelicals' view of him, for he feels he cannot stomach a God who can be violent. I wonder if McLaren has come by this attitude because as a pastor he has counseled many people who struggled with reconciling evil and God's goodness, knowledge, and power. Or, perhaps he has struggled up close and personally with such painful situations. He has been impacted (perhaps *very* deeply) by that pervasive issue that haunts us all—the problem(s) of pain and evil.

God's Solution: The Atonement, and Authentic Forgiveness

Again, we may see a threefold type of reasoning regarding the atonement:

1. The priority is on living in relationships, which is the new given (orthopraxis).

---

64. McLaren cannot seem to allow for any kind of essences, even for God. He rejects essences in part because they would be fixed, static, timeless, and perfect, and that would mean stories also would be forced, determined, etc. But now consider God: if he has an essence and is perfect (morally, in power, etc.) then apparently his story will also be forced, determined, etc., and it seems he may well have to force our stories to conform to his essential traits. Instead, just as all of us are prone to do (Gen 3:5), McLaren seems to have to adopted a view of God that will be like him—developing, emerging, and so forth. This leaves us with a God who is not truly perfect, purely good, utterly holy, and, ultimately, not worth worshipping.

2. Since (a) we are already in relation with God, and (b) God is good and loving (and therefore not violent), Jesus' death on the cross could not have been a substitutionary atoning sacrifice to propitiate the wrath of God against sin (as on the received view).

3. Instead, his death was an example of kingdom living—i.e., it is the greatest example of humility and nonviolent resistance, which is how we too are to live.

Yet, from what we have explored, we have seen that God is love, as well as holy, just, and good. If we separate out any of these qualities from his being, we end up with a deficient God who is not worthy of worship. We also end up with a God who can blow up in rage, which, ironically, is exactly what McLaren and our authors want to avoid. But, due to God's character, and our condition, humans need God to provide an atoning, substitutionary sacrifice for our sins. By his being love *and* holy *and* just, God's character as love is preserved. His character is truly good, and thus he is truly balanced and able to respond in full moral appropriateness to what any situation needs.

Moreover, God the Father did not victimize his Son. Jesus knows nothing of this view, nor does the rest of Scripture. No one takes my life from me, he taught; rather, he laid it down on his own initiative. He taught in John 3:16–21 that God so *loved* the world that he gave his one and only son, yet in the same context, he also taught about God's judgment upon those who do not believe in him. And, just as Moses lifted the serpent in the wilderness, so would he be lifted up (vv. 14–15). In Moses's case, Israel had sinned, and the only way to check God's judgment and certain death was to do what God said—look upon God's provision, a bronze serpent (Num 21:9). This implies that with Jesus, unless we "look to" and trust him as God's provision for our sins, we will face death and not enter the kingdom. Moreover, Jesus defined the mind of Christ in terms of his love for the Father (see John 8:29, 17:26; compare 17:4–5). Whatever he saw the Father do, he did likewise, out of his knowledge of the deep beauty and fulfillment of abiding in the Father's love (John 5:19–20). So, it is false that he was a victim of a vengeful, abusive God.

All this is not to say that other views of the atonement have no insights to offer. For instance, that Jesus died as an example for us to follow is true: "For the death that He died, He died to sin once for all; but the life that He lives, He lives to God. Even so consider yourselves to be dead to sin, but alive to God in Christ Jesus" (Rom 6:10–11). We his people have been crucified with him (Gal 2:20), and since he now lives in us, we are to follow his example. We have "been buried with Him through baptism [identification with him] into death, so that as Christ was raised from the dead through the glory of the Father, so we too might walk in newness of life" (Rom 6:4, bracketed insert mine).

Moreover, the ransom theory does point to the importance of a ransom being needed to free us from our sins. However, it is not a ransom paid to Satan, but the price God had to pay to satisfy his justice and holiness (Matt 20:28; Mark 10:45; 1 Tim 2:6). Or, consider Girard's scapegoat theory, at least in terms of how Jones portrays it. We do want what others have, and we become violent to obtain this. But, on this theory, it does not seem to be due to an inherited, deep depravity. It is a much more of a naturalistic kind of explanation of our behavior. Again, it does not address our deepest needs, to be reconciled to God. Last, the solidarity theory is right in that God demonstrated his solidarity with the human race by the incarnation of God the second person of the Trinity, who became fully human while remaining fully God. And, he bore our sins. But he did more than just beckon and call, set an example, and invite us into the life of the Trinity;[65] he provided a propitiatory sacrifice for our sins, as well as his righteous life, for us when we needed both.

But, before we move on to address the issue of hell, let's consider one more crucial factor. Jones claims God could forgive our sins in any way he would choose. And McLaren claims that God names, "absorbs," and then forgives our sin. Are these adequate views of real forgiveness? I think we can approach this from two standpoints: biblically, and from what we understand from our own experience.

Consider first Luke 7:36–50, where Jesus enters the home of Simon the Pharisee, and a woman who was a "sinner" entered.[66] She then violated several customs by touching Jesus, weeping on his feet, wiping them with her hair (which she had let down), and pouring perfume on them. As Gary Inrig explains, this was socially outrageous behavior.[67] When Simon recoils in self-righteousness against both the woman and Jesus, who did not rebuke her, Jesus tells a parable about two men who owed money to a lender. One of them owed five hundred denarii, which was about two years of wages. The other owed fifty denarii, which was about two months' wages. Neither one had the funds to repay their debt.

But the lender graciously forgave their debts as a free gift. Here is where an interesting insight surfaces. Inrig observes that the lender chose to *pay himself what they owed*. Indeed, he argues that "this is at the very heart

---

65. That is, on their view, by living the way of Jesus . . .

66. Inrig describes her as most likely being an adulteress, prostitute, or promiscuous woman. See his *Forgiveness*, 57.

67. Inrig, *Forgiveness*, 57.

of forgiveness. The one owed the debt pays the debt and the debtor goes free. . . . At the heart of all forgiveness is a substitution. The offended pays so that the offender goes free."[68]

Second, this same principle recurs in another parable, found in Matthew 18:21–35. There, a servant owed the king ten thousand talents, an astronomical sum in the billions of dollars.[69] To accumulate such a massive debt must have required his misappropriating large sums over a long time. Yet, he exhausted his resources and was unable to reply. Begging for mercy, the king pities him and cancels his debt.

Here again, the one who forgives, the king, pays what the debtor owed. Inrig puts it well: "By forgiving the debt, he [the king] forfeits all claims on it. In fact, he is paying the debt so the offender can go free. . . . The king, in fact, absorbs the loss. He doesn't establish any kind of repayment plan. He takes the cost on himself. *Forgiveness is free to the forgiven, but costly to the forgiver, because the forgiver pays.*"[70]

In our human relationships, we can see the same principle at work. If someone sins against me, they have harmed me and thus have incurred a debt that they now owe to me—to make right what they have done wrong. To forgive that person, I "take the cost on myself" by forfeiting all claims to cash in on that debt. In my late teen years, I was falsely accused by two men where I worked, just to test me (I think), to see if I was loyal to them as my leaders. Whenever something brings that situation back to mind and I feel my anger again, I need to refresh my forgiveness of them, give up my own vengeance, or even refuse to coddle my anger toward them.

But, couldn't Jones or McLaren reply that God could do the same? That is, he could pay the price of forgiveness by giving up his claim of vengeance, without a need for a penal substitutionary atonement. In reply, first, he wouldn't have a *morally just* claim to vengeance in the first place (for a violation of his holiness) unless he himself is holy and just, as we have seen. Second, the just recompense for sin is death (what we earn, deserve; see Rom 6:23). This is what happened with Adam and Eve in the garden; in dying spiritually, in terms of no longer being in relationship with God, they also thereby would die physically (Gen 2:17). And, as we have seen, to be truly holy and just, God must punish sin, which is by death of the one who sinned. But, there is no way we can be forgiven and God's justice be met unless God provides a substitute for us.

---

68. Inrig, *Forgiveness*, 60.

69. See Inrig, *Forgiveness*, 95.

70. Inrig, *Forgiveness*, 97 (emphasis in original).

Third, and relatedly, real forgiveness does not minimize the reality of evil. Therefore, "forgiveness does not involve excusing an act. If it can be excused, it needs to be understood, not forgiven."[71] Nor does forgiveness simply involve forgetting, as though wounds caused by sin could be healed in just that way. Neither does it involve ignoring, burying, or trivializing sin. God knows the horrific nature (and effects) of sin, and so he hates it.

John Ensor illustrates very pointedly these findings on forgiveness, in relation to God's love and justice:

> If I come across a man raping a woman, I cannot love both of them in the same way—and neither can God. Love is inherently *moral* in character. I can't go up to the struggling, terrorized woman and the overpowering assailant and say, "I love you both just the same, and so does God. He does not want you to harm this girl, but please do not think he is angry at you right now. Because God is love, he doesn't get mad. Isn't such a love amazing?" The woman would denounce my love as sick and worthless, even cowardly and evil. She would know that love must have a *passionate commitment* to right over wrong. It must be willing to vindicate and disarm; to reward and punish. To act in love in this situation I must *hate* what the attacker is doing and push him aside, scream my lungs out for help, grab the woman, and run.[72]

More Christological Violence—Jesus as Our High Priest

We have already seen ways in which these emergents' views do violence christologically. Nevertheless, there is yet another way to consider. This view of humans as physical also undermines the traditional, orthodox view of the unity of Christ's two natures. In turn, it also undermines his work as our great high priest. David looked ahead to the incarnation of the Logos, who is a priest forever, according to the order of Melchizedek (Ps 110:4). Hebrews 7:24 says Jesus holds his priesthood forever, and in 9:11–28, the author explains how he appeared as our high priest and entered the greater tabernacle through his blood. But, Jesus was already exercising his high priestly office during his life on earth (see his prayer in John 17).

Now, if Jesus cannot maintain his own personal identity through time and change in their physicalist view, then the one who was the great high

71. Inrig, *Forgiveness*, 113.

72. Ensor, *The Great Work of the Gospel*, 53. Originally, I came across this quote (as it appeared in Ensor's *Experiencing God's Forgiveness*) in Inrig, *Forgiveness*, 113.

priest in John 17 is not the same person as the high priest who officiates now. That, however, has horrific ramifications for those who hold on to Jesus' atonement as a propitiatory offering. The offering he made for sin apparently could not meet the righteous requirements of God, since God would not (even *could not*) have raised him (the same person) from the dead. That means we all are doomed to death, the penalty of sin (Rom 6:23), and left without any hope in this world. And there will be no hope for us beyond the grave, since we cannot maintain our personal identity through time or change.

On Heaven, Hell, and Other Religions

Our findings thus far have great import for the question of the reality of heaven and hell. If God is just, and he cannot look upon evil with approval (Hab 1:13; lit., *to look at evil*, NASB), then he must punish sin. What then should we make of the hope for followers of other religions to be in heaven too? And, would God send people to eternal, conscious torment in hell?

Will Followers of Other Religions be in Heaven?

While McLaren has said that this question is only important in the six-line, Greco-Roman narrative, and not his three-line story, nonetheless I think we can see the question does matter, due to some faulty reasons on his part. We may state the reasoning of our authors in response to this question in a threefold way:

1. The priority is on living in relationships, which is the new given (orthopraxis).

2. Since (a) we are already in relation with God, and (b) God is good and loving (and therefore not violent), we are not separated from God.

3. So, we need to embrace living the way of Jesus (as a moral transformation). But to do that, you don't have to be a Christian.

McLaren likes to talk of Muslims, Christians, and others throwing a party in the kingdom one day. Bell talks about how everyone has been reconciled to God, and even though they may not yet have been wooed by his saving love, they still have been reconciled.

What happens then to those who decide that they don't really want to take Jesus' story too seriously, but instead just want to be "good" people? It seems they too will be "in" the kingdom, since they already are in relationship to God. Indeed, it seems in their views that no one really has to take Jesus' story all that seriously to be "in."

But, is it really true that given enough time and opportunities, sooner or later *everyone* will respond positively to God's love? Will his love win, in Bell's sense? In light of the extraordinary degrees and amounts of evil even ordinary humans perpetrate upon others, I have to say *no*—not everyone will respond to God's call, even though he desires for none to perish, but all to be saved (2 Pet 3:9). Moreover, due to our deep bent from the heart to do evil and rebel against God, it seems God would have to *coerce* us to change our hearts to respond to his love.

Still, these preliminary points should not detract us from the main one: that Jesus offered himself as the perfect, spotless Lamb of God, to take away our sins. And just as in the Old Testament sacrifices, the worshipper's main need was not met just by going through the motions of bringing a sacrifice; then, as with Jesus, the one who comes to God is justified by faith, by the person's *trust* in what God has done on his or her behalf (cf. Heb 11:6, Hab 2:4b, and Rom 4:16: "For this reason it is by faith, that it might be in accordance with grace, in order that the promise may be certain to all the descendants, not only to those who are of the Law, but also to those who are of the faith of Abraham, who is the father of faith"). So it is not the case that Jesus' offering of himself in our place unilaterally is necessary *and* sufficient to reconcile all people to God. We must still receive his offer of salvation and forgiveness by faith (i.e., trust).

Furthermore, with our need for a substitutionary atoning sacrifice on our behalf, one that is unblemished, undefiled, and acceptable to God, in order to make it possible to have our sins punished and yet we be forgiven, there simply is no other way to the Father than through Jesus. *We need much more than just a moral transformation. We also need to be forgiven of our sins and then made alive to God (be born again, "from above," by the Spirit).* So McLaren's and others' views separate out the members of the Godhead as not needed in their fullness in some key ways: Jesus is not needed as our substituted sacrifice; the Father is not truly holy and good in his attributes; and we do not need to be born of the Spirit to be in a relationship with God, or even to be good enough before the Father.

But, isn't this traditional, evangelical position just a *radical exclusivism*, one that ostracizes others who are not part of their "in group"? If it were just up to us who gets to be part of God's family, then, yes, we would be biased in our choices, being selfish, fallen, and more. But it is God who has set these limits. Moreover, while reconciliation to God is *exclusive*, in that it can happen only through Jesus, nonetheless the gospel also is *radically inclusive*. Whoever trusts in him is welcome into his kingdom. God graciously wants to share his wide-open invitation with everyone, for the riches of his grace have been made abundant through Jesus' once-for-all perfect offering.

This discussion now leads us to perhaps the biggest question of all, as posed by Bell.

Will God Really Send People to Eternal Conscious Torment in Hell?

We also might ask a corollary: will only a select few be "in" heaven? Again, their answers seem to take a threefold reply:

1. The priority is on living in relationships, which is the new given (orthopraxis).

2. We are already in relation with God, and God is good and loving (and therefore not violent).

3. So, God would not punish people in hell with eternal conscious torment. (That is a Greek idea!)

But as I have argued, since we are deeply fallen and dead to God, rebellious and bent on usurping his place as God, and God must punish our sin, we stand in need of a Savior to take the punishment for our sins in our place, so we can be forgiven and have a relationship with God. But if there are people who will not respond to his love (since they are deeply bent from their hearts on rebelling against him), then what is God to do with them? Yes, he wants them to repent and receive his forgiveness and grace, but what if they refuse?

Perhaps God will not "re-member" them, to play off of McLaren's own ideas. That is, if we do not have an immortal soul as our essence, and our story is what gives us unity through time, then maybe God just shouldn't re-member us after we die. For why should he remember our story and then re-member our bodies, if only to cast us into hell forever? That would seem immoral.

But there is a problem with this suggestion too. God has made us in his image, thereby making us intrinsically valuable. That is, we are valuable not merely for what we do, but simply for who and what kind of thing we are, for that is how God has made us. Now, that has implications, namely, that we should never be treated merely as a means to an end, but as ends in themselves (on which Kant was right). So, treating us simply as a means to the end of reaching a pain-free state would be immoral; this would apply readily to assisted suicide, for example. But it also applies here; by annihilating us (or, on McLaren's view, by not re-membering us), God would be immoral for treating us merely as a means to cease to exist. At the same time, being intrinsically valuable does not mean that we also are supremely valuable; while we are valuable for who and what we are, it does not follow that we can never be treated violently, such as with punishment.

But, as I already have argued, we are more than just bodies; we are a deep unity of body (which is material) and soul (which is immaterial). Now, as such, our souls are immortal, *not* due to some special property we have, so that we could boast in ourselves, but due to how God has made us. God has made us such that we can survive the death of our bodies, which is why Paul can say that if he were to die, he'd be with the Lord, a state much better than living this life in his mortal body (Phil 1:23).

Now, if we are intrinsically valuable, and our souls are immortal, then at death, though the body has died, the soul still lives. And, one day our bodies will be resurrected and glorified. But what should God do with the person who has not repented from his or her rebellion against him, from that person's sins committed while in this life?[73] Since annihilation is not an option, and God is just for separating people from the lived experience of his presence due to their sin, then it seems that they have one option: hell, which was intended for the devil and the demons.

We have come to the end of my considerations of their views about the Bible and its evolving interpretations, which focused largely on implications for key areas of doctrine. Before we leave our assessment of the views of McLaren, Pagitt, Jones, and Bell, now I will return to address a subject I focused on in my *Truth and the New Kind of Christian*—their views about how we have knowledge (or, epistemology).

A Reconsideration: Is Everything Interpretation?

In *Truth*, I had developed an interpretation of the emergents' views that posited that we do not have direct access to reality, to know it as it truly is, in itself. There, I had understood McLaren and Christians who embrace more postmodern, philosophical views as advocating that we are somehow "inside" language and cannot escape those limitations. But, from interactions, I now realize that this is not really what these authors are intending to say. Instead, *everything is interpretation.*[74] To put this idea differently, Merold Westphal claims that "being must always already be conceptualized,"

73. The author of Hebrews says that God has appointed for us to die once, and after this comes judgment (Heb 9:27). Jesus' parable about the rich man and Lazarus is entirely consistent with this view, too (Luke 16:19–21).

74. For example, see Smith, "Who's Afraid of Postmodernism?," 222.

because we do not have direct access to things as they really are.[75] Thus, to even have an experience requires interpretation.

McLaren, Jones, Pagitt, and Bell have also embraced this position.[76] For them, there is no neutral place to stand to interpret anything, and we all have limited perspectives, due to our situatedness and finitude.[77] We cannot "shed" or "escape" our perspectives, backgrounds, and historically situated, conditioned experiences; so, no one is purely objective, or neutral.[78] All truth is contextual, and meanings cannot be pried off, or abstracted from, their place within a story and a community.[79] I also shared James K. A. Smith's criticisms of my earlier understanding with McLaren, who replied that he deeply resonated with Jamie's view that everything is interpretation.[80]

We might approach the claim that everything is interpretation in a couple different ways. First, we can focus on what is before our minds in conscious experience, to see if descriptively it fits with our experience. Second, we can consider logical implications of the view.

Before I examine some cases, though, I want to give examples of some things we do seem to know about reality, such as the following in science: 1) SSRI medications work on a neurochemical basis for depression; 2) nuclear fission involves the splitting of the nucleus of an atom into smaller parts; and 3) breathing in too much CO can kill you. We also have mathematical knowledge: 1) pi is the ratio of a circle's circumference to its diameter, and it equals 3.14, rounded to two decimal places; and 2) $2 + 2 = 4$. Moreover, we have historical knowledge: 1) Japan attacked Pearl Harbor on December 7, 1941; 2) Barack Obama was a two-term president; and 3) Napoleon Bonaparte was emperor of France. So, surely we do have knowledge about reality itself. These cases seem to support a *particularist* strategy in epistemology. On that, we start with cases of knowledge, and then we work from there to develop theories of how we know them.[81]

Now, the question arises: how then do we have knowledge? Here I will examine various cases, most of them everyday ones. Suppose we are in a

---

75. Westphal, "Hermeneutics as Epistemology," 430.

76. For some indications on Bell's views, see *What We Talk About*, 47–48, where he discusses our *involvement*.

77. McLaren, *More Ready*, 76.

78. McLaren, *More Ready*, 94.

79. McLaren, *A New Kind of Christian*, 106.

80. E-mail correspondence from McLaren to myself, July 17, 2006.

81. This is opposed to an epistemological methodist's approach, in which to know anything, one first has to have a criterion to know that. But, this seems doomed to an infinite regress: to know a, I must first know b. But to know b, I must first know c, and so on, without a way to get started.

worship gathering, and someone reads a passage of Scripture, namely Rom 9:13. Suppose the person reads it as follows: "Just as it is written, 'Esau I loved, but Jacob I hated.'" Now, since people can follow along in their own Bibles, some of them may look as though they are puzzled. Some might even utter "Jacob I loved, but Esau I hated" (which is how it actually appears in the text).

How would the people know whether what that person read was right or not? They have to hear the sounds uttered for what they are, see what the words on the page actually are, compare the two, and then they could express their thoughts in language (for example, "you misspoke," or "it reads, 'Jacob I loved . . .'"). I have used this kind of exercise intentionally in classes, to get students to pay attention to what was before their minds in conscious awareness—what they heard, what they read, their comparison of the two, and their judgment. Indeed, if we could not access these things as they really are, how could we correct anyone who misspeaks?

Here's a second case, which involves the ubiquitous PIN (personal identification number) pad for making a transaction by a debit card. If you want to make a purchase with a debit card, you have to determine whether the device is one that allows you to just slide your card, or if it requires you to insert your card. You can determine this by reading words on the screen. Then, you may have to choose whether the purchase is a debit or credit. After that, you may be prompted to enter your PIN. Next, you may be asked if you want cash back. If you press "yes," then you have to select the amount of cash you want from the options presented. Finally, you may have to verify that the total amount is okay.

At each step, there is a computer display, with buttons to push. You have to see the words on the screen for what they are, and that they match up with a certain button, and not another. Suppose you get an unexpected, confusing message on a screen; you have to see those words for what they are, comprehend them, and then press the appropriate button that will proceed with what you want to do.

In all steps, it seems you have to see things *for what they are* (the words, e.g.), match up other items with them (e.g., buttons), and recognize if you did or did not press the right one. If you did, or even didn't, make a mistake, you can know that by comparing what was before your mind consciously with the displayed results. You act by pressing certain buttons (which, in order to try to accomplish your goal, requires having formed and using concepts), and then you can compare your intended result with what is before your mind in conscious awareness. For instance, you need the concept that to proceed to a next step, you have to press the button aligned with the option you desire. You can check up on the results at any step by paying attention to the words displayed and see if they do or don't match up with what you expected. And, you can check the final result by reading the receipt.

Third, consider how a toddler learns to identify an apple. When my daughter was very young, often I would show her a book that had lots of pictures of different fruits inside. After separate pages for many individual fruits, the book displayed about twenty-four pictures of various fruits on two adjacent pages. I would point to a picture of an apple on one page, and I would say the word "apple." Then I would do this again with another picture of an apple (which sometimes varied from the type in the other picture) until we went through all the pictures of apples. Maybe another evening, I would open the book to those two pages and ask, "Where are the apples?" She would point to one, and then another, until finally she could identify all the apples pictured there. Moreover, she would see real apples at home, and many more varieties at the grocery store.

What was going on? From many opportunities to pay attention to what was before her mind in her conscious awareness, I think she was able to develop a concept of what an apple is. She then could use that concept to identify totally new kinds of apples when they appeared in the store. To first develop that concept, though, she had to see each apple picture (and actual apples) for *what they are*, hear the word "apple" uttered for *what it is*, learn to associate the apple with the word "apple," and develop a concept of what an apple is from many noticings.

There are many other kinds of cases we could consider. But now let me turn to consider some logical implications of the view that everything is interpretation, and that to even have an experience requires interpretation. If this were so, then it seems all our experiences are "theory-laden"; that is, they necessarily involve concepts. Now, in terms of philosophy of perception, this can be stated in terms of *seeing as*; we see something under an *aspect*, or *interpreted* in light of a concept. In contrast, there is another view, that of *seeing*, or *direct seeing*. According to this view, we can experience something directly, or immediately, without having to involve concepts.

Now, of course, our emergents' view rejects *seeing*. For them, there is only *seeing as* or *seeing that* (forming a belief in light of an experience, and beliefs involve concepts). Nevertheless, it seems mistaken descriptively, as I tried to show in the case studies. Moreover, it also seems mistaken "logically." That is, if their view is true, then we never can access anything without interpretation. If so, what are we accessing when we experience something? It cannot be the "thing" (object, person, belief, concept, etc.) itself, for that has been ruled out. It seems then the best candidate is that we are experiencing an *interpretation* of that thing. Yet, that raises a problem:

how can we get started in forming a concept of a thing if we can only access it via interpretation?[82] It seems we lack any way to get started and encounter reality at all.

Now, I have defended the view that we can have direct access to reality in many other places, and in more detail.[83] But, surely McLaren and our other emergents could object from the standpoint that I am ignoring our "situatedness," that is, the situating factors (historical location, ethnic heritage, family upbringing, language, culture, religion, and so forth) that shape how we "see" (i.e., interpret) life and the world in which we live. Part of the factors influencing this position is that they have embraced nominalism in this regard; we all have particular standpoints, and there isn't a universal standpoint that many (or all) can have, for that would be a universal vantage point. Still, perhaps I am committing a quintessential modern mistake of trying to escape my situatedness and gain an ahistorical, neutral, unbiased, God's-eye view of reality, which only God can have.

On the contrary, being able to access reality directly does not require that one shed his or her situatedness. There is a helpful sense of situatedness that J. P. Moreland has discussed, calling our situating factors ones that impact our "attentive influence." That is, they affect us in terms of how we tend to pay (or not pay) attention to what is available to us in conscious awareness. For him, as a descriptive matter of fact, we can compare our concepts with things as they truly are, just as in the apple example above, and adjust our concepts as needed to better fit with reality. Moreover, we can know this to be so, if we pay careful attention to what is consciously before our minds.

Yet, Moreland notes that over time, "people fall into ruts and adopt ways of seeing things according to which certain features are noticed and others are neglected."[84] For instance, I tried to notice many things when I first watched the series reboot of the movie *Star Trek*, which presents an alternate future for the main characters from the original series. What I noticed in part had to be assimilated in light of my understanding of the original series and its movies. But, when I watched it for the second and third times, I started to notice more subtleties that helped make the story based on an alternative timeline more coherent. Something that helped me

---

82. For surely we do form interpretations and concepts. It does not seem we come "preloaded" with all our concepts. Consider the Kalahari bushman in the movie *The Gods Must Be Crazy*, who needed to develop a concept of a Coke bottle, even though he had never seen anything like one before.

83. For example, see *In Search of Moral Knowledge*, ch. 12; "Nonfoundationalism, Postfoundationalism, and the Truth of Scripture"; and "Finitude, Fallenness, and Immediacy."

84. Moreland, "Two Areas of Reflection and Dialogue with John Franke," 311.

do that was observations my daughter made, who was not as familiar with the original series as me.

So, I think Moreland wisely suggests that "situatedness functions as a set of habit forming background beliefs and concepts that direct our acts of noticing or failing to notice various features of reality."[85] Our "situatedness" affects how we attend to reality, but, with effort and sometimes help, we can change how, and to what, we pay attention.[86] This change may require forming new habits, but it can be done. If it could not occur, then I think things like therapy, or even coming to see the extent to which language and culture influence us, would not be possible.

Now, let's apply this epistemology to McLaren's view of what the various religions are. As I have noted earlier, his views seem very similar to those of John Hick, who was a pluralist and Kantian in his epistemology.[87] (On Kant's view, we cannot know things as they really are, in themselves, but only as they appear to us.) For Hick, the world religions are various responses to the "Real" (ultimate religious reality), which we cannot know as it truly is, apart from how we experience and interpret it. Moreover, the goal of the world religions (including Christianity, properly understood) is moral transformation, much like what McLaren has said. Furthermore, "in light of the wildly different local conditions in which they encounter the same Spirit, we might interpret some religious differences in a new light: rather than saying different (contradictory) things about the same thing, various religions could sometimes be saying different (complementary) things about different (complementary) experiences entirely."[88] Moreover, on nominalism, these are particular interpretations, without a universal one in common.

Now, this claim might seem to have some plausibility to Christians, since *they* believe that there is but one Holy Spirit, and no other gods. Moreover, we are affected by our cultural and religious backgrounds in terms of how we understand God. But if we take McLaren's epistemology consistently, his claims are *his* interpretations, which he has drawn from *his* framing story, which I have described at length. But, what is he interpreting to give us this account? It does not seem he can get started in that interpretation process. *Moreover, it is his interpretation that all people encounter the same Spirit, but that may not be the case in reality. It is also his particular*

---

85. Moreland, "Two Areas of Reflection and Dialogue with John Franke," 311.

86. I will discuss my own story in the last chapter as another case study of changing my situatedness. There, it involves how I became better able to pay attention to the voice of the Lord, and his presence.

87. For an example of Hick's views, see "A Pluralist's View," 27–59.

88. McLaren, *Why Did Jesus*, 152.

interpretation that all religions aim at moral transformation, which is made possible by what *he* calls and identifies as the way of Jesus. But if it is just his *particular* interpretation (of what?), and he cannot base that claim on knowledge of reality itself, why should anyone accept his views?[89] Moreover, on a consistent nominalism, it is literally impossible for us to share McLaren's interpretation, for it is particular and discrete, and not something that others can have, too.[90]

Finally, McLaren's evolving interpretations of the Bible trade upon the idea that even if there were a meaning in the text that the human author, as well as the Divine Author, had in mind, we could not know it as such. So, Scripture readily becomes a set of interpretations of humans' experiences of what they consider to be "God." Now, postmodern thought continues the same trajectory that we saw developed in chapter 2, that there are no essences or universals. Instead, literally everything becomes particular, which is a nominalist view.[91]

So, applied to McLaren, it becomes impossible to have the *same* meaning in mind as he did when he wrote any of his many books. But that view is absurd and, frankly, shown to be something he himself doesn't believe, since he has written and published for large audiences. Nor can we have in mind what the Apostle John meant when he wrote the words of Jesus that are recorded in John 3:16. Nor can we have in mind what the Spirit is saying to us, whether through Scripture, or his still, small voice today. To have the author's (or speaker's) meaning in mind requires the reality of a *universal* (like Plato thought) and an *essence* to the author's meaning. So, on postmodern views, there are (at best) just particular interpretations, with no essential meaning of the author being conveyed by the grammatical-linguistic conventions used in a text. If so, why should anyone bother to listen to them?

Now, we should notice something else in McLaren's, Jones's, Pagitt's, and Bell's appeal to the ubiquity of interpretation. Interpretations require intentionality, as do concepts, which are needed in making interpretations. For a concept is always of or about something, and so is an interpretation. Since this is the case, it is impossible on a physicalist view of creation to have any interpretations or concepts. However, that makes their

---

89. Including those of other religions . . .

90. Indeed, I think on nominalism, there cannot even be resemblances between particulars. For a detailed argument against nominalism in this regard, see my "Craig, Anti-Platonism, and Objective Morality." Further, this problem of being unable to share concepts and interpretations applies to any of their views, including their version(s) of the gospel story, the conventional Greco-Roman story, etc.

91. Or, for postmoderns, even if essences may exist, they do not do any work for us. See Moreland and Craig, *Philosophical Foundations*, 147.

epistemological appeals, as well as all their many claims and writings, exercises in self-contradiction.

Conclusion

While I have stressed many concerns I have with McLaren's, Bell's, Pagitt's, and Jones's views, even so, *in many ways they are right on target in their criticisms of all too many evangelical churches.* In general, evangelicals in the West have been deeply affected by the mind-sets and attitudes of naturalism, and the result has been fleshly living, which is ugly and (frankly) evil. No wonder then that many are put off by such evangelicals!

But, the emergents' "solution," to embrace a new kind of Christianity, is no solution at all. *In light of their attempts to reconceive the faith in today's context, what was their hoped-for gain?* It seems it was to gain intimacy with God, and to stress as the new given the importance of living as we should in relationships with one another, both within the body of Christ and beyond. *These are good, important goals, but ones that cannot be achieved on their reformulation of the faith.*

By trying to reconceive the faith, instead it seems they have fallen into the same besetting sin and weakness of all humans (including their evangelical contemporaries): they have elevated their hearts and minds over the Lord's, and they are not ending up in a deep unity with him in those ways. So, I believe they, too, have fallen for the same lie that evangelicals have, and so they too need to repent and return to the Lord in the fullness of the Spirit and truth. There is no other way to live in fullness of life as promised in the gospel.

So, it is important to observe that these problems seem to be more than just intellectual mistakes, ones that come from mistakenly embracing a potentially viable, alternative paradigm. Why do I say that? There is a singular pattern at work in their many questions and their answers, which tries to bypass (or obscure, perhaps?) God's requirement for holiness of person, to come into his presence. All these threefold answers to their questions, while highlighting an important aspect of truth (such as the importance of orthopraxis), also introduce distortions, in particular in regard to the important unity of God's holy, just, good, and loving character. The emergents end up losing the very attributes they want to preserve. Far from drawing us closer in relationship to God, their answers will actually keep us distant and walled off from being in relationship with God, much less enjoying him.

Indeed, with orthopraxis as the new given, how is it that we can have any precise measurement of what is good behavior, or our faithfulness?

Instead, with right living as the starting point, we are led to think that core doctrines can be revised, when in fact that is very mistaken, as we have seen. This approach leads to our being able to rationalize all sorts of beliefs that seem to make sense to us (with ourselves as the measure). We end up thinking we can reconstruct a theology that will remain faithful in terms of actions without starting as first in priority with what *is* the case in reality. But this is utterly mistaken; it is to try to do ethics and develop norms without first asking what *kind* of thing we are, and what *the standards for our behavior are*. But mere behavior will not touch the deep needs of the heart to bow, in fullness of Spirit and truth. *That* is what we need, and if we reverse the priority, then truth becomes something we (subtly) think we can manipulate and construct.

These attitudes, of distancing us from God; of denying our need for being born from above; of God's requirement of holiness for us, and so on, are much older than McLaren and others today. Indeed, they match the very patterns of the one in Scripture who is called the enemy, the evil one, a liar (and father of lies), a thief, and a murderer, who wants to glorify himself and accuse God, and separate our hearts and minds from him.

While quite accurate in terms of their diagnosis of how evangelicals have bifurcated orthodoxy from orthopraxis, actually, *I think their diagnosis misses the mark at an even more fundamental level.* Compare below the effects of the inherited evangelical mind-set with the effects of McLaren's (and others') views:

Practical Effects of Cultural, Historical, and Philosophical Factors on Western Evangelicals	*Practical Effects of A New Kind of Christianity*
Very knowledge focused (i.e., as mental assent), with high confidence in human reason	*Our* interpretations (justified by the "turn to interpretation") become *the* focus, thereby still placing much confidence in our reasoning abilities. (It is what *we* think about God, life, church, etc., that counts)
Bible is seen as a perfect encyclopedia, or collection, of objective facts; all-sufficient	Bible is a collection of human interpretations of God and their experiences
Distrust, discount experience in theology (too subjective), and for rationality	While experience (in relationships) is valued, still this view distances God (or anyone else) from us by their being unable to be experienced.

Disciplines develop autonomously; little need to integrate	Disciplines develop in light of a Christian "holism," but still according to *our* interpretations, and not what God has to say about them.
Such a strong emphasis upon the mind that the heart (understood in terms of the emotions) is discounted, often leaving them bifurcated within ourselves, from one another, and from God	Though a renewed emphasis is upon embodied living in community (and thus living out our relationships), we end up being separated from God's heart and mind, that of others, and (perhaps) even within ourselves.
God is distant (functional deism); God doesn't give personal communication other than in Scripture; little expectation of miracles, or of demonic activity	While personal relationships and orthopraxis are stressed, they become impossible. God cannot communicate with us, and we cannot receive his communications (whether metaphysically or epistemologically). There is no real acknowledgement of divine miracles or demonic activity.
Universe is seen as mechanistic and closed; we too are seen as mechanisms; input-output methodology for sanctification	We are physical beings, embedded in creation and already in relation to God (turn to relationality)

Just as we have seen with the traditional evangelical churches, the practical effects of McLaren's and others' ideas all seem to fit closely with the broader definition of naturalism: they too all serve to make God irrelevant practically to our lives. *For just as naturalism has largely assimilated the traditional, inherited evangelical mind-set, so too it is the case with this "new kind" of Christianity.* It cannot hope to meet the deep needs of Christians, even those who have been burned by evangelical churches. For on it, too, there are three deeply naturalistic kinds of beliefs: 1) it suggests that we can go beyond any "limitations" on our authority and freedom (such that we are adequate in basically all respects, even to live the way of Jesus); 2) it steals our *focus* away from God's authority, love, and power, thereby distancing us from God; and 3) it denies (or undermines) God's personal investment in each heart, soul, and mind. *This "new kind" of Christianity is deeply naturalistic and undermines the Christian life, including our personal, intimate relationship with God and others.*

I also think the Lord has been trying to help me see some heart kinds of issues in relation to what we have seen in this new kind of Christianity. God is the perfecter of love, who alone is the fullness of peace and joy, and he alone provides faith and hope for something better than this temporal world. But, the enemy of our souls, the devil, has a threefold strategy to keep us separated from fully loving, and being fully loved by, God. He uses doubts, denials, and self-promotions to achieve this goal. In this, he attempts to substitute his thoughts for God's, in part by 1) declaring God is unable to hate what has nothing to do with the Way, the truth, and the life; and 2) denying God is absolutely good (and holy) by inferring that God must look upon sin yet with eyes that are blinded to sin's rebellion. Additionally, he insinuates that God's requiring someone to die for sin is not really loving. Yet, undefiled, true love takes our place, as sinners, in holy judgment in order to bring the only reconciliation possible between humans and God. Therefore, we should beware of a heart attitude that is intent on bypassing God's holiness that it must make itself feel acceptable in all of its choices.[92]

As with the evangelical churches, does one (or more) of the churches in Revelation 2 and 3 apply to McLaren, Pagitt, Bell, and Jones, and their views? They remind me of people in one of those churches, namely, the church in Sardis. These are not easy words, yet I think they are ones the Lord wants me to stress as I wrap up this portion:

> And to the angel of the church in Sardis write: He who has the seven Spirits of God, and the seven stars, says this: "I know your deeds, that you have a name that you are alive, but you are dead. Wake up, and strengthen the things that remain, which were about to die; for I have not found your deeds completed in the sight of My God. Remember therefore what you have received and heard; and keep it, and repent. If therefore you will not wake up, I will come like a thief, and you will not know at what hour I will come upon you. But you have a few people in Sardis who have not soiled their garments; and they will walk with Me in white; for they are worthy." (Rev 3:1–5)

If this "new kind," along with the received evangelical kind, of Christianity in the West is deeply affected by naturalism, then to what do we turn? Fortunately, Christianity (or, better, the Lord himself) has *far deeper* riches upon which we can draw. What then might authentic Christianity look and be like?

---

92. Perhaps ponder the following passages with these ideas: John 3: 16–17, Lev 19: 1–3, Deut 9: 3–5, John 8: 43–45, Rom 5: 7–9, 2 Tim 1: 6–9, and 1 John 5: 1–12.

6

A Faithful Way Forward

Something seems terribly amiss for both evangelicals in the United States and the West, and also for the emergents. I have contended that *both* groups have been shaped deeply by naturalism, which marginalizes God, making him irrelevant to varying extents, and elevating ourselves. Putting the point very directly, these effects are sinful. To the extent that Christians are living in such ways, they cannot please God. Nor will they be marked by the *fullness* of God's Spirit.

Yet, evangelicals have been trying to hold fast to God's specially revealed truth, found in the authoritative, infallible, and inerrant Bible.[1] And, the emergents also have been stressing truth, or maybe better, truthful living. Since both seem to be succumbing to a non-, even anti-, Christian set of values and mind-sets, perhaps we had better return to the basis (or, as my emergent friends might say, the story) of the Christian life, and Christianity itself. That is, it seems we need to return to, and search again, the Scriptures, to see what they teach about the faith, and what the Christian life should look and be like.

As I argued earlier, naturalism yields a heart and mind attitude toward God that fits with the portrait found in Genesis 3:5. Now, we have already seen aspects of the Bible's story line from Genesis, Exodus, the prophets, and more. Here, my goal is to explore and develop somewhat more deeply

---

1. A reminder and comment to my emergent readers: I am an evangelical, and here I am assuming these positions about inerrancy, etc. I have not made arguments for them in this book. So, I am speaking here especially to my fellow evangelicals. But, for some further essays on these kinds of topics, consider Carson, ed., *The Enduring Authority of the Christian Scriptures*.

the biblical and theological picture of how God intends for us to be in a deep heart and mind unity with him, but that sin has corrupted that, and therefore what God's solution involves. This study will try to develop more fully a picture of God's overarching theme (story line) in the Bible, and what the Christian life should be like. If the Bible is true in its claims, it should provide solutions and alternatives to the naturalized aspects of the faith in the West (and, again, particularly the States). Along the way, I will sprinkle in aspects of my own story, to help illustrate how God has been working out these solutions and correctives in my own life, thereby setting me more and more free from forms of bondage.

Biblically, Christianity is to be a supernatural religion, and if the Christian God really exists and the Bible is true, Christians' lives should be marked by *the supernatural power and presence of the risen Lord*. Yet, it seems that in far too many churches and believers' lives, that is not the case. What then should be done?

With that, let me turn now to explore major points of emphasis in Scripture.

The Bible's Overarching Story

God's purposes in Scripture surely are to redeem a people for himself. But his plan is far deeper than just to make us holy in our standing, or position before him. From the beginning of the Old Testament, culminating in the end of Revelation, and throughout the books in between, God is continually working out his consistent plan, which I think can be expressed as follows: *I will be your God, you shall be My people, and I will dwell in your midst.*[2] God wants to "tabernacle" and be deeply intimate with us. In the garden, Adam and Eve enjoyed intimate fellowship with God, as he dwelt in their midst. After the fall, God set out on his plan of redemption, to redeem a people for himself. So God chose Israel so that he would dwell among them first in the tabernacle and then the temple, and through them his fame and glory would spread to the nations. This theme becomes pronounced in the promised new covenant, as given through Jeremiah: "I will be their God, and they shall be My people" (31:33c). In God's plan to fulfill his new covenant, Jesus came and "moved into our neighborhood," so to speak, when he "became flesh and dwelt [tabernacled] among us" (John 1:14). Jesus asked the Father to give his disciples another helper, the Spirit, to *be with them* forever (14:16). And, Jesus said that "if anyone loves Me, he will keep My word; and My Father will love him, and We will come to him, and make Our

---

2. Compare, for instance, Exod 6:7; Lev 26:12; Jer 7:23, 11:4, 30:22; Ezek 36:28.

abode [home] with him" (14:23). That is, the Spirit of Christ would come and *dwell* in Christians forever (14:17; Rom 8:9; Eph 1:13).

However, this is not merely a truth to be taught and believed, but one to be lived. The promised new heart in the new covenant comes after being cleansed of our sin, by being sprinkled with water (Ezek 36:25; cf. John 3:5) as a symbol of forgiveness. It also comes from the Spirit's coming to live in us. Jesus explained that we must be born from above, by the Spirit, for "that which is born of the Spirit is spirit" (John 3:5–6). Jesus has in mind the promised new covenant as explained in Ezekiel, where God promises to give us a new heart and a new spirit, and that he would put his Spirit in us and cause us to walk in, and obey, his statutes and ordinances (36:26–27). Moreover, God reiterates his overarching plan, that the house of Israel (and by extension all others who trust in Christ as Savior) "will be My people, and I will be your God" (v. 28).

Furthermore, the Spirit's living in us is to accomplish God's great purpose, to be deeply *intimate* with us, so that we may know (not just as a fact, but as part of our experience) his deep love, beauty, splendor, majesty, holiness, and more, and that we can make him known to others, so they too can enter into the *beauty and fulfillment* of the Father's love. Consider the intimacy of God with his redeemed people portrayed in Revelation 21:3–5: "Behold, the tabernacle of God is among men, and He shall dwell among them, and they shall be His people, and God himself shall be among them, and He shall wipe away every tear from their eyes; and there shall no longer be any death; there shall no longer be mourning, or crying, or pain; the first things have passed away. And He who sits on the throne said, 'Behold, I am making all things new.'"[3]

Consider also the beauty and intimacy depicted in the heartfelt desires of David, the man after God's own heart. In Psalm 27, David's one desire is to behold God's beauty (or delightful loveliness) and dwell in his presence (v. 4). His heart's response to God's gracious invitation was to seek God's face (v. 8).[4] In Psalm 25, he knows (from experience, I think) God's "secret" (or, counsel, intimacy) which is "for those who fear Him." Indeed, David experienced God's intimacy with him on several occasions, such as when he

---

3. This is one of my favorite, deeply meaningful passages, especially in light of the many tears and pain I have experienced in my life, whether from rejection fears, anxieties, or (especially) being exposed often to death at an early age and later on.

4. Once, while meditating on this passage, I had a sense of being in the Lord's lap while he was on his throne, at peace and feeling completely safe in his holy presence. Like that "sense," there is a real beauty and intimacy portrayed in this psalm, which David experienced with the Lord.

asked God for his specific guidance in light of what Saul would do (1 Sam 23:9–13).

Or, in Exodus 33, consider Moses' heart's cry to know God intimately. There we are told that the Lord "used to speak to Moses face to face, just as a man speaks to his friend" (v. 11). But then Moses intercedes on Israel's behalf, for God had just told him that he would not go up in their midst, due to their great sin, especially after their rebellion with the golden calf. Instead, he told Moses to lead the people to the promised land, along with an angel he would send before them (vv. 1–3). But Moses intercedes, knowing he and the people need God's presence: "Now therefore, I pray Thee, if I have found favor in Thy sight, let me know Thy ways, that I may know Thee, so that I may find favor in Thy sight" (v. 13). God then responds in grace, promising his presence will go with him, which in turn encourages Moses to reiterate his request for God's presence. For how else will he and the people of Israel be distinguished from all other peoples, unless God's presence goes with them? God replies with more gracious favor, that Moses has found favor in his sight, and God knows him by name (personally). Then, Moses asks for something amazing, which for many years has expressed my own heart's cry: "*I pray Thee, show me Thy glory!*" (v. 18, emphasis added), a request that God delights in and honors (34:6–8).

God's great plan is for us to see his face (Rev 22:4) and dwell with him, beholding his glory, glorifying him, and enjoying him forever. For now, we see partially, getting glimpses of God's great love, intimacy, and wonderful power on our behalf (see 1 Cor 13:12). We also look back at wondrous miracles he has done for us, supremely in raising his son to life from the grave, thereby conquering death on our behalf. But one day, we will see his face (1 Cor 13:12, which is like the face-to-face, intimate relationship of the Father and the Word [the Son] in John 1:1), and we will be with him forever, untainted by sin in all the ways it distorts and twists our souls and our perceptions of him. We will have it supremely better than the sons of Korah, who wrote Psalm 84, which expresses the beauty and joy of being in God's presence in the temple. Even now we are the temple where the Spirit of Christ dwells (1 Cor 3:16), far more intimately than Old Testament believers could experience.

Now, there is another dimension to God's intimacy that I often think western believers can overlook. In 1 Corinthians 2:16, Paul makes the incredible claim that we have been given the very mind of Christ. This does not mean he has "replaced" our minds with his own, as though we no longer exist, but rather that our minds now have been redeemed and can be transformed by their renewal (Rom 12:2). So, we still live, but now in vital union with Christ. This makes sense in light of the new covenant, in which the Spirit of Christ actually lives in us.

Also, in Ezekiel 36:26–27, God promises to give us a *new* heart and spirit, ones that will respond to and obey him. The "heart of stone" (which is hardened against God) that he "removes" is not replaced with his own heart, as though I no longer exist, but with a "heart of flesh" (one that is tender and responsive to him). And the new "spirit" that he gives us must be from the Spirit (cf. John 3:6). He promises that his Spirit will be in us. Now the Spirit "bears witness with our spirit that that we are children of God" (Rom 8:16), and we know the Father as *Abba*, Daddy—a deeply intimate term.

What differences should these truths make in our lives? First, regarding having the mind of Christ, Paul asks rhetorically, "For who among men knows the thoughts of a man except the spirit of the man, which is in him? Even so the thoughts of God no one knows except the Spirit of God." (1 Cor 2:11) At first, this might seem a bit unusual statement, but Paul is observing that no other human being has access to my thoughts like I do—I alone have a unique, first-person perspective. For instance, if I pay attention to what is before my mind in conscious awareness, I can be directly aware (in a way no other human can) of my thoughts, feelings, beliefs, intentions, etc. My wife knows me very well, but at best, she can access my thoughts by observing me—my words, my mannerisms, expressions, and more. But she cannot read my mind. She does not have direct access to my thoughts. Likewise, while I can infer what she is thinking (or feeling, wanting, etc.), I am dependent upon her self-disclosure to truly know what is on her mind.

So it is with God's thoughts, too. Under the old covenant, God's words were written down on tablets and scrolls, having been given through Moses and the prophets. Those believers knew God's thoughts in a third-person kind of way, by reading (and hearing) what he had to say. Now, no one can know his thoughts in a first-person way, either, except the Son and the Spirit, who have such access to the mind of God the Father.[5] But then Paul extends his point: "But now we have received, not the spirit of the world, but the Spirit who is from God, that we might know the things freely given to us by God" (v. 12). Then he sums up this section by stating we have been given the mind of Christ.

What is the implication? We have been given an awesome, even deeply intimate, privilege—since we have the mind of Christ (by his Spirit living in us), we have been given an additional kind of access, not just to our own minds, but to the very mind of Christ *in a first-person way*, i.e., *directly*. Again, this does not mean that somehow our minds have been replaced

---

5. This also seems to me to be a helpful argument for the deity of the Spirit.

by his mind; rather, Christians now have access directly to the very mind (and thoughts) of Christ through his Spirit living in us. We no longer have access in the same way as under the old covenant, which involved God's laws given to us that yet remained externalized to us. And, his Spirit did not come to indwell believers permanently under that covenant. But now, we have been given a deeply personal and intimate relationship with the living God, such that our access to him is not externalized (and thus distanced, relationally speaking) even by his words written on the pages of Scripture, but is internalized and to be lived out in deep unity and intimacy. His laws have been written on our hearts by the Spirit (2 Cor 3:3; cf. Jer 31:33), and his Spirit speaks to us.

Having such access to the mind of Christ does not mean I can know all that is in his mind; he alone is omniscient. Nor am I infallible. Nor can I "search" his mind like I would do an Internet search, to obtain information. Access to his mind is not subject to my whims or demands; rather, it comes from abiding in him, in relationship with him, and his word abiding in me. And, it depends upon his choice to share his thoughts with me.

Now, consider the heart. Under the new covenant, when born from above, by the Spirit, we are given a new heart, one that is supple and responsive to God. No longer do we have to live in that old, hardened heart, which had been set on usurping God's throne. Now, we can live in a deep, intimate heart unity with the Lord, for he has given us a "hearing heart," one that will obey him and love him (just as with Solomon's request, 1 Kgs 3:9).

So, what God has done in the new birth is to give us not only access directly to the mind of Christ, so that our minds can be renewed, but also a new heart. He also has given us himself, through the Spirit, who now lives in us. We now have restored to us what Adam and Eve lost in that we can live in a deep heart and mind unity with his very heart and mind. Thus, we can listen to his voice, since he lives in us and has given us his very mind. So, while our hearts and minds have not been replaced by his, we now have the incredible privilege of thinking *with* his mind (or, in unity with his mind), and living in unity with his heart.

The Human Heart and Mind, and the Flesh[6]

As Jesus taught us, the greatest commandment is "you shall love the Lord your God with all your heart, and with all your soul, and with all your mind, and with all your strength" (Mark 12:30). Here, "strength" is *ischus*, which is

6. This section is adapted from part of my "'Emergents,' Evangelicals, and the Importance of Truth."

our ability or power to love God. Although "soul" (*psuche*) may be used to refer to an immaterial aspect of ourselves, it also can be used to refer to the person's vitality, or life, which makes sense here.

"Heart" and "mind" receive important, detailed treatments in Scripture. The mind seems to be an intellectual kind of faculty, something which is to be renewed and transformed, so that we can prove what the will of God is (Rom 12:2). Indispensably, this requires meditation upon, and the practice of, the word of God. It requires having knowledge, which biblically is not opposed to faith. We are to grow in the grace and knowledge of the Lord Jesus (2 Pet 3:18), so that we may experience his grace and peace (2 Pet 1:2). Knowledge of God and his word enables us to keep our ways pure (Ps 119:9). Knowledge of his will enables us to walk with understanding and all spiritual wisdom (Col 1:9). Growth in knowledge of his will (as revealed in Scripture) enables us to trust him.

So, the mind seems to be a faculty of understanding. On the road to Emmaus Jesus needed to open the minds of disciples to understand the truths in the Old Testament about him (Luke 24:45). We have received the mind of Christ (1 Cor 2:16), so that we may know his counsel. "Mind" can also refer to our thoughts, as in Ephesians 2:3 (there, evil thoughts) and their contents (Rom 8:6–7). But the mind also is capable of devotion, in that we are to love God with all our minds.

On the other hand, the biblical notion of the heart is quite unlike what our contemporary use might imply. In Britain during the Victorian era, Christianity was seen as being a religion of the heart, which seems to refer mainly to one's religious feelings, as distinct from knowledge. This seems to have been a fruit of the fact-value split, in which religion was relegated to the realm of mere opinion, preference, or feeling, but not knowledge. We may often use "heart" to mean such deep feelings, as in "my heart grieves for you."

But while biblically "heart" can refer to our deep feelings, it is not at all opposed to knowledge. The heart is the very core of our being and that from which we truly live. Thus, the heart seems to be our entire inner life, including our rational, emotional, and moral dimensions, and our will. We are to *trust* the Lord with all our hearts (Prov 3:5). If we confess with our mouths Jesus as Lord and *believe in our hearts* that God raised Jesus from the dead, we will be saved (Rom 10:9). Why? We believe from the heart, which results in righteousness (10:10). Here, belief is not to be identified with mere intellectual assent (as in the philosophical sense of "belief," which is a matter of cognition). While it involves cognitive content (and thus knowledge from mental assent to truth), it goes further and requires our placing our trust and allegiance in the Lord.

How did God intend for our hearts and minds to function? And, how do they in fact function? Let me start with the perfect God-Man, Jesus, to focus on the intimate relationship between the Father and the Son. In Jesus we see a deep unity with the Father, and not just in purpose. There is the deep love relationship between the Father and the Son, which shows their strong connection of both heart and mind. The Son is fully connected to the Father's will, and he knows the beauty and fulfillment of what it is to have the Father's love. We see that intimate relationship throughout the Gospels, but especially in John 17, where Jesus' intimacy with, and devotion to, the Father are showcased. His heart is set on doing the Father's will, thereby glorifying the Father (vv. 1–4), whom he knows so intimately that he would call him Abba, Daddy (Mark 14:36). There is a deep relationship of love, trust, intimacy, and obedience, for Jesus knows that the Father's will is indeed completely pure, loving, holy, and good. Thus, when the Father asks him to lay down his life, there is no fear of obeying the Father, even though Jesus fully knew the horrors and agony that awaited him. Importantly, then, *the mind of Christ is not merely a set of all true beliefs; rather, it is defined from his heart, by his love for the Father.*

In the garden, too, Adam and Eve enjoyed the beauty and fulfillment of the love of God, and they did not have any fear therein. Their hearts and minds were in unity with his. And, not only was that the case, their respective hearts and minds were deeply united within themselves. For instance, there was not an intrapersonal disconnection between what they knew to be true, and yet what their hearts would want to do, unlike what we see in Paul's description of the life of a Christian who experiences the war of the flesh (again, our sinful propensities, not the physical body per se) against the Spirit in his or her own life (Rom 7). Lastly, there was a deep unity of heart and mind interpersonally, between Adam and Eve. They did not experience the pull of the flesh in relationships that Christians experience today.

But, in stark contrast, consider the hearts and minds of the rest of human beings. Fundamentally, due to the fall, we are dead spiritually to God (Eph 2:1). Our hearts and minds have been severed from God and are bent on usurping him by worshipping ourselves.[7] To help unpack that, I will give a brief meditation on Genesis 3:1–13, along with some connections to a few other passages. There, Satan denies that Adam and Eve will die if they eat from the tree of the knowledge of good and evil, thereby claiming that God lied to them. Moreover, he accuses God of a will to power and of withholding something good from them: "For God knows that in the day you eat

---

7. Suppose (for sake of argument) that, as some argue today, we do not inherit this depraved condition from Adam and Eve. Even if this is so, all of us still sin and reap the same result.

from it your eyes will be opened, and *you will be like God*, knowing good and evil" (v. 5; emphasis mine). God cannot be trusted and does not want them to rival him. They would "know" (i.e., define, choose) good and evil, independently of God. In essence, they could usurp God by becoming their own gods.

It seems that Eve was mesmerized (1 Timothy 2:14 tells us she was deceived), but Adam disobeyed by eating. It seems he "suspended belief," in that he knew what God had told him, and that it was true, yet he chose to suspend that belief so he could have a moment of perspective from his own thoughts. Yet, both Eve and Adam were united in their will to become powerful over God Almighty by escaping the death sentence (2:17) and diminishing his absolute love. God did not truly love them absolutely, they thought, for he was withholding something good from them, and they could act in such a way as to not suffer God's stated consequences. Interestingly, they did not even consider asking God about the serpent's claims.

God gave them opportunity to choose freely to obey unto life, to enjoy a closer relationship with him. Instead, they chose to listen to deception and let Satan provide a definition of God and what he is like. They both sold their souls for a moment of perspective (of being like God) from their own thoughts. The key point of contention was to choose death or life, even in terms of who would be God.

They chose to silence God's Spirit by refusing to listen to and obey God, and instead they gave heed to the serpent's appeal and the desires of their own hearts. But in that, they became afraid of God's voice and of being seen by him, out of fear of his being able to override their desires for power and authority. Like Lucifer, they fell due to their arrogance and attempt to usurp God.

Thus, the core of sin depicted here is the attitude and willful choice to usurp God and worship a god of our own making, even ourselves. Moreover, these attitudes are replete throughout Scripture. For instance, out of envy the chief priests delivered Jesus to the Romans for crucifixion (Mark 15:10). Along with the scribes and elders, they had decided to reject and kill him, thus prompting his warning and declaration that he knew their intentions (Mark 12:1–12). In the parable of the Vine-growers, Jesus exposes their hearts as intent on usurping the inheritance of the owner's son, even by killing him (v. 7). Like Adam and Eve, the chief priests, scribes, and elders exhibit the same, willful heart to usurp God by grabbing for power and control and rejecting Jesus, whose words and miracles clearly attested to his being the Son of God. Compare v. 29, where Jesus exposes their duplicitous hearts by their unwillingness to admit that John was clearly a prophet; so too they were unwilling to acknowledge the clear witness of John's identity.

So, like Adam and Eve after their sin, the default condition of the human heart, the core of our being from which we truly live and choose, is dead to God, deeply rebellious, and intent on idolatrous self-worship.[8] Our hearts and minds, which were originally connected to God's heart and mind, were disconnected from him and instead united with Satan's. If this "connection with Satan" seems strange, consider the Pharisees' response to Jesus' speaking the words given to him by the Father. They were seeking to kill him (John 8:37), so Jesus tells them that since he was speaking the things he had seen with his Father, therefore they also were doing the things they heard from their father. They could not hear (take in) what he had to say because, as he said forcefully and clearly, "you are of your father the devil and you want to do the desires of your father. He was a murderer from the beginning, and does not stand in the truth, because there is no truth in him. Whenever he speaks a lie, he speaks from his own nature, for he is a liar, and the father of lies." (V. 44)

In light of our default condition, it makes sense that God needed to send his Son, who is fully connected to the Father's heart and mind, and yet who also, as a human, was connected to us in our hopelessness, in order to atone for our sins, break this disconnect of our hearts and minds from God, and supersede all our efforts at having control. Therefore, this discussion suggests a crucial question: What is in our hearts? Are we willing to humble ourselves and really seek to know God? If so, he promises to disclose himself to those who love him (John 14:21).

We need humble hearts for a number of reasons, but most of all because otherwise we will keep living out of our fallenness, with hearts bent on usurping God's throne, even if subtly. And it is nothing that we can do for ourselves. On their own, our fleshly hearts are "more deceitful than all else" and "desperately sick" (Jer 17:9). Since the heart and the mind have been severed from God, we are utterly dependent upon God to reconcile us to himself through Christ, thereby enabling us to have renewed hearts and minds. This is why we must be born again, by the Spirit, who gives us a new heart (Jer 31:31–34; Ezek 36:25–28; cf. John 3:3–8) and the mind of Christ (1 Cor 2:16).

But, just because we may be in Christ and justified before God positionally, it does not follow that we thereby are walking *in* that new heart and a renewed mind, under the Spirit's direction and power. As is abundantly clear, we can still be seduced and live in our flesh (cf. 1 Cor 3:1–3), according to the old desire to control and usurp God's throne. In that case, it is

8. So, obviously, this sense of "heart" is not the same as our organ that pumps blood.

crucial that we realize that it is not sufficient for one to be a true follower of Christ simply to have *knowledge* of truth. Demons know the truth about God, but reject it. Likewise, the Pharisees had a clear witness that God in Christ was standing before them and speaking to them, yet they rejected him. *So, only those who humbly submit to the Lord, in all their thoughts and ways, and with all their hearts, can stand in the place of truth.*

With that in mind, we can see that *the art of persuasion predominately by way of reason is not the essence of truth, unless the persuasion comes by way of his Spirit's infilling of the entirety of our being*—all our souls, minds, strength, and, in particular, our hearts. So, for instance, if we lean into humanly based reasoning processes in order to persuade people that they should follow the Lord, we miss out on fullness of truth. *For if the heart is not right, the thoughts will then go astray.* (For that matter, too, if the mind's thoughts and beliefs are not right, they can provide the heart with rationale to deviate from God's ways.) Anything less is prone to deception, due to the weakness of our thoughts and our flesh, and the deceptiveness of the devil. For he will seek to have us welcome indirectly his suggestions, which will enforce our own assumptions, thereby attempting to bind us into their "accuracy" as being even the very word of God. This approach appeals to us with our fleshly hearts' condition.

Therefore, it makes sense why the Lord would stress Deuteronomy 6:5 (as Jesus restated it) as the greatest commandment, for it confronts precisely, and is designed to overcome, the sinful bents of our flesh, particularly of our hearts and minds. It is crucial that we as Christians love the Lord with all our hearts, souls, minds, and strength, lest we be like Solomon who, although he was granted wisdom by God unlike anyone else, still had, at best, half a heart. It also is instructive to see that when Solomon asked God for *wisdom* (an *"understanding heart,"* 1 Kgs 3:9), he literally asked him for a *"hearing"* heart, one that would *listen to* (and, it is implied, *do*) what God would have to say. A heart that listens to God is one that should also obey him. Yet, early on, we see a pattern that would mark Solomon's life: he married foreign women who eventually turned his heart away to their gods. He stands in marked contrast to David, the greatest king thus far of Israel or Judah. The quality that most marked him was that he was a man after God's own heart, despite his great sins and lack in parental disciplinary skills. David would repent after being confronted with his sin (e.g., 2 Sam 12:13, and 24:10). But Solomon did not repent after God confronted him in 1 Kings 11 with his great sin.

Deuteronomy 30 underscores this connection between our hearts, our listening to God's voice, and our obeying him. Consider 30:2: if "you return to the Lord your God and obey Him with all your heart and souls according to all that I command you today," God would restore Israel from captivity. Interestingly, "obey" literally means "listen to his voice." To love him will require that he circumcise our hearts (30:6). Now, "listen" easily connotes to us these days that we simply "hear," that we notice audibly (and maybe also pay attention to) what is being said. Yet, that is not merely what Scripture means. "Listening" involves both paying earnest heed to *and* obeying what God says. It involves the mind, since we need *knowledge* of what he says, and it involves a heart that *obeys*; otherwise, we are hearers who deceive ourselves (Jas 1:19–26). And obedience only comes about when we are filled with his Spirit. As Jesus explained in John 15, unless we abide in him (through his Spirit), and his words abide in us, *we can do nothing* (vv. 5–7) —an extremely sobering reminder of our *complete* dependence upon him for our very lives, witness, power, and the ability to do anything of kingdom value.

Importantly, then, there is a danger for all of us, especially for church leaders and Christian educators. In the fleshly whims of our hearts, and our common tendency to want to usurp God, even leaders in Christian institutions (academia, churches, and parachurches), who have been taught much knowledge, can create untruth as an elevated, arrogant thought to explain (or rationalize) things in a way that fits with our hearts' desires to control all things. No one is immune from self-deception and the heart's desire to usurp God. Plus, knowledge without humble hearts before him actually betrays a lack of a fear of (i.e., reverence for) the Lord, which shows that we really lack wisdom and understanding. Knowledge can puff up, leading to idolatry, especially for academics, not to mention church leaders. Indeed, the fear, or reverential awe, of the Lord is the beginning of knowledge (Prov 1:7, written by perhaps the wisest man who, apart from Jesus, ever lived). But it also is needed *throughout the process of growth* in knowledge, lest subtly we think that in ourselves we are wise and not really in need of God, thereby reliving the arrogance in the fall all over again.

If these things were not enough to give us a sobering picture of the human heart, we also should consider Jesus' explanation of what defiles us. It is not certain foods but instead "the things that proceed out of the mouth [which] come from the heart, and those defile the man. For out of the heart come evil thoughts, murders, adulteries, fornications," and much more, to which we could add idolatries and attempts to elevate our hearts and minds over his (Matt 15:18–19a, bracketed insert added). So, while the mind needs to *know*, the heart (as the core of our being from which we truly live, reason, feel, and decide) is of utmost importance in our need for transformation— and it needs to *bow* before him. So, even as Christians who stand justified before God positionally, we still can live out of our old, fleshly hearts.

Fortunately, God says that in the new covenant, he will give us a new heart (Ezek 36:26–27; cf. 2 Cor 5:17), and he will write his laws upon our hearts (Jer 31:33). Merely being declared righteous by trusting in Christ's atoning sacrifice on our behalf is not enough to rescue us from living in the depraved condition of our hearts and minds. For us to be his redeemed sons and daughters *and* enjoy fellowship with him, we desperately need a new heart and a renewed mind.

Being Intimate with God

Now, for some time, I have wondered in what way(s) it really could be "better" for Christ to have left his disciples, and for his Spirit to come. Yet, that is what he told them (John 16:7). Often, I have felt like I would love to have been able to see his face while he was on earth, to be able to experience firsthand Jesus' facial expressions, smiles, tone, feelings, touch, and more—in short, his nonverbal communication. It is one thing to read his words and what others wrote about him, but that still can leave a sense of distance, a lack of other important cues as to what someone is really like. For instance, it is one thing to know that as a matter of fact I am loved by my wife, but it is another to experience that, perhaps through her tone of voice when she says something, or the way she touches me, or demonstrates that she empathizes with me.

This has been a challenging area with truly experiencing God's love for me. I grew up knowing that, as a matter of fact, God loves me, and I could explain a primary way I knew that to be true, by his Son's death and resurrection on my behalf. But cognitive assent only sinks in so far, especially since in my case I had other factors affecting my abilities to receive and experience his love for me. Looking back, I now understand that while growing up, I knew my dad (who was a Christian) loved me—he was a good provider and a faithful husband in an intact family; he could talk with me about many things, such as about good life skills and wisdom; and we could enjoy fishing and sports together. But I have realized as an adult that emotionally, he could not meet me in the ways I needed and wanted. I "caught" fears of being rejected and other anxieties, which I think both my parents carried, and when I tried to express my feelings with him, I often felt rebuffed, that he just couldn't identify with me. I also "caught" the anxiety that unless I was perfect, I would not really be accepted.

So, after becoming a Christian at age twenty, unconsciously I projected those same traits of my dad upon God as my Father. I just "slid" into those same habituated patterns and fears that I had to be perfect, too. I wanted to experience intimacy and closeness with God, but I now realize that I was basically perceiving his love for me through my own habituated "grid." So, I wished I could have been able to experience Jesus' nonverbal expressions, and not just the content of his verbal ones, so that they could help sink into my heart and help me experience him as he is. Scripture seems to set expectations that he wants to be intimate with his people, but I seemed unable to experience that.

Now, the Lord has met me in special ways since then to help bring healing to me and my heart, in ways that have revolutionized my walk with him. But my point for now is that Scripture helps create, and even encourages, those expectations that he wants to be intimate with his people. So, how then can it be to our advantage that he is not bodily present with us now, but his Spirit lives in us, since we cannot experience his nonverbal expressions?

Surely there are several advantages that Scripture discusses. These would include the benefits of the Spirit's indwelling us, such as his giving us new life (John 3:5; Rom 8:11); sealing us for the day of redemption (Eph 1:13); giving us power to be Christ's witnesses (Acts 1:8); producing his fruit in us, that we may bear it (Gal 5:22–23); giving us spiritual gifts (e.g., 1 Cor 12, Rom 12, Eph 4, 1 Pet 4); and much more. *But one thing that seems all too neglected is that he lives in us and gives us access directly to the mind of Christ, and even to his heart.* That is an incredible kind of intimacy with him that the disciples did not have with Jesus while he lived bodily on earth. In that key, relational way, it truly is to our advantage that Jesus left and sent his Spirit.

So, having new hearts and renewed minds blesses us by being able to live now in deep intimacy with those of the Lord himself. But this is not the only blessing; we can also experience the fruits of this newness by having a deep unity *intrapersonally* in ourselves, between our own hearts and minds. Jesus himself is the perfect God-man. He is our goal (or, *telos*) in every sense (and not just morally); we are to grow up in *all* aspects into him (Eph 4:15). We are to will from a heart that is in sync with his. We are to live with minds that are being renewed, and are in deep unity with his mind. We are to love what he loves, which involves training our affections and desires according to his will and what he has revealed in Scripture. And, surely we are to honor and live like him with our bodies. So, through good habits we need to develop dispositions to behave in ways that please him.

As our exemplar for what real human life is to be like, Jesus was (and is) perfectly whole. That is, in all respects as a human being, Jesus' traits are fully integrated, balanced, and in harmony. John 1:14 helps illustrate this fullness of both heart and mind in him, yet in perfect harmony—he was "full of grace and truth." Luke 2:52 describes how the young man Jesus grew up as a whole person, by "increasing in wisdom and stature, and in favor with God and men." Indeed, his person was so compelling to people that they were drawn to him like a magnet, for they could see what authentic human life is to be like.

Such living should be so for us, too, for we are made to live holistically; we have been made to be whole, integrated people. But, it is all too easy to become imbalanced, with hearts divided to various extents from our minds, and/or vice versa. For example, if we live too much out of our minds, even if they are well-grounded in the truth in Scripture, so that we are imbalanced and not also living from our hearts, we can fall into all sorts of excesses. For instance, we could start to emphasize truth yet without compassion and grace, which could set us down a path to be legalistic and like Jesus' enemies, the Pharisees, who were the religious conservatives of his day. Out of their zeal to protect the law of Moses (and desire to usurp God's throne), they could not, even would not, recognize God's being in their very midst. But on the other hand, if we tend to live too much from our hearts and not as well from our minds, then our desires and choices can be untutored by knowledge of God's word, leading us instead to rationalize all sorts of behaviors that are not of God.

Personally, in my family upbringing, I was not taught (or encouraged, I think) to be listening to what my feelings were telling me. So, if I were to be dealing with fears of rejection (also from my experiences and upbringing), my way of handling that was to try to remind myself of truth, over and over again, to try to control my feelings by willing them to stop. But the fears kept recirculating, and that method would not really deal with the roots of why I was feeling that way. So, though I knew truth (even after I became a Christian), those fears would still resurface. It wasn't until I was able in counseling (and with the Lord) to identify and then deal with those roots that I began to be set free of them in my experience. Especially, it took the Lord saying to me in a personalized way that he loves me with all his heart, and I have begun to experience at my own heart level his deep love and joy. That has released my heart to experience freedom from those old wounds and forms of bondage, now to love him more completely from my heart (and mind), and to love others more so too.

And, *interpersonally*, relationships can be affected by whether we are living excessively by our minds or our hearts. As an example, I know of a young teenager growing up in the late 1950s who wanted to please God, but was sensitive and therefore struggling with some aspects he felt were sinful. He wanted help in addressing them. In his evangelical church, he approached a leader for advice, vulnerably telling him his story. But the man's response was one that left that young man feeling judged and condemned, telling him that he didn't know he was such a sinner. Before that meeting, that young man's heart was sensitive and wanting to know how he could please God. But that reply was a more rigid, legalistic one, and not one of a compassionate shepherd, and it hurt his heart, inclining him to turn away from such people and perhaps also evangelical forms of Christianity. Here, living too much from the mind, without a balance of compassion and grace (since we know we all struggle with sin), inflicted harm upon that youth. And, such an excessive devotion to biblical truth (here, knowing what was considered sin) led to distortions of that truth.

Today, we live in a society that has deeply imbibed of ethical relativism (ER), and it should not surprise us that it affects God's people, too. Now, I think ER serves as a justification that allows us to pursue our own hearts' desires, which, if leaning into our sinful propensities, will be displeasing to God.[9] Indeed, ER is a perfect expression of the core, now default human attitude depicted in Genesis 3:5, that we, not God, will define what is good and evil, right and wrong.

The effects of this mind-set lead to all sorts of damage in relationships. With people living largely from their own hearts' desires, without being balanced and tutored by God's truth, they engage in behaviors that undermine committed relationships. ER deceives us into thinking we can live autonomously, but that really lets us rationalize behaviors that serve our selfishness, leading to broken marriages, damaged children, distrust in personal and business relationships, and more wreckage.

Also, consider the impact of the bifurcation of the heart from the mind within the body of Christ. As members of his body, we are to live in deep unity with the heart and mind of Jesus, which will lead us then to truly love, serve, build up, and care for one another. But all too often this is not happening, at least in evangelical churches in the United States. For instance, we tend to see deep distrust between cessationist believers (by which I mean those who believe the so-called "miraculous" gifts of tongues, prophecy, and the working of miracles have ceased), versus continuationist Christians (those who hold those gifts continue today), even if in the same evangelical local church. And, there can easily be suspicion between those who are officially

---

9. Philosophically, ER can be argued for as follows: (1) Moral values and principles vary from culture to culture (a descriptive thesis of anthropology, etc.). (2) What *makes* some moral principle or value right is *dependent upon* some culture (or person) accepting it as right. Thus, if both (1) and (2) are valid, then (3) there are no universal, objective morals binding upon all people at all times. (By "objective" here, I mean the idea that something is what it is metaphysically—i.e., the way something is in reality—regardless of what we believe or think about it.) If ER is true, then all morality is up to us.

"open," yet are very cautious, about these gifts and continuationists. At the risk of stereotyping this distinction, it easily can seem like the former place a focus upon the intellect (knowledge of Scripture), whereas the latter stress the heart (here, understood as experience, especially in terms of ecstatic feelings). But to the degree that actually happens, there could be leaning too much into the mind or the heart, one at the expense of the other. Now, the issue does come down to which view is more biblical; if these gifts have ceased, then continuationists are mistaken and need to change. But if these gifts still apply today, then they need to be embraced in order to experience more of the fullness of Christ and the deep unity, mutual love, and care he wants among the all members (1 Cor 12:14–26).

Now these scriptural (and experiential) considerations should point us to a solution to the ways evangelicals have deprived themselves of their birthrights as Christians. And, though differing in particulars, yet by following in much the same naturalistic trajectory, emergents' thought also cannot offer the fullness of life that Jesus Christ offers to all those who have been born from above, by the Spirit. Now I will look somewhat briefly at that fullness he offers.

The Solution: Fullness of Spirit, and Fullness of Truth

The New Testament authors and early Christians testify to the amazing truth that God dwells in the midst of all those who have been born again by the Spirit. Moreover, they knew experientially the reality of his promised power and presence, and they turned the world upside down. Can we too know and experience that deep unity with his heart and mind, and live in the power of his resurrection life? The Bible surely indicates that that is our birthright.

However, as we have seen, the practical effects of naturalism serve to make God irrelevant and corrode the Christian life, shaping it into a fleshly, all too often de-supernaturalized faith for both emergents and evangelicals. Crucially, then, the solutions to a preternaturalized Christianity include 1) repentance from the heart, 2) changing our minds, and 3) embracing the Lord in all his fullness (the threefold cord of being deeply united with his heart and his mind, and living in the fullness of the Spirit).

What should the fullness of the Spirit look like? To help show this, I will give a brief meditation on the fullness of Christ in Ephesians, making connections to what I have laid out in this chapter so far, and extending it. Paul mentions the fullness of the Lord many times in his letter to the Ephesians. I think this emphasis is not minor; rather, it is one of vital importance to the Christian life. But I also think too many Christians, particularly in the States, do not really appreciate it. Paul explains how we, even in the increasingly secular West, can know and experience God's amazing power and presence. If so, this will be of vital importance to overcome the grips of naturalism upon believers in the West.

Paul has much to say in Ephesians about our relationship with Christ, especially along the themes of intimacy and power. God loves us lavishly (e.g., 1:3–13), and he wants us to live out the richness of this new life, so that we may have "[deep and intimate] knowledge of Him" (1:17, AMPC).[10] He also wants us to know (not just intellectually, but also by experience) the surpassing greatness of his power toward us who believe (1:19). Notice that Paul illustrates this power by appealing to Jesus' resurrection, a miracle par excellence, and not bearing the fruit of the Spirit, though that too utterly depends upon God.

Paul also explains how God is making a people for himself by uniting all who trust in Christ in his body, which is "the fullness of Him Who fills all in all [for in that body lives *the full measure of Him* Who makes everything complete, and Who fills everything everywhere with Himself]" (1:23, AMPC, emphasis mine). In the body, Jesus is present now, with all his power.

In 3:14–21, Paul gives us a much more detailed look into this fullness. It includes his great plan, with him dwelling in us (v. 17), and his great power (v. 18), so that we would be able to experience his great love (v. 18, AMPC). Then, almost in a crescendo, Paul explains that God really wants us to come "to know [practically, through experience for yourselves] the love of Christ, which far surpasses mere knowledge [without experience]; that you may be filled [through all your being] unto all the fullness of God—[may have the richest measure of the divine Presence, and become a body wholly filled and flooded with God Himself]!" (v. 19, AMPC). God doesn't want us to have mere "head" knowledge of him; he also wants us to *experience* his love and fullness. Paul is not afraid of rich experiences of the Lord in the Christian life. Yet, they should be rooted in knowledge of God and Scripture.

But, what does his fullness look like and include? What should we expect that to look like today in our contexts in the west, including the States? Scripture, our standard, depicts the Christian life as a *supernatural* one, the very antithesis of the kind of one we have been led to believe is "godly" for today under the influences of naturalism. So, suppose Jesus was living on earth with us today; how would he live? It seems to me that he would do similar things as he did during his thirty-plus years on earth. For example,

---

10. "AMPC" stands for the Amplified Bible, classic edition.

he would preach the gospel, make disciples, live in unity with the Father and in the Spirit's power, and perform miracles out of compassion (cf. Matt 14:14).

But, here's a *crucial* point: *Jesus is here now* in the body of Christ (Eph 1:23). So, it seems that we should see God doing these things through us. But that raises the question: shouldn't we expect him to be doing miracles amongst us? And wouldn't he address the specific beliefs people (Christian and non-Christian) today have that blind them to God?

That raises the issue about whether the miraculous gifts are for today. So, it is intriguing that Paul broaches the gifts in the context of fullness of Christ within the passage that spans 3:14–21 through 4:13, where he instructs that we are to reach maturity by attainting to "the measure of the stature of the fullness of the Christ" (AMPC). I do not think this positioning of the gifts is accidental. Paul discusses the gifts again in 1 Corinthians 12:7, where he indicates that the gifts are a *manifestation* of Christ until they are no longer needed (see 1 Cor 13:8–10). That is, the gifts are to demonstrate and make plain the presence and power of Christ—even Christ himself—in us. This should not surprise us, since Scripture indicates that Jesus Christ lives in believers now. Since Christ is to be manifested in all his fullness through his body, and he would be speaking truth to us today in our contexts and (it seems) also showing his power through miracles, it seems the miraculous gifts (miracles, prophecy, etc.) are actually critical for today.

It is also interesting to observe that while humans can attempt to counterfeit some of the gifts, such as showing hospitality, mercy, or serving, the "miraculous" gifts are ones that seem the most difficult, if not impossible, for humans to counterfeit. We simply lack the abilities in our own strength to perform miracles or give messages actually from God. Those gifts are the ones that most clearly indicate the supernatural power and presence of the Lord. Yet, not surprisingly, they also would be the ones most likely to disappear if the church is living all too naturalistically.

Without all the gifts, it seems to follow that Christ will not be manifested in all his fullness through his body. Yet, so often, that result seems to be the case. But Paul clearly commands us to be filled with his Spirit (Eph 5:18). In order for Christ to be made fully manifest to the watching world, it seems we should not refuse the full measure of him. In Ephesians, at least, that seems to require the "miraculous" gifts.

Of course, though, one of the major concerns for cessationists is that more words from God would mean Scripture is not closed. That is, claims to more words from God could lead to excesses and abuses, or additions to the canon. This is an *important* concern. Still, it seems that if God were to speak specifically to us in our contexts now, it would not add to Scripture since, *according to Scripture itself*, the canon is closed (Heb 1:1–2; Jude 3; Rev 22:18–19). Yet, from Paul's stress on the unity of the body of Christ in Ephesians, it seems unity of *both* groups (continuationists, and cessationist (or open but cautious)) are needed. Satan has divided and withered the whole body by sowing distrust in both groups. The result is an anemic, divided body, which cannot stand. That is a condition from which believers in the US must urgently repent.

Moreover, the Bible is God's universally applicable, inerrant, infallible word. Where it does teach, it teaches authoritatively. But, it does not seem that the Bible is intended to be a *textbook* on many subjects—science, philosophy, art, political science, and many more. So, at least for those aspects of our lives that are not directly addressed by Scripture, what should we do?

Clearly, we are to have renewed minds and live in dependence upon him. We are also to ask him for wisdom (Jas 1:5). But God never intended for us to live out aspects of our lives in which we did *not* depend upon him and his mind. Indeed, Jesus is to be Lord of *all* of our lives. Furthermore, he has given us access to the mind of Christ, and in him are hidden all the treasures of wisdom and knowledge (Col 2:3). So, to be able to serve him in areas not addressed directly by Scripture, it would seem that God wants us to come, humbly seek, listen, and expect him to speak into our lives. (Otherwise, it would seem that Jesus just speaks into our lives in terms of spiritual and moral matters, as the naturalistically inspired fact-value split suggests.) Yet, his speaking into our lives in such ways does not add to Scripture. If so, then this concern about adding to Scripture seems misplaced.

That does not mean, however, that today we should not test any putative "word" from God. All of us are probably aware of various people making claims to further revelations, including, but not limited to, Mormons. Surely there are abuses done in the name of God. John MacArthur raises good concerns about such claims made by some more popular people today that are clearly unscriptural.[11] So, how do we examine and test them, per 1 Thessalonians 5:21? The primary way is by Scripture; if something contradicts, undermines, or does not fit well with Scripture, then it is not of God (cf. 2 Tim 3:16–17). Also, believers also should test any putative "word" by prayer, asking the Lord for guidance, and they should consult other mature, Spirit-filled believers.

I think Paul in Ephesians also has Christ's fullness in mind when he discusses the armor of God. At the start, he tells us to be strong in him and his strength (6:10). Interestingly, often the various "pieces" of armor are treated as largely defensive, and one or two being offensive—the word

---

11. That is the emphasis of his book *Strange Fire*.

of God (v. 17), and prayer (v. 18). I think, though, that this treatment can tend to minimize something crucial—the power of Christ. How did Jesus deal with spiritual battles? Consider Luke 11:14–26; Jesus cast out a demon by his power (v. 22). Jesus went on the offensive against demons, but he did not utilize just prayer and the word of God. Though they imply use of God's power, this text indicates explicitly that he drew upon the *power* of the Spirit. Yet, too often, I am afraid evangelicals in the US do not stress this because they do not expect God to show up supernaturally in power. Nor do they seem to expect to encounter real demons.

Now, someone might say I have read Ephesians too selectively. For in 2:20, Paul taught that the foundation of the faith (i.e., Scripture) has been laid. Since we have the completed canon of Scripture, there is no more need for the miraculous gifts. However, I think this objection misses the point of God's great plan throughout Scripture, to be intimate and live in the midst of his people, so they may know and experience his presence and power. *Knowing and obeying the written word of God is utterly important; it is God's authoritative, inerrant teaching for all. But, it is not intended to substitute for the manifest, intimate presence of the living Word, Jesus himself.*

In sum, we need to repent from the many mind-sets and practices that have been shaped by naturalistic influences. This applies equally well to evangelicals and emergents. *The solution to these de-supernaturalized versions of Christianity is repentance from their naturalistic ways. We must acknowledge, confess, and repent of these idolatrous mind-sets and patterns that make God practically irrelevant and elevate ourselves over him.*

Indeed, God is not dead; he is alive and well and very much able and willing to pour out his Spirit in all his fullness on humble, obedient sons and daughters of the King.[12] If so, we can see the supernatural power and presence of the Lord manifested in our midst today, the very "things" that believers *and* a watching, secularized world need to see. In that, we can experience a deeply authentic Christian life, one that would emerge from the

12. To read some stories of what God is doing around the world (and recently in the West, too), which are quite encouraging, consider (for example) looking into Keener's two-volume set, *Miracles*. In it, he provides painstaking, detailed evidence for God's miraculous activity in recent times around the world. These miracles are of such quality, and extent in location and quantity, that they seem to support strongly that New Testament-quality miracles are indeed happening. With many miracle reports, Keener refers to documentation (e.g., X-rays before and after a healing) that can serve as an audit trail for independent verification. Also, for decades, Paul Eshleman of Cru's "Jesus Film Project" has reported numerous examples of how God has shown up personally and powerfully through the showing of the *Jesus* film around the world. Some videos of him are available online, where he recounts such events. For example, see "Jesus and the Healing Torch."

distorted, naturalistic forms we experience all too often today. Such a life would be deeply progressive, in all the freshness and fullness of life that comes from abiding richly in the Spirit of Jesus.

Bibliography

Albright, William Foxwell. *Yahweh and the Gods of Canaan: A Historical Analysis of Two Contrasting Faiths.* Garden City, NY: Doubleday, 1968.

Alston, William P. "What Euthyphro Should Have Said." In *Philosophy of Religion: A Reader and Guide*, edited by William Lane Craig, 283–98. New Brunswick, NJ: Rutgers University Press, 2002.

The Amplified Bible. Classic ed. La Habra, CA: The Lockman Foundation, 1987.

Aristotle. *Metaphysics.* Translated by W. D. Ross. http://classics.mit.edu/Aristotle/metaphysics.html.

———. *The Nicomachean Ethics.* Translated by David Ross. Revised by J. L. Ackrill and J. O. Urmson. Oxford: Oxford University Press, 1980.

"The Assyrians." *The Jewish Virtual Library.* http://www.jewishvirtuallibrary.org/jsource/History/Assyrians.html.

Balakian, Peter. "Armenians in the Ottoman Empire." In *Encyclopedia of Human Rights*, Vol. 1, edited by David Forsythe, 92–103. Oxford: Oxford University Press, 2009.

Baxter, Craig. "Bangladesh/East Pakistan." In *Encyclopedia of Genocide and Crimes Against Humanity*, vol. 2, edited by Dinah Shelton, 115–19. Farmington Hills, MI: Thomson Gale, 2005.

Beecher, Henry Ward. "The Mission of the Pulpit." In *History, Essays, Orations, and Other Documents of the Sixth General Conference of the Evangelical Alliance*, edited by Philip Schaff and S. Irenaeus Prime, 392–96. New York: Harper and Brothers, 1874.

Bell, Rob. "Rob Bell's Practical Guide to Finding Joy and Meaning in Everyday Life." http://www.oprah.com/app/rob-bell-joy-meaning.html.

———. *Love Wins: A Book About Heaven, Hell, and the Fate of Every Person Who Ever Lived.* New York: HarperOne, 2011.

———. *What We Talk About When We Talk About God.* New York: HarperOne, 2013.

Bernstein, James. "The Original Christian Gospel." 2009. https://preachersinstitute.com/2014/09/22/the-original-christian-gospel/.

Bozeman, Theodore Dwight. *Protestants in an Age of Science: The Baconian Ideal and Antebellum American Religious Thought.* Chapel Hill, NC: University of North Carolina Press, 1977.

Bradley, Anthony. "Farewell Emerging Church." *World Magazine* (April 14, 2010). https://world.wng.org/2010/04/farewell_emerging_church_1989_2010.

Brink, Jonathan. "A State of Emergence 2010." 2010. http://jonathanbrink.com/tag/emergent-village/; originally posted at http://www.emergentvillage.com/weblog/brink-state-of-emergence-2010.

Brower, J. E. "Aquinas on the Problem of Universals." *Philosophy and Phenomenological Research* (2015) 715–35. doi: 10.1111/phpr.12176.

Brown, Callum. *The Death of Christian Britain.* 2nd ed. New York: Routledge, 2009.

Burson, Scott R. "Apologetics and the New Kind of Christian: An Arminian Analysis of Brian D. McLaren's Emergent Reconstruction of the Faith." PhD diss., Brunel University, 2014.

———. *Brian McLaren in Focus: A New Kind of Apologetics.* Abilene, TX: Abilene Christian University Press, 2016.

Carson, D. A. *Becoming Conversant with the Emerging Church.* Grand Rapids: Zondervan, 2005.

Carson, D. A., ed. *The Enduring Authority of the Christian Scriptures.* Grand Rapids: Eerdmans, 2016.

Chalmers, A. "Atomism from the 17th to the 20th Century." *Stanford Encyclopedia of Philosophy,* October 9, 2014. https://plato.stanford.edu/entries/atomism-modern/.

Chang, Iris. *The Rape of Nanking: The Forgotten Holocaust of World War II.* New York: Basic, 1998.

"Convention on the Prevention and Punishment of the Crime of Genocide." Article II. United Nations Convention No. 1021, December 9, 1948. http://treaties.un.org/doc/Publication/UNTS/Volume%2078/volume-78-I-1021-English.pdf.

Copernicus, Nicolaus. *On the Revolutions of the Heavenly Spheres.* On the Shoulders of Giants series, edited by Stephen Hawking. Philadelphia: Running Press, 2002.

Courtois, Stéphane. "Introduction: The Crimes of Communism." In *The Black Book of Communism: Crimes, Terror, Repression,* edited by Stéphane Courtois et al., 1–32. Translated by Jonathan Murphy and Mark Kramer. Cambridge, MA: Harvard University Press, 1999.

Craig, William Lane. "God Directs All Things." In *Four Views on Divine Providence,* edited by Dennis Jowers, 79–100. Grand Rapids: Zondervan, 2011.

Craine, Patrick B. "Shock: No jail time for woman who strangled newborn because Canada accepts abortion, says judge." September 12, 2011. http://www.lifesitenews.com/news/judge-rules-no-jail-time-for-infanticide-because-canada-accepts-abortion?utm_source=feedburner&utm_medium=feed&utm_campaign=Feed%25253A+LifesitenewscomLatestHeadlines+%252528LifeSiteNews.com+Latest+Headlines%252529.

Del Soldato, E. "Natural Philosophy in the Renaissance." *Stanford Encyclopedia of Philosophy,* August 30, 2016. https://plato.stanford.edu/entries/natphil-ren/.

Dennett, Daniel C. "Dennett, Daniel C." In *A Companion to the Philosophy of Mind: Blackwell Companions to Philosophy,* edited by Samuel Guttenplan, 236–43. Oxford: Basil Blackwell, 1994.

Ehrman, Bart. *Forged: Writing in the Name of God—Why the Bible's Authors Are Not Who We Think They Are.* New York: HarperOne, 2011.

Ensor, John. *The Great Work of the Gospel: How We Experience God's Grace.* Wheaton, IL: Crossway, 2006.

Eshleman, Paul. "Jesus and the Healing Torch." 2013. http://legacyccc.com/?s=eshleman.

Etcheson, Craig. "Khmer Rouge Victim Numbers, Estimating." In *Encyclopedia of Genocide and Crimes Against Humanity*, vol. 2, edited by Dinah Shelton, 613–15. Farmington Hills, MI: Thomson Gale, 2005.

Firestone, Chris. E-mail correspondence to Scott Smith, January 22, 2013.

Firestone, Chris, and Nathan Jacobs. *In Defense of Kant's Religion*. Indiana Series in the Philosophy of Religion. Bloomington, IN: Indiana University Press, 2008.

"Four Spiritual Laws." Cru. http://www.crustore.org/fourlawseng.htm.

Galilei, Galileo. "*Il Saggiatore*" ("The Assayer"). In *Discoveries and Opinions of Galileo*, 231–80. Translated by S. Drake. New York: Doubleday & Co., 2005. https://www.princeton.edu/~hos/h291/assayer.htm#_ftn19.

———. "Letter to the Grand Duchess Christian of Tuscany." http://www.fordham.edu/halsall/mod/galileo-tuscany.asp.

Gay, Craig. *The Way of the (Modern) World: Or, Why It is Tempting to Live as if God Doesn't Exist*. Grand Rapids: Eerdmans, 1998.

Gilkey, Langdon. *Shantung Compound: The Story of Men and Women Under Pressure*. San Francisco: Harper and Row, 1966.

Girard, René. *Things Hidden Since the Foundation of the World*. Translated by Stephen Bann and Michael Metteer. Redwood City, CA: Stanford University Press, 1987.

———. *Violence and the Sacred*. Translated by Patrick Gregory. Baltimore: John Hopkins University Press, 1979.

The Gods Must Be Crazy. Directed by Jamie Uys. 1990. Bloemfontein: Mimosa Films and C.A.T. Films.

Green, Joel B. *Body, Soul, and Human Life: The Nature of Humanity in the Bible*. Grand Rapids: Baker Academic, 2008.

Grenz, Stanley. "The Relational God." In *Theology for the Community of God*, 77–95. Grand Rapids: Eerdmans, and Vancouver, BC: Regent College Publishing, 2000.

Grudem, Wayne, ed. *Are Miraculous Gifts for Today? Four Views*. Grand Rapids: Zondervan, 1996.

———. *Systematic Theology*. Grand Rapids: Zondervan, 1994.

Hare, John. *The Moral Gap: Kantian Ethics, Human Limits, and God's Assistance*. Oxford Studies in Theological Ethics. Oxford: Oxford University Press, 1996.

Hatfield, Gary. "René Descartes." January 16, 2014. *Stanford Encyclopedia of Philosophy* http://plato.stanford.edu/entries/descartes/.

Hauerwas, Stanley. *A Community of Character*. Notre Dame, IN: University of Notre Dame Press, 1981.

———. *Dispatches from the Front: Theological Engagements With the Secular*. Durham, NC: Duke University Press, 1994.

Hick, John. "A Pluralist's View." In *Four Views on Salvation in a Pluralistic World*, edited by Dennis Okholm and Timothy Phillips, 27–59. Grand Rapids: Zondervan, 1996.

"Influential Evangelicals: Brian McLaren." *Time*, February 7, 2005. http://content.time.com/time/specials/packages/article/0,28804,1993235_1993243_1993300,00.html.

Inrig, Gary. *Forgiveness: Discover the Power and Reality of Authentic Christian Forgiveness*. Grand Rapids: Discovery House, 2005.

Jones, Andrew. "Emerging Church Movement (1989–2009)?" December 30, 2009. http://tallskinnykiwi.typepad.com/tallskinnykiwi/2009/12/emerging-church-movement-1989-2009.html.

Jones, Clay. "We Don't Hate Sin So We Don't Understand What Happened to the Canaanites: An Addendum to 'Divine Genocide' Arguments." *Philosophia Christi* 11:1 (2009) 53–72.

———. "We Don't Take Human Evil Seriously So We Don't Understand Why We Suffer." 2009. http://www.clayjones.net/wp-content/uploads/2011/06/Human-Evil-and-Suffering.pdf.

———. *Why Does God Allow Evil? Compelling Answers for Life's Toughest Questions.* Eugene, OR: Harvest House, 2017.

Jones, Tony. *A Better Atonement: Beyond the Depraved Doctrine of Original Sin.* Kindle ed. Minneapolis: The JoPa Group, 2012.

———. *The Church is Flat: The Relational Ecclesiology of the Emerging Church Movement.* Kindle ed. Minneapolis: The JoPa Group, 2011.

———. E-mail correspondence to Scott Smith, February 28, 2006.

———. *Postmodern Youth Ministry.* Grand Rapids: Zondervan, for Youth Specialties, 2001.

Kallenberg, Brad. *Ethics as Grammar: Changing the Postmodern Subject.* Notre Dame, IN: University of Notre Dame Press, 2001.

Kant, Immanuel. *The Critique of Pure Reason.* In *The Philosophy of Kant: Immanuel Kant's Moral and Political Writings,* translated and edited by Carl J. Friedrich, 25–42. New York: Modern Library, 1993.

———. "What is Enlightenment?" In *The Philosophy of Kant: Immanuel Kant's Moral and Political Writings,* translated and edited by Carl J. Friedrich, 145–53. New York: Modern Library, 1993.

Keener, Craig S. *Miracles: The Credibility of the New Testament Accounts.* Vol. 2. Grand Rapids: Baker Academic, 2011.

Klein, J. "Francis Bacon." *Stanford Encyclopedia of Philosophy.* December 7, 2012. https://plato.stanford.edu/entries/francis-bacon/.

Kren, George M., and Leon Rappoport. *The Holocaust and the Crisis of Human Behavior.* New York: Holmes & Meier, 1980.

Lewis, C. S. *The Problem of Pain.* New York: HarperCollins, 2001.

Lewis, Kevin. E-mail correspondence with Scott Smith, November 9, 2009.

———. "Hamartiology II." Essential Christian Doctrine I, Biola University, Fall 2011. http://people2.biola.edu/faculty/kevinl//cdf11.htm.

MacArthur, John. *Strange Fire: The Danger of Offending the Holy Spirit with Counterfeit Worship.* Nashville: Nelson, 2013.

MacIntyre, Alasdair. *After Virtue.* 2nd ed. Notre Dame, IN: University of Notre Dame Press, 1984.

Margolin, Jean-Louis. "China: A Long March into Night." In *The Black Book of Communism: Crimes, Terror, Repression,* edited by Stéphane Courtois et al., 436–546. Translated by Jonathan Murphy and Mark Kramer. Cambridge, MA: Harvard University Press, 1999.

Marsden, George. *Fundamentalism and American Culture.* 2nd ed. New York: Oxford University Press, 2006.

———. *Understanding Fundamentalism and Evangelicalism.* Grand Rapids: Eerdmans, 1991.

Marty, Martin. *The Modern Schism: Three Paths to the Secular.* New York: Harper & Row, 1969.

May, Henry F. *The Enlightenment in America.* New York: Oxford University Press, 1976.

McLaren, Brian. "A Cordial Response to R. Scott Smith. Letter to R. Scott Smith, July 11, 2006.

———. E-mail correspondence to Scott Smith, July 17, 2006.

———. E-mail correspondence to Scott Smith, November 10, 2009.

———. *Everything Must Change*. Nashville: Thomas Nelson, 2007.

———. "Five Questions You Might be Asking." In *Brian McLaren in Focus: A New Kind of Apologetics*, by Scott Burson, 13–17. Abilene, TX: Abilene Christian University Press, 2016.

———. *A Generous Orthodoxy*. Grand Rapids: Zondervan, 2004.

———. *More Ready Than You Realize*. Grand Rapids: Zondervan, 2002.

———. *A New Kind of Christian*. San Francisco: Jossey-Bass, 2001.

———. *A New Kind of Christianity*. New York: HarperOne, 2010.

———. *The Secret Message of Jesus*. Nashville: W Publishing Group, 2006.

———. *The Story We Find Ourselves In*. San Francisco: Jossey-Bass, 2003.

———. *Why Did Jesus, Moses, the Buddha, and Mohammed Cross the Road? Christian Identity in a Multi-Faith World*. New York: Jericho/FaithWords, 2012.

Moreland, J. P. *Kingdom Triangle: Recover the Christian Mind, Renovate the Soul, Restore the Spirit's Power*. Grand Rapids: Zondervan, 2007.

———. "Two Areas of Reflection and Dialogue with John Franke." *Philosophia Christi* 8 (2007) 307–12.

———. *Universals*. Central Problems in Philosophy series, edited by John Shand. Montreal: McGill-Queen's University Press, 2001.

Moreland, J. P., and William Lane Craig. *Philosophical Foundations for a Christian Worldview*. Downers Grove, IL: InterVarsity, 2003.

Mueller, John Theodore. *Christian Dogmatics*. St. Louis: Concordia, 1934. https://archive.org/stream/Mueller/Mueller_djvu.txt.

Murphy, Nancey. *Beyond Liberalism and Fundamentalism: How Modern and Postmodern Philosophy Set the Theological Agenda*. Rockwell Lecture Series, edited by Werner H. Kelber. Harrisburg, PA: Trinity Press International, 1996.

———. *Bodies and Souls, or Spirited Bodies?* New York: Cambridge University Press, 2006.

———. "Human Nature: Historical, Scientific, and Religious Issues." In *Whatever Happened to the Soul?*, edited by Warren S. Brown et al., 1–30. Minneapolis: Fortress, 1998.

Murphy, Nancey, and Warren Brown. *Did My Neurons Make Me Do It? Philosophical and Neurobiological Perspectives on Moral Responsibility and Free Will*. Oxford: Oxford University Press, 2007.

New American Standard Bible. Anaheim, CA: Foundation, for the Lockman Foundation, 1977.

Nietzsche, Friedrich. *The Gay Science*. Cambridge Texts in the History of Philosophy Series, edited by Bernard Williams. Cambridge: Cambridge University Press, repr. 2003.

Noll, Mark. *The Scandal of the Evangelical Mind*. Grand Rapids: Eerdmans, 1994.

Pagitt, Doug. *A Christianity Worth Believing*. San Francisco: Jossey-Bass, 2008.

———. "The Emerging Church and Embodied Theology." In *Listening to the Beliefs of Emerging Churches*, edited by Robert Webber, 119–43. Grand Rapids: Zondervan, 2007.

———. *Flipped: The Provocative Truth that Changes Everything We Know About God.* Kindle ed. New York: Convergent, 2015.

Piper, John. "John Piper—The Emergent Church." March 24, 2010. https://www.youtube.com/watch?v=MkGq5A4QEjg.

Plantinga, Alvin. *God, Freedom, and Evil.* Grand Rapids: Eerdmans, 1977.

Plato. *The Republic.* Translated by Benjamin Jowett. http://classics.mit.edu/Plato/republic.7.vi.html.

Richardson, Don. *Peace Child.* Ventura, CA: Regal, 1975.

Rummel, R. J. "Genocide." http://www.hawaii.edu/powerkills/GENOCIDE.ENCY.HTM.

———. *Lethal Politics: Soviet Genocide and Mass Murder since 1917.* New Brunswick, NJ: Transaction, 1990.

Sagan, Carl. *Cosmos.* New York: Ballantine, 1980.

Saucy, Robert L. "An Open but Cautious View." In *Are Miraculous Gifts for Today? Four Views,* edited by Wayne Grudem, 95–148. Grand Rapids: Zondervan, 1996.

Schaeffer, Francis. *How Should We Then Live?* 50th L'Abri Anniversary ed. Wheaton, IL: Crossway, 2005.

Sellars, Wilfrid. *Science, Perception, and Reality.* Atascadero, CA: Ridgeview, 1991.

Shults, LeRon. *Reforming the Doctrine of God.* Grand Rapids: Eerdmans, 2005.

———. *Reforming Theological Anthropology.* Grand Rapids: Eerdmans, 2003.

Smith, George. "Newton's *Philosophiae Naturalis Principia Mathematica.*" *Stanford Encyclopedia of Philosophy,* December 20, 2007. http://plato.stanford.edu/entries/newton-principia/.

Smith, James K. A. "Who's Afraid of Postmodernism? A Response to the 'Biola School.'" In *Christianity and the Postmodern Turn,* edited by Myron B. Penner, 215–28. Grand Rapids: Brazos, 2005.

Smith, R. Scott. "Craig, Anti-Platonism, and Objective Morality." *Philosophia Christi* 19:2 (2017) 331–43.

———. "Are Emergents Rejecting the Soul's Existence?" *Knowing and Doing,* C. S. Lewis Institute Magazine (Fall 2009) 1–4.

———. "Emergents and the Rejection of Body-Soul Dualism." *Christian Research Journal* (September–October 2009). http://www.equip.org/article/emergents-and-the-rejection-of-body-soul-dualism/.

———. "'Emergents,' Evangelicals, and the Importance of Truth: Some Philosophical and Spiritual Lessons." In *Evangelicals Engaging Emergent,* edited by William Henard, 128–57. Nashville: Broadman and Holman, 2009.

———. "Emerging Church." In *Encyclopedia of Christian Civilization,* edited by George Kurian, 824–26. Malden, MA: Blackwell, 2009.

———. "Finitude, Fallenness, and Immediacy: Husserlian Replies to Westphal and Smith." *Philosophia Christi* 13:1 (2011) 105–26.

———. "God and Relationships on the 'New Kind' of Christianity: A Doctrinal Update on Brian McLaren and Other Emergents." *Christian Research Journal* 39:4 (2016). http://www.equip.org/PDF/JAF5349.pdf.

———. *In Search of Moral Knowledge: Overcoming the Fact-Value Split.* Downers Grove, IL: InterVarsity, 2014.

———. "Joel Green's Anthropological Monism: Biblical, Theological, and Philosophical Considerations." *Criswell Theological Review* 7:2 (Spring 2010) 19–36.

———. *Naturalism and Our Knowledge of Reality: Testing Religious Truth-Claims.* Aldershot: Routledge/Ashgate, 2012.

———. "Nonfoundationalism, Postfoundationalism, and the Truth of Scripture." In *The Enduring Authority of the Christian Scriptures,* edited by D. A. Carson, 831–71. Grand Rapids: Eerdmans, 2016.

———. "Reflections on McLaren and the Emerging Church." In *Passionate Conviction: Contemporary Discourses on Christian Apologetics,* edited by Paul Copan and William Lane Craig, 227–43. Nashville: Broadman and Holman, 2007.

———. *Truth and the New Kind of Christian: The Emerging Effects of Postmodernism in the Church.* Wheaton, IL: Crossway, 2005.

———. *Virtue Ethics and Moral Knowledge: Philosophy of Language After MacIntyre and Hauerwas.* Aldershot: Routledge/Ashgate, 2003.

Solzhenitsyn, Aleksandr. *The Gulag Archipelago: 1918–1956.* Vol. 1. Boulder, CO: Westview, 1974.

Thorp, John P. "Bangladesh, Genocide In." In *Encyclopedia of Genocide and Crimes Against Humanity,* vol. 1, edited by Dinah Shelton, 115–16. Farmington Hills, MI: Thomson Gale, 2005.

Torrey, Reuben A. *What the Bible Teaches: A Thorough and Comprehensive Study of What the Bible has to Say Concerning the Great Doctrines of which it Treats.* 17th ed. New York: Fleming H. Revell, 1933.

The Trial of Galileo: Essential Documents. Translated and edited by Maurice A. Finocchiaro. Indianapolis: Hackett, 2014.

Tye, Michael. *Ten Problems of Consciousness: A Representational Theory of the Phenomenal Mind.* Cambridge: Bradford, 1995.

Ugaritic Narrative Poetry. Translated by Mark S. Smith. Edited by Simon B. Parker. Atlanta: Society of Biblical Literature, 1997.

Volf, Miroslav. *Free of Charge: Giving and Forgiving in a Culture Stripped of Grace.* Grand Rapids: Zondervan, 2005.

Warfield, Benjamin B. "Introduction." In *Apologetics, or The Rational Vindication of Christianity,* vol. 1, by Francis R. Beattie, 35–47. Richmond, VA: Presbyterian Committee of Publication, 1903.

Westphal, Merold. "Hermeneutics as Epistemology." In *The Blackwell Guide to Epistemology,* edited by John Greco and Ernest Sosa, 415–35. Malden, MA: Blackwell, 1999.

———. "Phenomenologies and Religious Truth." In *Phenomenology of the Truth Proper to Religion,* edited by Daniel Guerrière, 105–25. Albany, NY: State University of New York Press, 1990.

Willard, Dallas. *The Divine Conspiracy.* New York: HarperCollins, 1997.

William of Ockham. *Quodlibetal Questions.* Translated by Alfred Freddoso and Francis Kelly. New Haven, CT: Yale University Press, 1991.

Witherspoon, John. "Lectures on Moral Philosophy." In *The Works of the Rev. John Witherspoon,* vol. 3. Philadelphia: William W. Woodward, 1802.

Yakovlev, Alexander N. *A Century of Violence in Soviet Russia.* Translated by Anthony Austin. New Haven, CT: Yale University Press, 2002.

Index

Made in the USA
Las Vegas, NV
02 September 2021